Battlefield Pennsylvania

Battlefield Pennsylvania

A GUIDE TO

The Keystone State's
Most Sacred Ground

Brady J. Crytzer

WESTHOLME
Yardley

Facing title page: The meadow at Gettysburg battlefield over which the 2nd Massachusetts and 27th Indiana charged on the morning of July 3, 1863, toward the woods occupied by Confederate general Edward Johnson's Division. (*Library of Congress*)

First Westholme Paperback 2022

©2018 Brady J. Crytzer
Maps by Paul Dangel
Maps © 2018 Westholme Publishing

Westholme Publishing, LLC
904 Edgewood Road
Yardley, Pennsylvania 19067
Visit our Web site at www.westholmepublishing.com

ISBN: 978-1-59416-379-1
Also available as an eBook.

Printed in the United States of America

For Braddock James

Contents

PART THREE
THE REPUBLIC'S FIRST TESTS (1794–1844)

PART FOUR
THE CIVIL WAR ERA (1861–1865)

PART FIVE

THE MODERN ERA

LIST OF MAPS

Introduction: Scars

Pennsylvania is a battlefield. In many ways, battlefields are like scars on the landscape of a nation. They remind us that history is real and that its effects stay with us forever. They also remind us that no matter how painful they may be at the time, wounds will heal. The pain is temporary and dissipates slowly, and all that replaces it is the memory of the moment itself. The preservation of a battlefield serves many different purposes for the collective national consciousness of a people, but at its core it is all about memory. How do we remember the past? What lessons can we learn from it? How can we avoid those same problems again? History is filled with clichés like "Those who do not know history are doomed to repeat it" and "How can we know where we are going if we do not know where we have been?" Those ideas have merit to be sure, but history is more than a lesson to be learned. History is at its best and most useful when used as a mirror to reflect on ourselves. After all, history does not repeat itself; contingencies exist all around us. But when used properly, it can reveal a great deal about human nature in the face of a momentous decision.

Battlefields are also about competition. Of course, there is the obvious competition between two armies, but there are bigger struggles as well. When the forces of Britain and France met on the battle-ground of North America, they each waged war in the name of a vision, a defense of the future of the continent, not merely the present. The same can be said for the Indian warriors and settlers of the back-country and the striking workers of the industrial age. When the young men of the American Civil War era donned the Butternut and Blue, they were not just fighting over a hill or a railroad junction but in the name of an American future deemed unacceptable by their opponents. While these visions may have been different depending on the time and the place, they all had one stunning feature in common: they were worth killing and dying for. There are few political ideals in the twenty-first century that seem to meet that unthinkable standard—until those ideals are threatened.

When you consider all the battles that took place in the Keystone State over the last three hundred years, it can seem like a constant war was being waged in Pennsylvania. It wasn't. We must remember that by and large, William Penn's dream of establishing a "Peaceable Kingdom" has remained intact. Political debates and neighborly disputes have been present throughout the history of the common-wealth, but battles are not the natural resolution of these conflicts; they are a failure of the system. Understanding how these systems break down and descend into violence and chaos is the most critical purpose of this book. Remember, context is critical to truly under-standing an event. Battles are easily understood with helpful maps and knowledgeable guides familiar with the landscape, but unless we can fit them neatly into a larger story, we can never truly grasp the importance of the moment. This book sets out to fill in those vital details of the battlefields that scar Pennsylvania's landscape.

When I first developed *Battlefield Pennsylvania*, I did so with a clear purpose. I wanted my friends and neighbors to see their home state the same way I did—as a living monument to the past. Rather than viewing its battlefields as places to be visited and forgotten or bypassed altogether, Pennsylvania should be seen as a great inheri-tance provided by past generations. Just as they entrusted it to us, we will entrust it to those who follow us. Only by understanding the full breadth of our history can we truly grasp the magnitude of the legacy we are paying forward. As a lifetime resident of Pennsylvania, I revel in the amazing history that swirls all around us every day, and along with my previous books, *Battlefield Pennsylvania* is another way to share that passion that has become such a special part of my life.

To quote two-time British prime minister Benjamin Disraeli, "When I want to read a book, I write one." I knew that the Pennsylvania Cable Network (PCN) was one of the few broadcasters willing to dedicate hour-long blocks of programming to deep historical topics; I knew this because I watched it regularly. As I perused the recent docket of historical programming on other networks, I saw few options: too short, too vague, and too far out. When history did receive a one-hour show, it was typically given over to the realm of conspiracy and was a great disservice to the brilliant men and women who have dedicated their lives to studying professional history (not to mention the people who fought and died on the battlefield). PCN had a long track record of providing quality programming that was unafraid to dig deep into the archives of the past. When I was offered high-definition cameras, a full crew, and a one-hour time slot, the series *Battlefield Pennsylvania* had found its home.

A person can spend his life studying a historic event using primary sources in archives and carefully preserved survivor accounts, but there is nothing like visiting a battlefield. To see the plunging valley near Bushy Run or the pleasant flow of the Brandywine River offers a perspective that simply cannot be gained from afar. When one steps into the open air and feels the timeless breezes that wash over a battlefield or sees the setting sun, there is the distinct feeling of connection to the past. The commonwealth has over fifty battlefields within a day's drive for anyone from parts of the Midwest, South, and Northeast. While this book does not cover them all, it does include the sites featured in the first three seasons of *Battlefield Pennsylvania*. When it comes to battlefields, being there is important, and having

the chance to visit these sacred sites has been a tremendous honor. I am even more grateful for now having the opportunity to share them with you. Thank you for bringing me along.
Let's hit the road!

Brady J. Crytzer
Pittsburgh, Pennsylvania

PART ONE

THE SEVEN YEARS' WAR ERA (1753–1765)

IN THE EIGHTEENTH CENTURY, North America was a battleground of empires. For much of the previous six centuries, the armies of Great Britain and France had fought wars for political dominance of Europe. As the kingdoms grew into empires, however, so did the scope of their influence. By the seventeenth century, both had added North American colonies to their imperial domains, and they had very different designs for the future of the New World. As colonists and settlers flocked across the North Atlantic to build lives in America, these longtime rivals began to carve out their own realms of control across the continent. The French claimed the St. Lawrence River valley, the Illinois Country, and Louisiana, while the British held near total control of the Atlantic Seaboard with its thirteen colonies. The styles of these empires varied greatly in North America.

The British colonists' vision of empire was one of permanent control through the calculated ownership of land and property. As the colonies grew westward from the East Coast, they engaged in a type of clear-and-hold strategy of influence. For every tree cut down and inch of soil tilled, the British legitimized their claims through deeds and surveyors. With land being held at a premium, the colonists fully intended to keep the area they settled and for their plantations to be permanent additions to the landscape of the New World.

The French, however, had a very different perspective on imperial control and implemented their unique vision differently. They viewed the continent as a wild fortress of impassable mountains, dense forests, and many unknowns. To negotiate these factors, they avoided wasting money and resources on taming the land and instead focused on locating the easiest routes into the heart of the continent. Viewing North America as a type of circulatory system with its heart in the city of Quebec, French forces took advantage of Mother Nature's natural superhighways that already existed: the rivers and lakes of the New World. Placing a special emphasis on sending canoes and bateaux far into the west via this interconnected network of waterways, the agents of New France reached the Rocky Mountains before the British even reached the Appalachians.

Standing in the way of these two competing visions of empire were the people who lived in the New World long before any European ships arrived. The native population of the continent thrived under an ancient, trade-based economic system; if the British or French wanted to truly own North America, it became clear they would need to weave themselves into the complex fabric of the existing Indian world. By the eighteenth century, both empires flooded the backcountry with commercial agents and trade goods, and so started the great race for the control of the western frontier and the future of the continent.

In the middle of the eighteenth century, the rival empires Britain and France were poised to collide in spectacular fashion. For the first time, the English-speaking colonies of the Eastern Seaboard were beginning to spill over the Appalachians, and this development was viewed as a direct threat to New France's existing claims; the most contentious area of conflict was the region of modern western Pennsylvania known as the Ohio Country. With a fortune in trade and the future of the New World at stake, both sides were prepared to go to war to control it.

George Washington's Mission to Fort Le Boeuf

(OCTOBER 31, 1753–JANUARY 16, 1754)

BACKGROUND: In June 1749, a military expedition under the command of Pierre Joseph Celeron de Blainville ventured deep into the Ohioan frontier to claim the contested region for King Louis XV. Celeron buried lead plates along the way at vital intersections of rivers and creeks, and his efforts served as the basis for New France to claim the entire Ohio Country in the emerging 1750s. Fearing the expansion of the British colonies from their coastal hubs along the Atlantic Seaboard, administrators in Quebec undertook the construction of a series of forts in spring 1753 to further solidify their claims. Beginning with Fort Presque Isle near modern Erie, Pennsylvania, building crews pressed farther south to the banks of the French Creek; the fortification completed there would be known as Fort Le Boeuf, the modern site of Waterford, Pennsylvania.

Despite the monumental costs of the project, British officials were not to be outdone. Robert Dinwiddie, colonial governor of Virginia, also sought control of the Ohio Country. As a colonial official and member of the Ohio Company of Virginia, a land-speculation group,

Dinwiddie desired both imperial and financial gains in the disputed region. Remembering his late associate and fellow Ohio Company member Lawrence Washington, Dinwiddie called on Lawrence's twenty-one-year-old younger brother, George, to lead an expedition to the distant Fort Le Boeuf. Once there, his mission was to formally deliver a letter to the French commandant requesting that he abandon the Ohio Country at once. Accompanied by a party of experienced frontiersmen, including Christopher Gist of Maryland, Major Washington left the colonial capital of Williamsburg on October 31, 1753.

BATTLE: On the last day of October, Washington took his first steps on the journey of a lifetime that led to the presidency of the United States. In fall 1753 however, the American republic was only a distant possibility, and the young Virginian was a dedicated follower of King George II. While Washington had only limited experience in the wild, his previous time as a surveyor proved to be invaluable. He was green to be sure, but he had a keen eye for detail and a natural ability to see the potential that a landscape as wild as the Ohio Country had to offer. Although he was determined, ambition alone was not enough to survive the harsh journey ahead. Aiding him on this expedition was a team of scouts led by Christopher Gist. Gist was a hardened frontiersman but by no means a roughneck. He was a member of a prominent Maryland family of considerable wealth, and he, too, had designs on profiting from the tree-covered ridges of the West. Washington kept a detailed journal throughout the nearly three-month expedition, and his commitment to the cause of the Crown was unmistakable.

By November 23, Washington's team had reached the fabled Forks of the Ohio, the site of modern Pittsburgh. He noted in his journal that the location had considerable advantages, most notably its total command of the mouth of the Ohio River. He believed the Ohio to be a superhighway to the interior of the North American continent and suggested the spot as an ideal location for a fort. Indeed, a fort was constructed there, but it was swiftly overtaken by the French and claimed for King Louis XV. Washington was comfortable surveying, but his mission was far greater in scope. Along with taking copious notes on the landscape, the young Virginian was also assigned to foster alliances with the native Ohioan tribes en route to Fort Le Boeuf. His first stop was the bustling village of Logstown.

Washington was new to diplomacy, and he struggled to master the art. Logstown was a tiny village along the Ohio River, and the residence of Tanacharison, the Iroquois half-king. Tanacharison was a throwback; as a representative of the imperial Iroquois, he was the leading viceroy among their Ohioan subjects. Administrators in Virginia believed that winning him to their side would ensure the allegiance of the various native peoples who lived under his jurisdiction. They were wrong. The power of the Iroquois had slipped considerably in the Ohio Country, and the half-king had lost much of the prestige and respect that came with his title. The Shawnee, Delaware, and Mingo had historically been ruled by the Iroquois, but the political grounds within the region were shifting, and neither Washington nor Tanacharison knew what would come next. Despite his waning influence, the half-king steadfastly pledged his hand in friendship to Washington, and in a greater sense, the British Empire.

Tanacharison assembled a party of his own and agreed to accompany the Virginians to their destination. En route to the French fort, the Anglo-Indian force made essential stopovers in a number of important Ohioan villages along the Venango Trail. By far the most critical was the one that bore the same name: the village of Venango. This was a crossroads of the Indian world, and for that reason, agents of New France had frequented the site. It sat at the confluence of the French Creek and the Allegheny River, and the smoking fires of Venango were visible for miles. When Washington arrived on the scene, he received his first taste of French hospitality in the wilderness. Officials in Quebec had planned on constructing a fort at Venango, but by 1753, the lateness of the season literally froze their plans. Instead, they dispatched one of their most prominent diplomats, Philippe Chabert de Joncaire, to the village. On the cold night of December

4, Joncaire invited Washington into his cabin to dine and proceeded to drink himself into a stupor. While he was intoxicated, Joncaire liberally discussed the French plans for the region. In a show of drunken disrespect, he insulted Washington and belittled his countrymen.

Leaving the sour taste of his meeting with Joncaire behind him, Washington and his team set out for Fort Le Boeuf. As was the custom of the time, the British expedition was treated with a modicum of hospitality by the French in the region. While the Virginian described the ground as "good" despite the deep snow and icy streams, their journey was made easier by an escort from Fort Le Boeuf named Michel Pépin, a.k.a. "La Force." La Force was an experienced woodsman and took special care to ensure that the visiting diplomat reached his destination unharmed. Washington described Fort Le Boeuf:

> The Bastions are made of Piles driven into the Ground, and about 12 Feet above, and sharp at Top, with Port-Holes cut for Cannon and Loop-Holes for the small Arms to fire through; there are eight 6 lb. Pieces mounted, two in each Bastion, and one Piece of four Pound before the Gate; in the Bastions are a Guard-House, Chapel, Doctor's Lodging, and the Commander's private Store, round which are laid Plat-Forms for the Cannon and Men to stand on: There are several Barracks without the Fort, for the Soldiers Dwelling, covered, some with Bark, and some with Boards, made chiefly of Loggs: There are also several other Houses, such as Stables, Smiths Shop.[1]

Washington promptly delivered his secretive letter from Governor Dinwiddie. Although he was received kindly by the commandant, a provincial officer from the wilds of western Canada named Jacques Le Gardeur Saint-Pierre, it was made clear that the French were not leaving the Ohio Country. Saint-Pierre gave the Virginians ample supplies for their return voyage and promptly sent them on their way. With his mission now complete, Washington had no idea that the most dangerous part of his journey was about to begin.

---

1. "Journey to the French Commandant: Narrative," *The Diaries of George Washington*, vol. 1, 149.

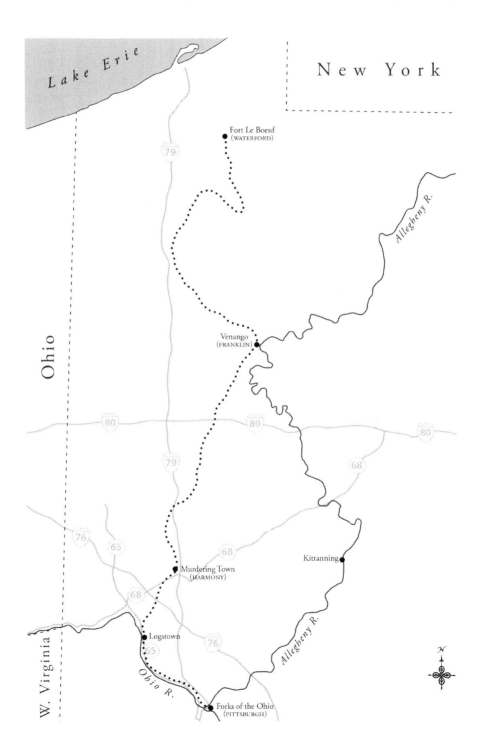

Lake Erie

New York

Fort Le Boeuf
(WATERFORD)

Allegheny R.

Ohio

Venango
(FRANKLIN)

Murdering Town
(HARMONY)

Kittanning

Logstown

Allegheny R.

W. Virginia

Ohio R.

Forks of the Ohio
(PITTSBURGH)

N

To expedite his southward trek, Washington ordered the bulk of his party to stay behind and move supplies while he and Gist pressed forward alone. Washington believed that his return to Williamsburg was urgent and sought any means of shortening the hike whenever possible. On December 27, Washington was approached by an unknown Ohioan guide in the village of Murderingtown. While Gist remained suspicious, the guide offered to show Washington a secret path that would skim days off his journey, and the young man accepted. This was a critical error, for after marching the men hours in the wrong direction, the Indian guide suddenly turned and fired his musket at Washington. The musket ball whizzed harmlessly by, the treacherous guide escaped, and the twenty-one-year-old learned a valuable lesson about naivete in the wilderness.

Just two days later, Washington and Gist reached the banks of the Allegheny River and were crushed to see that it had not frozen over as they hoped. With few options, the two men fashioned a raft out of logs with a single hatchet and proceeded to push themselves across the icy river with long poles; for the second time in three days, Washington's inexperience nearly cost him his life. As they attempted to navigate the flowing waters, Washington lost his footing and plunged into the depths of the Allegheny. Though the water was less than six feet deep, the icy conditions could have been a death sentence in the far-off reaches of the distant frontier. Gist swiftly pulled the hypothermic Washington from the water and pulled him back toward shore. His quick thinking saved the young man's life. On January 16, Major Washington reported back to Governor Dinwiddie in Williamsburg, having survived his first treacherous excursion into the wilderness. It would not be his last.

LEGACY: Although his mission appeared to be unsuccessful, in reality it accomplished precisely what Dinwiddie had hoped. The eighteenth century was an era of gesture politics, and although they could be cumbersome, formalities such as delivering a letter were often deemed essential during the buildup to war. It is unclear whether the inexperienced Washington understood this, but despite his own feelings, he was certainly rewarded for his efforts. On his return to Williamsburg, his detailed journal was published and read across British North America, eventually landing in some newspapers as far away as London. He became a rising star in the elite classes of the Virginia Tidewater and was on the radar of imperial forces an ocean away. More importantly, he was promoted to lieutenant colonel and was sent back into the wilds of the Ohio Country just four months later.

Historians balk at speculation, but Washington's mistakes in western Pennsylvania could have had tremendous consequences in the great span of American history. Had the renegade musket ball of his treacherous Ohioan guide found its mark outside of Murderingtown, or had he not survived his unexpected dip into the icy Allegheny River, George Washington would be only a minor footnote in the greater story of British North America. Washington returned to the Ohio Country in 1754, 1755, 1770, and a final time as president in 1794, but visitors can be assured that the story of George Washington began in the frozen wilds of western Pennsylvania during winter 1753.

WHAT TO SEE: Washington's 1753 journey was vast, giving travelers an excellent opportunity to fuel up and hit the road. Beginning in Pittsburgh's Point State Park, read from Washington's journal describing the land as "extreamly well situated for a fort" and observe the natural advantages granted by the former Forks of the Ohio.[2] Next, travel across the Allegheny to Pittsburgh's North Shore, the former site of Lenape sachem Shingas's encampment. Travel along Route 65 about seventeen miles to Ambridge and the site of the Ohioan village of Logstown. Continue north a few more miles toward Conway, then north to follow the Venango Trail. (A detailed map of modern roadways is provided by the Butler County Tourism and Convention Bu-

2. "Journey to the French Commandant: Narrative," *The Diaries of George Washington*, vol. 1, 149.

Statue of George Washington in British uniform in Waterford, Pennsylvania, at the site of the old Fort Le Boeuf. The statue, dedicated in 1922, commemorates Washington's presentation of a message to the French at this site in 1753 demanding that they leave the Ohio Country. (*PNoble805/Wikimedia Commons*)

reau and is available at www.visitbutlercounty.com.) Continue about fourteen miles along Route 68 to the historic town of Harmony, then a few more miles toward Evans City; although its exact location is disputed, the site of Murderingtown in certainly in this vicinity. Drive north about fifty miles to Franklin and see the location of Venango, taking special care to note the confluence of the Allegheny River and French Creek as seen by Washington 250 years ago. Finally, finish your journey by visiting the Fort Le Boeuf Museum in Waterford, about fifty miles north of Franklin, and view its incredible collection of eighteenth-century frontier artifacts. Across the street you can see the statue of the young wilderness diplomat with letter in hand and the location where we filmed our episode on the 1753 expedition.

2

Firefight at Jumonville Glen

(MAY 28, 1754)

BACKGROUND: In January 1754, the colony of Virginia was preparing for war. Even before George Washington's 1753 mission into the Ohio Country was completed, Governor Robert Dinwiddie decided that provincial forces needed to be proactive to combat the French threat in the region. With French forces preparing to fortify the Indian village of Venango, Dinwiddie sent a newly raised Virginia regiment into the wilderness to establish a fort at the much-desired Forks of the Ohio (modern Pittsburgh.) Under the leadership of Colonel Joshua Fry, the Virginians promptly moved north. Before long disaster struck when Fry died after falling off a horse. Despite the loss, the regiment pressed on toward the forks and began construction on what would be called Fort Prince George or Trent's Fort.

For a brief time, the British held the forks, but that did not last long. On April 18, 1754, nearly one thousand French soldiers under the command of Captain Claude-Pierre Pecaudy de Contrecoeur swept down the Allegheny River valley and captured the British post commanded by Ensign Edward Ward. One hundred miles to the south, at Wills Creek (modern Cumberland, Maryland), Lieutenant

Colonel George Washington acted swiftly. Originally designated to survey a route through the wilderness to aid in Britain's new venture into the Ohio Country, the twenty-two-year-old immediately ordered his 150 men north into the contested area. While he needed reinforcements to make any legitimate stand against the French, he understood the situation to be dire and placed his men on war footing. Though the two massive empires remained at peace, Washington considered these actions by the French to be nothing less than an act of war.

Charles Willson Peale's 1772 portrait of George Washington in his colonel's uniform of the Virginia Regiment. (*Washington and Lee University*)

BATTLE: Despite his inexperience, Washington acted with confidence in late spring 1754. After seeing that the French capture of the Forks of the Ohio had unsettled the entire Ohio Country, the young Virginian moved a force of 159 deep into the region. His motivations were many, but one of the greatest was the direct result of his 1753 mission six months earlier. After forming an alliance with the Iroquois half-king, Tanacharison, Washington realized that each man had mutual interest in halting the French advance. For the half-king, the encroachment of the French meant that his Iroquois order was collapsing. The French were aggressively wooing the Iroquoian subjects to their side, and if the Shawnees, Delawares, and Mingos joined the forces of King Louis, it would result in nothing less than open rebellion in Indian country. Tanacharison understood that Washington's men were the only bulwark against the French conquest of the Ohio Country and that an alliance was critical to save the Indian system that had ruled it for decades.

Some of Washington's motives aligned with Tanacharison's, but not entirely. Washington was an agent of his home colony and, therefore, an agent of the Crown, but he also represented a private business interest. The Ohio Company of Virginia stood to make an untold fortune by surveying and selling plots of land along the frontier, and Washington's late half-brother Lawrence had been a prominent player in the investment firm. Washington was authorized to march his men into the Ohio Country and block any further French advance; even more, he was given permission to "defend the Possessions of his Majesty against the Attempts and Hostilities of the French."[1] Although the point would be minimized or totally missed by later generations, Captain Contrecoeur's hostile attack on Ensign Ward's men at the Forks of the Ohio geared Washington's mind entirely toward the possibility of open warfare in the near future.

The Virginians' potential route of response was limited by the harsh realities of Mother Nature. The Ohio Country was sprawling, and the land between Virginia and the newly established Fort Duquesne was unforgiving. The region of today's southwestern Pennsylvania and western Maryland was spiked with craggy mountains and sudden, pitched valleys. The forest was dense and, in some places, like the legendary Shades of Death, blocked out the sun altogether. Thus, as Washington moved his 159-man force north, his intended target was already decided on. After leaving Wills Creek, the Virginians proceeded to an open gap of clearing in the endless forest known as the Great Meadows. It was a welcome site; the Great Meadows was a natural stretch of prairie that allowed Washington's men the opportunity to rest, rehydrate, and consider their next moves. Although their final targeted destination was the established trading post known as Redstone Fort, the Virginians never arrived there.

By May 24, Tanacharison and his warriors encamped with Washington and his militiamen, but he brought troublesome news. The half-king declared that a sizable French force had recently left Fort Duquesne and was seeking Washington and his men. The French and British armies relied heavily on native spies to gather intelligence

---

1. "Expedition to the Ohio, 1754: Narrative," *Diaries of George Washington*, 174.

on their behalf. To confirm, Washington dispatched a seventy-five man reconnoitering party of his own, which soon left the Great Meadows under the command of Captain Peter Hogg. With almost half his manpower gone, Washington could only sit blindly and await their response.

As night fell on May 27, an Iroquois scout named Silver Heels rushed to Washington and Tanacharison to report that the French were nearby. In recent days they had been spotted at nearby settlements in the Youghiogheny River valley bullying British families under the pretense that the settlers were trespassing in land belonging to New France. Whetting Washington's appetite further, Silver Heels also claimed that the very same enemy army was encamped a mere six miles away in a dark hollow atop Chestnut Ridge. If they were in fact coming to strike Washington, this may have been his best chance to turn the tables on the much larger force. In the wee hours of the morning of May 28, a joint Anglo-Indian force consisting of forty militiamen and a dozen Iroquois warriors slowly crept through the wilds of the Ohio Country to confront their unsuspecting French nemesis for the first time.

What happened next remains lost to history. By most accounts (British, French, and Indian), the Virginians came upon approximately thirty-five French Canadians encamped in a deep gorge. Shots were fired, and a fifteen-minute skirmish ensued. The event was chaotic, but one thing remains certain: the French forces under the command of Ensign Joseph Coulon de Villiers de Jumonville were caught off guard. Taking fire from their rear and left, Jumonville's men rushed forward to escape the melee, only to be met by the warriors of Tanacharison, who charged into the gorge and brutalized their enemies with tomahawks and knives. For Washington it was a total victory, but what was at stake remained to be seen.

In the aftermath of the firefight came more shocking developments. As the survivors sorted out what had occurred, French troops maintained that they were merely a diplomatic party and Washington's attack was an illegal assault on their king and country. Some

The firefight at Jumonville
Glen. The action is sur-
rounded by controversy.
(*New York Public Library*)

sources indicate that Michel Pépin—La Force—was taken prisoner
as a survivor; Pépin is notable for having guided Washington to Fort
Le Boeuf six months earlier. What happened next, though, remains
a watershed moment in the history of the frontier. According to
Washington, the half-king arrested Jumonville and threw him to the
ground. To the young lieutenant colonel's horror, Tanacharison uttered the phrase "Tu ne pas encore mort, mon pere!" ("Thou are not
yet dead, my father") and viciously plunged his tomahawk into the
skull of the young officer. Though Washington did not fully understand it at the time, Tanacharison's macabre gesture was rife with
deep diplomatic and philosophical meaning. "Father" was a custom-
ary title for the French among his Iroquois people, and murdering
Jumonville was a symbolic declaration of war against the empire of
New France.

Washington may not have fully understood the horrifying spec-
tacle that played out that morning, but he knew that it would not
go unpunished.

LEGACY: Until only recently, the firefight at what came to be known
as Jumonville Glen was considered to be of questionable importance
and controversial. During the nineteenth century, historians were reluctant to be critical of George Washington, and many ignored the

event because of its specious nature. However, recent revelations have shown Washington's first true military action to be one of utmost importance.

The mysteries that swirled around the firefight were numerous. Did Washington attack a diplomatic party unprovoked? Were Tanacharison's actions the result of a personal vendetta or were they a greater declaration of war? Who shot first? As is so often the case in history, there did not appear to be a smoking gun to answer these burning questions. However, in 2015, historian David Preston discovered previously unknown documents from Indian warriors present at the firefight that shed new light on the events of May 28, 1754. As part of his research for his book *Braddock's Defeat,* Preston uncovered an account stating that the Virginians and Tanacharison's warriors were to begin their ambush of the French diplomatic party when they heard a signal in the form of a single gunshot. Interestingly, this warrior claimed that the shot was fired by Washington himself

For the last two centuries, the firefight at Jumonville Glen was considered to be at best a misunderstanding, at worst a serious blunder by Washington. But tried-and-true research methods and the dedication of determined historians like David Preston have helped us better understand this important event and answer questions that many thought would remain a mystery forever.

WHAT TO SEE: Jumonville Glen is part of Fort Necessity National Battlefield along Route 40 in Farmington, Pennsylvania. As you drive to the crest of a hill overlooking the city of Uniontown, note the tremendous elevation of the ground and imagine the logistics of moving men, supplies, and pack animals over the difficult terrain. After arriving at Jumonville Glen, read the informational signage at the top of the paved walking trail. Then look immediately to your left to see the trail previously used by guests that has since been converted to a maintenance road. Although the path is paved, be warned: it can be challenging and steep.

Looking down from the Virginians' position at the trail where Jumonville was shot. (*Author*)

Headed down the path, you will see previous generations' monuments and memorials and note how our understanding of the event has changed over time. Once you have reached the bottom of the trail, you are in what is believed to be the site of the firefight itself and the location of the French diplomatic party under Ensign Jumonville. To your left will be a large rock ridge believed to be where the Virginians under Captain Adam Stephen positioned themselves the morning of the battle. Under close inspection, one can see a set of steps carved into the rock face in the early twentieth century that granted visitors a better vantage point of the entire site, but they have since been closed off. To your rear is a much more gradual slope where Washington was believed to have been situated. Finally, in front of you will be a visible narrowing path where Tanacharison and his warriors rushed into the glen to overwhelm the French.

There has never been an adequate archaeological survey of the site, so its authenticity has never been confirmed. Tradition holds that this hollow is the location of the firefight. If genuine, one can marvel at the feeling of total hopelessness when considering the Anglo-Indian attack positions to your left, rear, and front. But tread lightly: French soldiers remain buried on the site, and the soil beneath your feet is their final resting place.

3

The Battle of Fort Necessity

(JULY 3, 1754)

BACKGROUND: By June 1754, the Ohio Country was preparing for war. In April, French forces under the command of Captain Claude-Pierre Pecaudy de Contrecoeur floated down the Allegheny River and forced a team of Virginians off the Forks of the Ohio; for the French, it represented the announcement of a new order on the frontier, but to the colony of Virginia it was an act of war. In response, George Washington, as we read in chapter 2, led 159 men into the wilderness in a show of strength. After establishing a base at Great Meadows, Washington and Iroquois half-king Tanacharison agreed on a plan of aggressive response to the growing French threat in the region. For the young Virginian, options were limited. He was given permission by Governor Robert Dinwiddie to confront French Canadian troops in the area, and it was recommended that he respond with force if they resisted his efforts. Although both sides seemed primed for conflict, these measures were unprecedented given that the empires of France and Great Britain were, and remained, at peace.

On May 27, Washington and Tanacharison received a valuable piece of intelligence stating that a French war party had departed

Fort Duquesne at the Forks of the Ohio and were headed in Washington's direction. Almost certainly viewing the Virginians as invaders, the French command under Ensign Joseph Coulon de Villiers de Jumonville proceeded through the forests, stopping at times to hassle and bully isolated British settlers they encountered. Finally, on May 28, the proactive strategy agreed on by Washington and Tanacharison was put into action. After finding the French war party encamped in a deep hollow on Chestnut Ridge, the Anglo-Indian force attacked. After a fifteen-minute firefight against an unsuspecting enemy, Washington was victorious. He soon departed for the Great Meadows to await a larger French response.

BATTLE: With the firefight at Jumonville Glen now complete, Lieutenant Colonel Washington had to prepare for the retaliatory strike that was all but certain to come from Fort Duquesne. He sent his men back to the Great Meadows, where the Virginia militia traded their muskets for picks, axes, and saws. Working around the clock in shifts, the men completed a fortification in less than a week, finalizing what would be known as Fort Necessity on June 3. Never in the history of colonial America had a post been more aptly named. It was primitive, even by frontier standards, and consisted of a circular wooden stockade of fallen trees surrounding a basic, cabin-like structure that served as a makeshift storehouse for powder and supplies. To further fortify the position, the men built earthworks around the outer perimeter to provide necessary cover and defensive maneuvering. Fort Necessity was insufficient by every measure, but given the circumstances, it was Washington's best effort.

The situation evolved rapidly. Shortly after the completion of the fort, the remainder of the Virginia regiment arrived to bolster Washington's numbers. But with these new soldiers came unexpected news: Colonel Joshua Fry had suffered a broken neck after falling from his horse, and his untimely demise suddenly catapulted Washington to the rank of colonel in his stead. With the weight of an upcoming engagement already on his shoulders, the newly minted colonel apparently had command of almost three hundred men. A short time later, a party of British regulars from South Carolina arrived on-site under the command of Captain James Mackay. Despite being on the same side, the redcoats clearly attempted to separate themselves from the provincial militias, and the two forces rarely mixed. It appeared that with a total force of nearly four hundred troops, Washington and Mackay would command their own parties separately.

Part of Washington's original mission was to expand a road that connected the Potomac River to the Monongahela River. Even under the threat of an oncoming invasion, Washington believed that completion of this objective would be a great boon to his overall mission. On June 16, he ordered his men to focus on the expansion toward Redstone Creek Fort, and he remained there for the next two weeks. Washington implored his Indian allies to remain at his side for the fight to come, but to no avail. Considering the meager defenses at Fort Necessity, the various sachems of the Ohio Country concluded it would be foolhardy to fight alongside the Virginians. Despite their reluctance, Washington was given a unique assurance from the Delaware Shingas, an old acquaintance from his 1753 expedition. Washington later wrote, "Though King Shingas, and others of the Delawares could not be persuaded to retire to our camp with their families . . . they nevertheless gave us strong assurance of their assistance and directed us in what manner to act in order to obtain our desire. . . . King Shingas promised to take privately the most subtle measures to make the affair succeed though he did not dare do it openly."[1] Time would reveal precisely how Shingas would aid the colonel.

By the end of June, the French had mobilized out of Fort Duquesne. Approximately six hundred French Canadians and one hundred Indian allies from myriad nations expertly made their way through the treacherous terrain of the Ohio Country. At the head of

1. *George Washington,* ed. J. M. Toner (Albany, NY: 1893), 123.

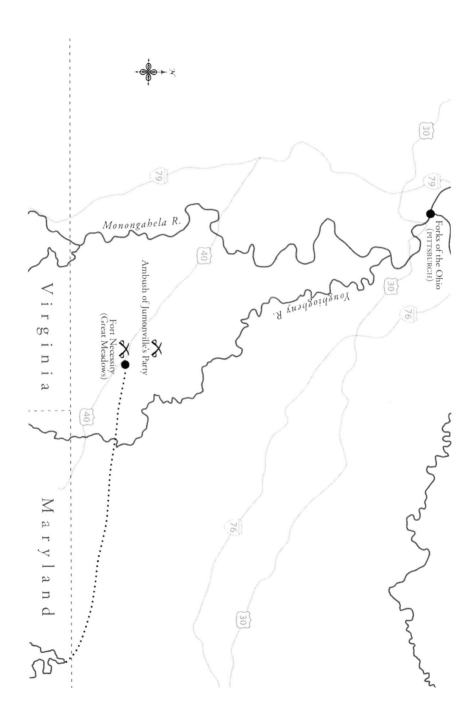

Forks of the Ohio
(PITTSBURGH)

Monongahela R.

Youghiogheny R.

Ambush of Jumonville's Party

Fort Necessity
(Great Meadows)

Virginia

Maryland

The modern reconstruction of Fort Necessity. Fort Necessity was aptly named . . . it was all that Washington could muster to defend against the French. (*National Park Service*)

the column was Louis Coulon de Villiers, the brother of the slain Ensign Jumonville. Washington correctly predicted that a response force would come following the events of May 28, but he could not have predicted that the murdered officer's brother would personally lead the charge. By July 1, Washington rallied his men hurriedly back to Fort Necessity, and it appeared that their fateful stand was about to take place.

Washington's men were badly undersupplied and terribly isolated. They lacked even basic provisions and hardly had enough powder for even a tolerable defensive stand. To illustrate the desperation of the Virginians' situation, the entire regiment had only three "worms" among them. This vital tool was a standard piece of equipment used to extract a musket ball from a gun that failed to fire. On July 2, a heavy rainstorm poured onto the Great Meadows and swamped Fort Necessity. Washington realized that the French were likely to hide in the tree line during the engagement; they would stay dry, and the British would be soaked to the bone. In a flash decision, the colonel ordered his men to build wooden breastworks atop the existing earthworks as an added defensive measure (two centuries later this decision befuddled archaeologists working at the site). Ready or not, Fort Necessity would have to be enough to hold off the oncoming French attack.

Early in the morning of July 3, Villiers and his men reached the site that would become known as Jumonville Glen. He saw mutilated bodies and a Frenchman whose head had been cut off by an Ohioan warrior and placed on a spike in a grizzly display. He spent the dawn hours mourning his countrymen and burying their bodies. By 11:00 AM, the French had arrived at the Great Meadows, and Villiers promptly ordered his men to march toward the fort. When he paused the advance to adjust its approach, Washington immediately saw an opportunity to order his men to meet them in the field. Villiers recognized the importance of staying under cover and aligned his men within the safety of the trees, where they could fire rounds into Fort Necessity at will. Washington responded in turn by ordering his men to form a line in the open field in an effort to remove the enemy from its protected position, but the rifts that existed within the British forces revealed themselves at a most inopportune time. Mackay's regulars stayed with Washington in the meadow, but his ill-trained Virginians scrambled for the safety of Fort Necessity. Washington was now badly outnumbered because of the insubordination of his men and could only fall back in the face of seven hundred Franco-Indian enemies. As the afternoon dragged into evening, Fort Necessity was pummeled by rainfall and gunfire, and the men inside became resigned to their fate. Some drank heavily, and others disobeyed their superior officers with little regard for traditional decorum. Finally, as midnight came, the French commander Villiers unexpectedly called for Washington to surrender, and the dejected and demoralized colonel accepted.

LEGACY: Washington was not aware of it at the time, but Fort Necessity revealed one of Tanacharison's and Shingas's last-ditch efforts at maintaining peace and relevance in the Ohio Country. As Louis Coulon de Villiers assaulted the British from the cover of the forest, he was repeatedly told by Ohioan spies that the sounds of drums could be heard in the distance. He was further informed that a large force of British reinforcements was approaching. Knowing that he could outmatch Washington's men but running too low on dry powder to compete with reinforcements, he decided that asking for the young Virginian's surrender was the best way to affirm his victory. Unbeknownst to the French commander, he was being intentionally deceived by the Ohioans, and no such reinforcement was coming. The scheme saved the Virginians and momentarily kept the French at bay. In the end, the Battle of Fort Necessity was a hard learning experience for Washington and Villiers regarding life on the American frontier.

Washington's defeat at Fort Necessity further advanced New France's efforts in the Ohio Country, but only slightly. When Washington signed the terms of surrender on July 4, 1754, he did so with the honors of war. This meant the colonel could return to Virginia with his men, flags, banners, and baggage. As a stipulation, they turned over their swivel guns. As Washington could not read French, he only loosely understood the document he signed that rainy night in the forest. While he did not know it at the time, he affixed his signature to a document that fully admitted to the "assassination" of Ensign Jumonville in May, and though Washington later denied it, the document became a critical piece of propaganda in the emerging blame game preceding the Seven Years' War.

WHAT TO SEE: The Fort Necessity Battlefield in Farmington, Pennsylvania, is a genuine treasure. Encompassing a state-of-the-art museum and interpretative facility along with the sprawling battlefield itself, the park offers guests a truly immersive experience. Included in the interpretative center are numerous models, dioramas, life-size statues, and maps that help explain the entire colonial period in the Ohio Country. Exit the back of the facility and follow the paved walking trail into the trees and you'll be rewarded with the stunning appearance of a reconstructed Fort Necessity as it looked in 1754. Archaeologists and historic builders took special care to reconstruct the fortification according to accounts written during the battle, but that was not always the case.

The state-of-the-art Fort Necessity Interpretive and Education Center is a must see for any visitor. (*National Park Service*)

For much of the twentieth century, Fort Necessity was interpreted to look like a traditional log cabin, despite period sources stating otherwise. Then, following an archaeological survey, the post was reconstructed in the shape of a large, square quadrilateral. This raised immediate objections from historians, as all of the firsthand accounts described Fort Necessity as a circular stockade. As the debate continued, further archaeology proved the historians correct. When the archaeological survey was undertaken, large timbers were found buried underground. Traditionally believed to be the original outer walls of a stockade, they were later discovered to be merely wooden breastworks built in support of the earthworks that encompassed the post itself. Sure enough, later studies found the imprint of the 1754 round stockade, leading to the reconstruction of the post as it appears now. Take special care to observe the tree line that envelopes the site; this does not match the eighteenth-century tree line, but the National Park Service has worked tirelessly to restore it to its original position by planting saplings.

4

The Battle of the Monongahela

(JULY 9, 1755)

BACKGROUND: The defeat at Fort Necessity sent shock waves through the British world and became a major force of change in the developing conflict. Until George Washington's surrender, the struggle against New France had been largely executed by colonial forces in North America, while the administration of the British Empire was only nominally involved. After Fort Necessity, however, the British played a much more direct role in guiding the war effort, as it appeared that a major conflict was about to occur. Because the British and French empires were global entities, the coming conflict would truly be a world war. King George II wasted no time getting the upper hand. In 1755, Major General Edward Braddock landed on North American shores with two Irish regiments; it seemed that what had started as a battle between the provincial powers of Virginia and New France had escalated to a new level.

Braddock was an experienced commander. At sixty years old, he had a long record of service to the British Crown and a reputation as a no-nonsense tactician. He was soon granted the title of commander in chief of all British forces in North America and became an integral cog in a massive war machine to wrest the continent away from the French. By striking at critical French posts across the Northeast, British policymakers believed that New France could be severely diminished in the event of a major global conflict; Braddock's role in this stratagem was to lead an army into the wilderness and reclaim the Forks of the Ohio in the name of Britannia.

BATTLE: Braddock's March on Fort Duquesne and eventual demise has become a sort of tragic mythology, but up until the very moment of his defeat, he had accomplished one of the great acts of modern military history. In order to move his two thousand one hundred men and enormous supply train from the settled plains of Virginia into the heart of the wild frontier, he needed to navigate some of the most treacherous lands on earth. Even more, he needed to move at a snail's pace to carve out an effective military road to further open the frontier. His column of men understood that if they survived the tremendously difficult march dragging along cannons and supplies, taking Fort Duquesne would be all but certain. There was no way they could have understood how horribly wrong they were, but it must be clear that until the very end, there existed a general sense of triumphant resolve among his entire force.

Using Fort Cumberland (modern Cumberland, Maryland) as a staging point, Braddock's army began its historic trek on May 29, 1755. The aspiring Virginian George Washington was present, one year and one day having passed since his firefight at Jumonville Glen. The land that stood between Braddock and his intended target of Fort Duquesne shocked his men; Highland Scotsmen marching compared the tree-covered peaks and valleys of the Ohio Country to an extreme version of their home country. The logistics of moving such a force as Braddock's were mind-boggling, but the army pushed forward at a pace that few expected. The most impressive aspect of the fabled march was its ability to drag heavy artillery through the mountains. Fort Duquesne was but a pittance compared to the large stone fortresses of New York and Canada. Prevailing wisdom was

A nineteenth-century illustration of Gen. Edward Braddock's troops marching through the Pennsylvania wilderness. The column built the road as they progressed toward Fort Duquesne. (*New York Public Library*)

that a single piece of heavy artillery would effectively neutralize the post; Braddock brought more than two dozen.

From the outset of the march, the general remained focused on managing his army's pacing. With 1,350 British regulars from the 44th and 48th Regiments of Foot, he rounded out his army with approximately five hundred troops from across British North America. Not only was Braddock's March a legendary feat, but it was one of the first truly pancolonial armies ever assembled on the continent. As his force approached the ruins of the year-old Fort Necessity at the Great Meadows, Braddock elected to split his army into two parts. The first consisted of one thousand three hundred men arranged in a "flying column" to move more quickly toward Fort Duquesne, while the second body marched more slowly with the supplies and draft animals. As they marched, they exchanged fire with French-allied warriors from the Great Lakes region; Braddock knew that with the element of surprise gone, at least he could shock them with his army's speed.

The situation at Fort Duquesne was one of readiness. As the French were still wooing the Ohioan peoples to their side, many re-

An early twentieth-century photograph of Braddock's Road showing the dense forest and undergrowth that confronted Braddock's expedition. (*Library of Congress*)

mained unconvinced. Therefore, nearly seven hundred warriors from across North America arrived in a show of solidarity. Men from a variety of tribal nations of the Great Lakes, or Pays d'en Haut (Upper Country), came in droves, and despite being far from home, they made up the vast majority of native warriors who would participate in the upcoming battle at the Monongahela River. If the battle went their way, French agents hoped, the Shawnees, Delawares, and Mingos could be persuaded to join their cause and give New France an iron grip over the future of the Ohio Country.

By July 9, the British force was within ten miles of Fort Duquesne. Having mastered some of the most dangerous and difficult terrain on the planet, Braddock's army approached the Forks of the Ohio like conquering Caesars. Their remaining obstacle to reaching the post and delivering a killing blow was a duel river crossing of the Monongahela. With over two thousand people in Braddock's army, the British line of march stretched for miles in a narrow formation. Despite never having been to the Ohio Country before, the major general recognized that this river crossing would be his most vulnerable position of the entire campaign. As the vanguard of the army

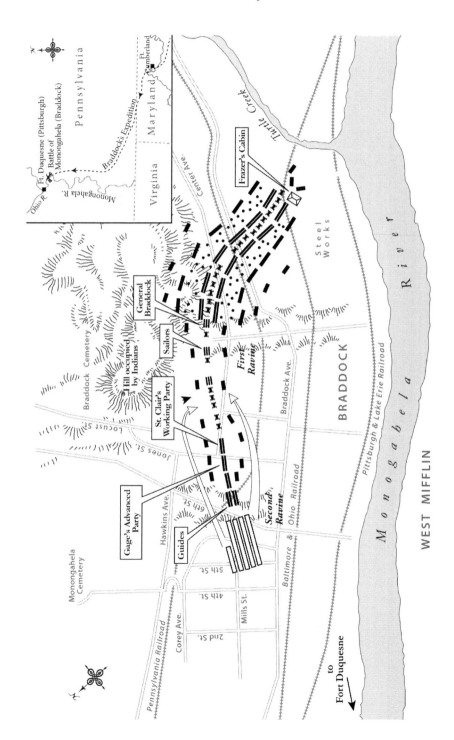

A nineteenth-century French illustration depicting the Battle of the Monongahela. Braddock's troops were decimated by a combined French and Indian force just miles from their destination. Note the musket fire from the cover of the woods.

reached the northern bank of the river, they began to ascend the heights that overlooked the valley. It was at this moment that disaster struck, and the Battle of the Monongahela began. As the forward soldiers reached a piece of high ground overlooking a ravine, they unexpectedly collided head on with a charging group of Frenchmen and their native allies. Though this moment would often be called an ambush, it was no such thing. Each army was caught off guard by the other, and combat began as a classic meeting engagement.

The battle quickly turned into a chaotic rout of the British. As the redcoats at the front tried in vain to establish a defensive line, the remainder of the army still filed unknowingly across the river. While the French played by the traditional rules of European warfare and lined up across from their enemies to exchange volleys of fire, the Indian warriors immediately took to the trees and situated themselves along the right and left flanks of the confused British. Now positioned skillfully in the cover of the trees, the warriors poured fire into the British column from the sides rather than from the front as Braddock anticipated. The veteran Englishmen had never experienced frontier warfare and had little answer for this new development. As the command fell apart, the Great Lakes peoples began to skillfully target the officer corps of their enemy, and without the necessary command structure in place, Braddock's entire venture fell to pieces.

It was in these moments that George Washington received numerous musket balls through his coat and even through his hat; miraculously, he suffered no injuries. In a revealing moment, the American provincials took to the trees to mirror the Indian fighting style that was so effective on the frontier, but the rigid tactical adherence of their British officers offered no support. With the tide turned well against them, the British turned in retreat, only to collide with their advancing rearguard. It was a scene of utter chaos, and all the while, the Great Lakes warriors inflicted more damage. Braddock was wounded during the battle and died shortly after. In a final desperate effort, the once-triumphant British army turned and ran in a disorganized retreat. The warriors of the Great Lakes put their stamp on the great victory by plundering all that remained on-site. Wounded were killed, supplies spoiled, trophies taken, and the greatest British force to ever march through the wilderness of North America was reduced to a pile of smoking wreckage along the banks of the Monongahela River.

LEGACY: Braddock's Defeat, as the event came to be known, was a linchpin moment in the history of the frontier and a stinging low point in British military history. From the French perspective, the victory gave them an unimpeachable sense of domination over the Ohio Country. They expanded their fortification efforts at Fort Duquesne and funneled a fortune's worth of trade goods onto the Ohio River and west toward the Illinois Country and Louisiana. The natives of the region also realized the importance of the Battle of the Monongahela, and many in the region saw it as undeniable proof that joining the French would be a winning proposition. For the British, the lessons of the Monongahela were many, and they were learned the hard way.

One of the steep streets in modern Braddock with the ridge line in the background. (*Thomas Crocker*)

The number of young officers and soldiers who participated in the fight and went on to illustrious military careers is impressive. Thomas Gage, who commanded British forces in North America at the start of the American Revolution, was there. The provincials were even more impressive, though: George Washington, Charles Lee, Daniel Morgan, Horatio Gates, and Daniel Boone all cut their teeth in the bloody melee, and all became legends in the decades that followed.

Aside from the deep roster on hand, Braddock's collapse also revealed some difficult truths. Had Braddock deviated from his inflexible interpretation of traditional warfare, he may have had a chance. Had he only allowed the provincials to fight in the manner they preferred, a wild guerrilla style considered deeply offensive to the sensibilities of the strait-laced major general, he might have survived. The logistical and diplomatic fallout was equally damaging. The victorious French captured all of Braddock's heavy artillery and used it in the years to come; they also recovered his headquarters papers revealing major British plots against New France despite the peaceful status between the two countries. Braddock himself died of wounds suffered along the Monongahela, and despite his long career of service, his legacy was defined there.

WHAT TO SEE: In the words of one visitor, "if this battlefield was in a nicer area, it would be one of the most visited in the country." Today the battlefield sits under the modern steel town of Braddock, Pennsylvania. Braddock has fallen on hard times with the loss of the steel industry, but this tough city embodies the spirit of the men who fought on its grounds more than 260 years ago. Braddock's streets are going through a renaissance of sorts and are quite walkable, but its steep hills are the same ones the major general's army trekked in 1755. The highlight of the battlefield is without question the Braddock Battlefield History Center on Sixth Street. Founded by Robert Messner, a retired attorney and devoted historian, the facility is situated directly at the point of first contact between British and Franco-Indian forces on July 9, 1755. As recounted by eyewitnesses, the combatants first met on opposite sides of a creek bed; standing in the history center parking lot, one can still see the path of that stream in the form of a modern culvert. Likewise, directly across Sixth Street, one can see a rising piece of ground ten to fifteen feet above street level. Using the mind's eye to eliminate a modern high rise that currently occupies it, the elevated ground that is mentioned by period sources as being used by an advanced British guard is still visible. The history center is filled with archaeological remnants from the engagement and even houses a document signed by King George. Take a quick stroll to Jones Avenue to view noted sculptor Frank Vittor's statue of a determined George Washington standing tall over the battlefield. For the adventurous, be sure to purchase Norman L. Baker's book *Braddock's Road,* which will allow you to follow the 289-mile route from Alexandria, Virginia, to the fateful conclusion at the Monongahela.

5

The Kittanning Raid

(SEPTEMBER 8, 1756)

BACKGROUND: In the aftermath of Braddock's Defeat, the Ohio Country went through a political transformation. British influence among its native peoples was virtually erased, and the war machine of New France flooded its freshly allied Ohioan warriors with goods, weapons, and powder. For the Shawnees, Delawares, and Mingos of the Ohio Country, an alliance with New France represented a way to escape from the imperial yoke of the Iroquois; as their "masters" would certainly side with the British, the French were the only true route to freedom for the Ohioans. In October 1755, the Ohioans finally took up the hatchet with the French, and the Pennsylvania settlement of Penn's Creek was devastated and burned as a result. Over the next year and a half, Ohioan raiding parties terrorized the Pennsylvania frontier, kidnapping dozens and killing hundreds more. Indian combat was terrible and brutal, and the frontier became a nightmarish wasteland when the natives took to the warpath.

Pennsylvanians stood aghast at news of atrocities coming from the west, and most believed that the large village of Kittanning (Kit-ha-nee, or "at the Great Stream") was the origin of the Ohioan raiders.

The frontiers demanded revenge, but the politics of colonial Pennsylvania stalled the measure. Because the colony was founded by nonviolent Quakers in the 1680s, William Penn's Peaceable Kingdom never had a standing army before. Creating one was a fight in itself, a struggle I write about in my book *War in the Peaceable Kingdom*. Finally, as death tolls mounted along the frontier, both parties compromised in August 1756. Colonel John Armstrong of Carlisle was selected to lead three hundred Pennsylvania frontiersmen into the west at the helm of the colony's first true armed militia, and their target was Kittanning.

BATTLE: John Armstrong was not a military leader but a numbers man. He was the surveyor general of Pennsylvania, and his military service consisted of overseeing the construction of a road in support of Braddock's expedition a year earlier. The road was never finished, but Armstrong did learn a great deal about crossing the wilderness of the Ohio Country. As the Scots-Irish of the frontier had suffered most of the losses at the hands of Kittanning's Ohioan warriors, colonial administrators believed that a Scots-Irish commander would drive recruitment efforts to build Pennsylvania's first military force. Given his experience and the fact that he was born in Ireland, Armstrong was the natural choice to lead. He hoped to raise seven companies totaling 350 men by late August, but he was disappointed that he mustered only three hundred volunteers. Many farmers were hesitant to leave their families unguarded to march into the dark frontier, and others worried that given the lateness of the season, their harvest would suffer. By the time the expedition began its march on August 31, Armstrong believed his men to be nothing more than a motley collection of unemployed scoundrels.

Armstrong's penchant for logistics was a great boon to his command. Knowing that no east-west road existed from the Allegheny Mountains into the Ohio Country, he instead opted to follow existing Indian hunting paths. He could have taken the Raystown Path, which offered a shorter route to Kittanning but over much more un-

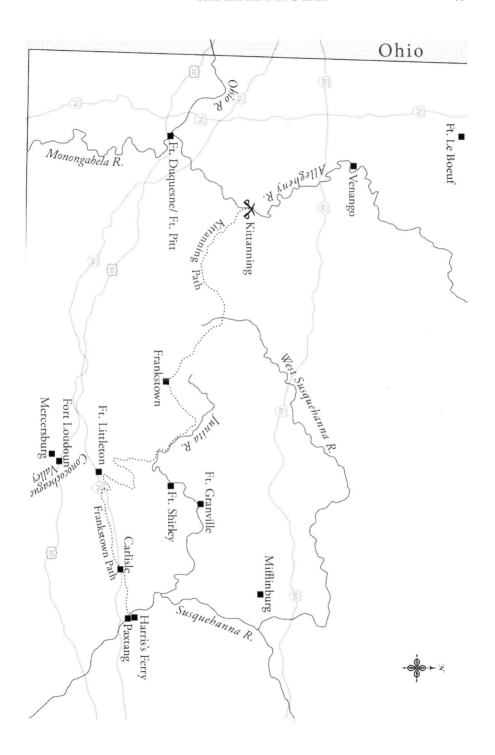

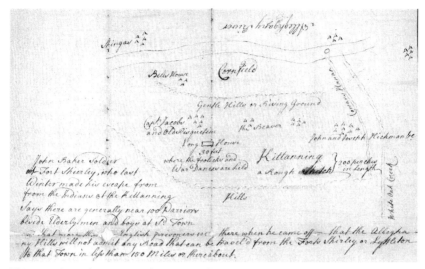

This map drawn by an escaped captive is the only illustration we have of Kittanning in 1756. The Allegheny River is at the top. Shingas's settlement is located in the upper left opposite the large cornfield between the river and Kittanning. The settlements of Captain Jacobs (Tewea), the Beaver (Tamaqua), and "Delaware Jo" Hickman are identified from left to right, as well as the village's Long House. (*American Philosophical Society*)

even terrain. Instead, he elected to take the Frankstown Path. The latter was longer but mostly on level ground; he fully anticipated being ambushed en route and preferred to fight on flatter land. During the dark morning hours of September 7, Armstrong's three-hundred-man column had slunk its way to the Allegheny River valley and prepared for their assault. To his astonishment, it seemed that Kittanning's population had no idea he was coming. The Pennsylvanians hoped to execute a raid using the same tactics that had been used against their frontier settlements so effectively. They hoped to strike fast before dawn, rescue as many hostages as possible, round up the suspected ringleaders of the raids, and burn down the village. Armstrong depended wholly on the element of surprise and wanted no part of an extended firefight. With Kittanning in striking distance, Armstrong's men came upon a small party of warriors sitting around a campfire. If they had seen the militiamen, they would have alarmed others and disrupted the entire operation. As a precaution, Armstrong left a small detachment of troops behind under the command of Lieutenant James Hogg with instructions not to attack until the main operation began in the valley below.

If Armstrong was bothered by his enlistees' shortcomings, he was driven mad by the slowness of his approach to Kittanning. Because they were moving in darkness, the men were slowed by fallen trees and rocks that littered the forest floor; by the time they reached Kittanning, the sun had already risen. Starting the raid in the cornfield that ran parallel to the Allegheny River, Armstrong's men charged into the village as a ferocious blur. Most of the Indian warriors were indeed caught off guard, but the untrained frontiersmen scrambled to capitalize on their surprise attack. In the minutes after the raid began, Kittanning residents began moving their white captives across the Allegheny to the eastern bank. Waiting there were approximately sixty French soldiers from Fort Duquesne to aid in the captives' removal deeper into the Ohio Country. It seemed that the primary objective of Armstrong's raid would be its first failure.

Seven miles away, at a place that would be known as Blanket Hill because of the militia's decision to stash their packs on-site, Lieutenant Hogg began his secondary assault on the Indians who had been sitting around a fire along the path to Kittanning. Questions remain about what happened, but according to sources, Hogg charged what he believed to be only four warriors. In a drastic miscalculation, there were actually many more warriors nearby, and Hogg was soon overwhelmed. After an hour-long fight, many of his men simply fled, and Hogg was killed in the skirmish.

Several high-value targets lived at Kittanning who had bounties on their heads, most notably Shingas and a younger sachem named Tewea (also known as Captain Jacobs). Armstrong hoped to capture both men, but Shingas appeared to be absent from the village on the morning of September 8. Tewea was home at the time, and his fighting ability lived up to his reputation. As the shock of the Pennsylvanians' initial assault wore off, Ohioan warriors skillfully took cover in their log cabins to hold off their attackers. Just as Colonel Armstrong feared, the shock raid devolved into a long, drawn-out fire-fight. Kittanning had long been used a staging ground for Ohioan attacks on the Pennsylvania backcountry, and French agents out of Fort Duquesne had stockpiled weapons, gunpowder, and supplies at the village. Since the bulk of French troops were busy fighting the British in upstate New York and along the Canadian border, admin-istrators of New France depended on the Ohioans to wreak havoc in Pennsylvania as an extension of their own greater war effort. When the Pennsylvania militiamen exchanged fire with Tewea and his war-riors at Kittanning, they were shocked to discover large kegs of gun-powder stored in the homes of the village residents. For this reason, Armstrong ordered his men to set fire to the cabins of Kittanning in an effort to ignite the gunpowder. Shortly after Tewea's home was set ablaze, he boldly shouted that he could "eat fire,"[1] and his cabin sud-denly exploded, killing everyone inside. One by one the cabins at Kittanning began to ignite, and before long the Pennsylvanians watched from the cover of the forest as the village was reduced to ashes.

LEGACY: The Kittanning Raid was lauded as a great triumph for Pennsylvania, and more importantly, the British Crown. Kittanning itself was left in a pile of smoking ruins and never recovered, but the raid was far less effective than it first appeared to be. Pennsylvania's first military unit was a watershed moment in the history of what has been called William Penn's Holy Experiment, but it provided mixed results. The primary objective of Armstrong's raid was to res-cue the 150 hostages being held in the Allegheny River valley, but only seven were saved. Compounding the controversy was the fact that after Kittanning was burned, its resident warriors simply moved to other Ohio Country villages, including Venango (Franklin, Penn-sylvania), Logstown (Ambridge, Pennsylvania), Sawcunk (Rochester,

---

1. Robert Robison's testimony, in Archibald Loudon, *A Collection of Some of the Narratives of Outrages Committed by the Indians in the Wars with the White People, Vols. 1* (London: Loudon, 1808), 249.

Pennsylvania), and Kuskuskies (New Castle, Pennsylvania). In fact, over the next year, Indian raids along the Pennsylvania frontier actually increased, although the number of casualties did drop.

Despite these incontrovertible figures, the Kittanning Raid was lauded throughout the colonies as a major achievement on the frontier. With war officially declared between Britain and France in May 1756, the British populace desired immediate victories over

The commemorative medal presented to the Kittanning raiders by the city of Philadelphia. (*The State Museum of Pennsylvania*)

France, but they would not come. From 1756 to 1757, the British lost a series of important battles across five continents; the period was so dark that many called it "the Years of Defeat." Suddenly, with news of a successful raid in the depths of the American frontier, a spark of hope came to life, and that glimmer of light became a shining beacon to the men and women of the English-speaking world. Armstrong himself doubted the true impact of his attack on Kittanning, but the political agents of British North America propagandized it into a momentous event. A ceremony was held for the officer corps, Armstrong was considered a heroic conqueror, and the first military medal ever produced in North America was awarded in the raid's name.

WHAT TO SEE: The village of Kittanning is gone. It was destroyed that fateful day in September 1756. The modern town of Kittanning now stands in its place, and there are some distinct clues that allow the battlefield to reveal itself to travelers. Make your first destination Riverside Park, where the course of the Allegheny River remains roughly in place from the 1750s. Turn your gaze into town and take note of the three large, craggy hills that overlook the site; this is where Colonel Armstrong rallied his men after the raid had ended and where he watched the village burn. Across the river is a small settlement called West Kittanning, which was the location of the French soldiers who supported the Ohioans during the attack. Several markers and monuments run the length of Riverside Park, and one can take them all in during a leisurely stroll along its walking paths.

After leaving downtown Kittanning, drive on Route 422 East about seven miles until you encounter a blue Pennsylvania Historical and Museum Commission sign indicating the site of Blanket

The blue Pennsylvania Historical and Museum Commission markers are vital for navigating the Kittanning Raid battlefield. (*Author*)

Hill. The berm is very narrow and traffic is swift, but this is the site of the secondary skirmish between the forces of Lieutenant Hogg and the Kittanning warriors that occurred during the main portion of the battle. There is also a sizable stone marker placed by the Daughters of the American Revolution in 1934 commemorating the occasion. Like so many of Pennsylvania's Seven Years' War sites, the landscape is the battlefield, so take special care to seek out landforms and features that were mentioned by historic figures and proved decisive in their own time.

6

The Battle of Fort Duquesne

(SEPTEMBER 14, 1758)

BACKGROUND: From 1756 to 1757, Great Britain was losing the Great War for Empire, or Seven Years' War, across the globe. Stakes had never been higher in England, and political upheaval came in the form of William Pitt, Earl of Chatham. Upon his rise to leader of the House of Commons and secretary of state, Pitt promised a relentless war effort against New France that would stem the tide of defeat. As part of Pitt's new commitment to victory, Scottish brigadier general John Forbes was tasked with doing what the late Edward Braddock could not: capture Fort Duquesne. Given approximately six thousand soldiers, Forbes decided not to repeat the mistakes of his predecessor and elected to build a new road of his own into the depths of the Ohio Country. Despite his willingness to innovate, Forbes quickly discovered that the politics of colonial America were deep and passionate. Because he decided to build his road out of Carlisle, Pennsylvania, and not one of the major cities of Virginia, tensions arose among his command throughout the march. Both the Peaceable Kingdom and the Old Dominion fully planned on claiming the Ohio Country as their own after the war, and this choice was a perceived slight to Virginia and a show of favoritism toward Pennsylvania. Forbes's march was filled with important figures from both colonies. Among Virginia's many officers was Colonel George Washington, a rising star and local celebrity, who prepared to lead troops into the Ohio Country for a fourth time. A combination of wounded pride and clashing egos added yet another wrinkle to the logistical challenges faced by the Scottish general.

While he all but promised victory, Forbes did not guarantee expediency. Unlike Braddock, the Scotsman decided to carve out a road that would be wide and permanent. At specific intervals, he ordered the construction of fortifications to further solidify his hold over the region and bolster his cause. This included small stopover posts like Fort Dewart in the Allegheny Mountains, as well as much greater strong houses like Fort Ligonier on Loyalhanna Creek. Although it was slow going, it allowed for men and supplies to freely flow west in support and virtually guaranteed that the isolated post of Fort Duquesne would wilt upon Forbes's arrival. The Forbes Campaign worked throughout the heat of the summer, and by September his army had closed in on its target.

BATTLE: John Forbes was known as "Iron Head" among the native peoples of the Ohio Country, and he was a dedicated soldier, but by September he was in dire straits. His column was the greatest fighting force to ever march into the dark valleys of the frontier, but the brigadier general was slowly dying. When Forbes first launched his campaign against Fort Duquesne, he was not feeling well, and in time, the rigors of the frontier only exacerbated the symptoms of what was likely an advancing form of cancer. By the time his men reached Fort Bedford (site of the modern-day city of Bedford), he was so ill that he needed to be carried on a litter. For all of his personal obstacles, though, he encouraged his men to press onward, and he had full faith in his officer corps. By far his most trusted commander was Lieutenant Colonel Henry Bouquet, and as Forbes slowly deteriorated, he gave him more and more responsibility. Bou-

Pittsburgh's Point State Park was the home to a number of eighteenth-century forts, including Fort Duquesne, whose outline can be seen in the park. (*Author*)

quet was not British but Swiss. He was a mercenary in the British army and was the fine type of soldier only produced on continental Europe. Flexible, sharp, and dedicated, Bouquet had no problem taking up the mantle of command when his general began to slip away.

As the British forces moved west, inching closer and closer to Fort Duquesne, they continued to build impressive fortifications. Along Loyalhanna Creek, construction was under way on what would be called Fort Ligonier. From Bouquet's best estimates, this new post rested approximately fifty miles from the Forks of the Ohio, and he desired a full intelligence briefing before he was willing to move Forbes's six thousand men toward their destination. To gather information and scout out French strength at the forks, Bouquet called up Major James Grant of Ballindalloch, Scotland, to lead the reconnoitering party. Grant took with him a company of the 77th Regiment of Foot, also known as Montgomerie's Highlanders, as well as provincial troops under Virginian Andrew Lewis. If possible, Grant was to avoid a general engagement with the French and—though unlikely due to the heavy presence of native spies—return to Fort Ligonier undetected.

On the evening of September 13, Major Grant and his men arrived near the Forks of the Ohio. Things were quiet, and Fort Duquesne looked pitifully empty. Compared to his eight hundred troops, Grant believed that no more than two hundred Frenchmen were in the fort at the time. Sensing opportunity, and maybe chasing glory, Grant decided they would strike the post in the morning despite the orders from Bouquet to return unnoticed. As a morale booster to his men, Grant ordered an isolated supply storehouse burned that night.

The next morning, Grant put his plans into motion. He sat on a large hill overlooking Fort Duquesne that was heavily wooded; he had a commanding view of the entire three-river valley below. As a diversionary tactic, Grant ordered the company of the 77th Highlanders to march toward the unsuspecting fort with full fanfare. They were to beat their drums, play their bagpipes, and lure out any would-be attackers from inside Fort Duquesne. Once the Franco-Indian force took the bait, Grant would order the remainder of his men to charge down the hill and capture the highly coveted fortress. As a fallback, Grant also positioned Major Andrew Lewis's provincials near the rear of the army along its supply train. If the Ohioans tried to plunder their store, Grant thought, Lewis and his men could simply launch a secondary ambush there. Either way, Grant's positioning atop the large hill would allow his men to respond to wherever the fighting occurred with downhill momentum and bayonets fixed.

On cue, the drummers began their steady beats, and the wailing bagpipes splintered the morning stillness at the Forks of the Ohio. The Highlanders of the 77th Regiment marched forward steadily in their plaid kilts and willingly placed themselves in danger on the orders of their commander. As expected, a French and Indian war party spilled out of Fort Duquesne. As Grant was attempting to time his response, he noticed something unexpected: the war party was much

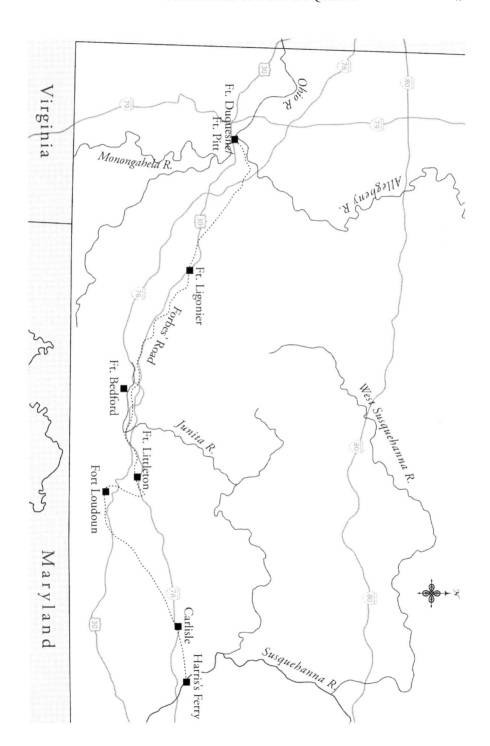

larger than he first believed. From his vantage point atop the large
hill, it appeared as if the flow of enemy combatants was endless.
While Grant believed that only two hundred men were inside Fort
Duquesne, he had grossly misjudged. In truth, there were over five
hundred French and Indian warriors in and around the post. The diversionary force of the 77th Highlanders were soon overrun and
mowed down where they played their fateful tune. In a panic, Lewis's
provincials abandoned their intended ambush site near the rear supply train and rushed forth to help the dying Highlanders. Before they
could reach the field, however, they began to take fire from a nearby
piece of high ground.

   As Grant tried to make sense of the chaos and probably wondered
how he could have been so off in his calculations, his column was
being decimated. The Ohioan warriors fired from the cover of the
trees and, aside from telltale puffs of smoke, were virtually invisible.
The British force quickly disintegrated, and many turned back east
to run for their lives; most were not so fortunate. Of Grant's eight-
hundred-man force, approximately 340 were killed or wounded, 230
of whom were from the doomed 77th Regiment. Lewis's provincials
lost six of their eight officers, but many of their men were able to
flee. The majority of the Highlanders, including Grant, were taken
prisoner. They were strangers in a foreign land, and were completely
unaware that the most terrible act in the drama of the Battle of Fort
Duquesne was still to come.

LEGACY: James Grant's army was annihilated by the collective forces
of the Ohio Country, and the results were nothing short of terrifying.
Many of the British soldiers involved were taken prisoner by the
Ohioans, including Grant. He was soon rushed to Canada as a high-
value prisoner of war, but he was one of the lucky ones. For the next
several nights, the victorious warriors of the Shawnee, Delaware, and
Mingo nations tortured and executed their captives in an ancient
form of macabre celebration. The scene at Fort Duquesne was hor-
rific, and eyewitnesses recount seeing the severed heads of their com-

The French burned Fort Duquesne before they abandoned the site to the British. (*Tuttle's Popular History of the Dominion of Canada, 1877*)

rades placed on spikes and lining both sides of the road into the fort. In one account, a Highlander was tortured so badly that he convinced his tormentor that he was actually immortal. When the Ohioan asked for proof, he dared his captor to try to split his skull with a tomahawk; the warrior did so, killing the Highlander instantly and bringing his pain to a merciful end.

More than the ritualistic torture that was so prevalent in Indian warfare were the greater consequences of the battle on their overall perception of the conflict. After defeating the British, the Ohioans understood that such a small force could not have marched all the way to Fort Duquesne on its own; instead, it had to be part of a greater attack force. When they discovered Forbes's army was within striking distance of Fort Duquesne, their fears were affirmed. A month later, a French and Indian attack was defeated at Fort Ligonier. In response, the natives immediately reconsidered their alliance with the forces of New France, and on October 26, 1758, the various sachems of the Ohio Country called a council at the Pennsylvania village of Easton. Joined by colonial administrators from Pennsylvania and New Jersey, the Ohioans agreed to abandon the French and stop fighting in exchange for the return of large tracts of land previously lost. It was a major diplomatic success for the colonial governments and a great relief for the war-torn frontier. As for the French inside Fort Duquesne, they were on their own.

WHAT TO SEE: The site of the Battle of Fort Duquesne has been long buried under the modern city of Pittsburgh. Although it's difficult to perceive to the naked eye, a walk from Point State Park to the aptly named Grant Street is a steep, uphill climb. For much of its history, the Forks of the Ohio was overshadowed by a massive hill, and it was on this hill that Grant suffered his terrible defeat. For much of the early history of Pittsburgh, this landform was called Grant's Hill, and today the Allegheny City-County Building rests at its peak on Grant Street. The best way to experience this battle is to begin at the City-County Building, going inside to see Sir William Reid Dick's 1922 bust of William Pitt. Also note that the city flag retains the symbol of the Pitt family crest, as well as his family colors, black and gold. Exit the building and walk across Forbes Avenue to the Allegheny County Courthouse to locate Pulitzer Prize winner Vincent Nesbert's breathtaking murals of the battle that dominate the grand staircase.

Now exit the courthouse and begin your march west toward the legendary Forks of the Ohio. Once you reach the green space known as Point State Park, look for the historic bronze plate and concrete outline that mark the exact position of Fort Duquesne. With the Allegheny to your right and Monongahela to your left, view the mouth of the mighty Ohio River, which the world's two largest empires fought so valiantly to control.

7

The Battle of Fort Ligonier

(OCTOBER 12, 1758)

BACKGROUND: In summer 1758, the new administration that governed Great Britain under Secretary of State William Pitt drastically escalated the empire's commitment to winning the Seven Years' War. As part of the strategic overhaul, Scottish brigadier general John Forbes was to march a six-thousand-man army into the heart of the frontier. Their target was the isolated post of Fort Duquesne, the centerpiece of the French occupation of the Ohio Country. Forbes's campaign would roughly mirror that of Edward Braddock's 1755 disaster, with one major exception: rather than marching posthaste toward his objective, Forbes would march his army gradually and carve out a major roadway as he moved west. In many ways the Forbes Campaign was both a military expedition and a massive infrastructure project. The roadway would be a permanent addition to the imperial framework of North America and ensure that troops, supplies, and settlers could move west unimpeded for generations to come.

To strengthen his effort, the brigadier general demanded that fortifications be constructed at specific intervals along what became known as the Forbes Road. Some were merely stopovers and storehouses, but others were massive. Two of the most impressive were Forts Bedford and Ligonier, and they not only bolstered British efforts to conquer the region but became de facto keystones for diplomacy and expansion. Fort Ligonier was an incredible structure. Made in a rough but practical way, it embodied the latest design features of military fortification and the innovative spirit of the frontier. Alongside the Loyalhanna Creek, Fort Ligonier was nothing short of an engineering marvel that projected bold strength and sent a clear message: the British were here to stay.

BATTLE: As part of Forbes's now legendary protected advance, fortifications and posts were constructed at intervals to ensure victory against the French at Fort Duquesne. None was as grand and impressive as the post at Loyalhanna. With victory in sight, Forbes planned to use Fort Ligonier as a launching point and primary supply depot. Appearing from above as star-shaped, it was a marvel of classical European defensive design. The sharp angles of the fort virtually eliminated blind spots and provided for enfilade fire, and an attacking enemy would need to confront heavy artillery blasts before ever reaching the post's outer walls. From Fort Ligonier's vantage point along the Loyalhanna Creek, Fort Duquesne was a scant fifty miles west, and Forbes wanted to make sure that unlike his predecessors, he would be facing the enemy at full strength. Although the post was to figure large in his plans, it was by no means a finished product. It was the start of a supply depot, and the noise of construction was a constant reminder that it was a work in progress; in fact, Fort Ligonier did not reach its final form until 1766, eight years later.

Fifty miles away at Fort Duquesne, the scene was growing desperate. A month earlier a force under Major James Grant had launched a surprise raid on the Forks of the Ohio, and though the Franco-Indian force beat it back, the attack was a bad omen. Aside from the looming sense of dread that an enormous invasion force was headed his way, Captain François-Marie Le Marchand de Lignery, the fort's commandant, was also contending with a starving garrison. Two

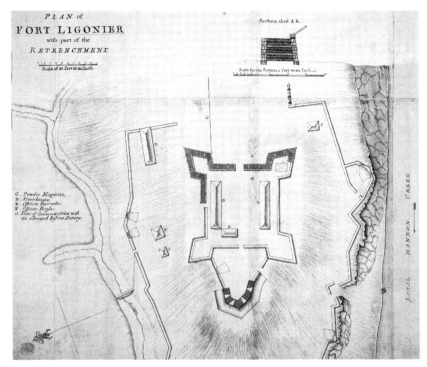

The plan of Fort Ligonier with part of the retrenchment, drawn in 1758. (*Norman B. Leventhal Map Center, Boston Public Library*)

months earlier, in late August, Fort Frontenac, in what is today Kingston, Ontario, was captured by British forces under Lieutenant Colonel John Bradstreet. New France envisioned its North American settlements as dependent on a circulatory system; it relied on moving goods and supplies down waterways to feed its southern posts, with furs and other raw materials returning by the same waterways. If Quebec was the proverbial heart of the empire, supplies trickled down the St. Lawrence River, into the Great Lakes, through rivers like the Allegheny, then to the Ohio, Mississippi, and ultimately Louisiana. When Fort Frontenac fell, it effectively severed the supply line that fed every fort and post south of it. After more than two months, Fort Duquesne was beginning to wither, and Captain Lignery needed to act to save his men's lives. While he knew the odds were against him, he recommended a raid on Fort Ligonier to plunder what valuable stores they could from Forbes's army. It was a long shot, but they were desperate. In a last-ditch effort, Lignery assigned an officer named Charles Phillip Aubry to lead nearly his entire garrison of 440 men along with 150 Delaware warriors to assault the British post.

As Forbes was suffering and unable to travel, day-to-day operations of his command were left to Lieutenant Colonel Henry Bouquet. Bouquet was fully invested in the campaign and regularly scouted future routes for the military road personally. On October 12, Bouquet was away and Fort Ligonier was left in the capable hands of Colonel James Burd. As Forbes's army was vast, its members were spread for miles around Loyalhanna Creek. Animals grazed in distant meadows and soldiers toiled nearby. While guarding livestock was not the most exciting assignment for these young troops, it was typically quiet—and very important. It was not unusual to wake up and find that an Ohioan band had stolen cows or horses during the night. As these soldiers stood guard that day, they were suddenly shocked when a force of almost six hundred French soldiers and Delaware warriors dashed from the forest, firing and overwhelming their positions. Almost a mile and a half away from Fort Ligonier, these men stood little chance against the surprise attack of the charging enemy.

The distant crack of gunfire raised alarms in Fort Ligonier, and Colonel Burd immediately dispatched two hundred men of the Maryland Battalion to reinforce whoever remained in the field. They arrived quickly but proved to be no match for the larger force out of Fort Duquesne. As the Marylanders fell back, Burd dispatched the 1st Pennsylvania Battalion as well as North Carolinian provincials. They likewise melted in the face of the charging Franco-Indian war party and retreated for cover into the safety of the post. In the first true test of the fort, Burd ordered artillery fire into the bulk of the enemy lines; it stopped their advance. Rather than daring to charge the fort's heavy guns, Aubry elected to hide in the tree line until nightfall when they could attempt another assault. Raids such as this

One of the angular redoubts of the reconstructed Fort Ligonier. During the eight years of its existence as a garrison, Fort Ligonier was never taken by an enemy, including a successful repulse of a Native American attack prior to the Battle of Bushy Run in August 1763. The fort was decommissioned from active service in 1766. (*Michelle A. Leppert*)

one depended on the element of surprise, and when the shock and awe wore off, the attacking force was usually stymied if its target survived the initial charge. From the tree line, the French command realized it had wasted its tactical advantage, as British troops arrived on the freshly cut road and were totally unimpeded by their enemy.

In a final attack, Aubry ordered his men to charge one of the angular redoubts of Fort Ligonier, but to no avail. They were able to close in on the position but were once again repulsed by artillery fire. While many of the French were actually native Canadians born on the frontier, they were repeatedly impressed and frustrated by the supreme marksmanship of the American riflemen. Because many of these frontiersmen were raised hunting small game from long distances, they were crack shots, as opposed to their classically trained British regular counterparts, who relied on imprecise volley fire to strike down opponents. From inside Fort Ligonier, the Americans could hunker down, take their time, and pick off any would-be at-

tacker who dared to peak his head out from behind a tree. As the
Franco-Delaware force retreated from its failed assault, it was clear
that the balance of power in the Ohio Country was about to change.

LEGACY: The Battle of Fort Ligonier was a flash point in the long
history of the Ohio Country. For the French and Indian forces, it
was a raiding expedition that failed to resupply Fort Duquesne. For
the British, it was a surprise attack that was easily fended off and a
validation of Fort Ligonier as the strongest post in the Ohio Country.
But the battle was a watershed moment in the history of the frontier.
As a result of the battle, Ohioan forces had a first-hand glimpse of
exactly what kind of firepower the British were bringing to the Forks
of the Ohio. From Braddock's Defeat until fall 1758, the British war
effort had been half-hearted, and the Ohioans reaped great benefits
in trade from their alliance with New France. In the wake of the Battle of Fort Ligonier, however, it became clear to the various sachems
of the region that the war would be very different moving forward.
Just two weeks later, the tribal leaders of the various Ohioan nations
made peace with Pennsylvania and New Jersey at Easton, Pennsylvania, and agreed to peace with the British Empire.

When the Ohioans abandoned the French at Fort Duquesne, all
hope was lost. For Brigadier General John Forbes, the peace agreement meant he could proceed to the Forks of the Ohio virtually
unimpeded. Although Forbes was dying, he sent his secondary officers to capture the post in his name. Sensing that the end was near,
Commandant Lignery, and the remaining garrison at Fort Duquesne
decided that resistance was futile and ignited their powder kegs,
blowing the coveted post to pieces. By the time Forbes's army arrived
on November 25, it found Fort Duquesne to be a pile of smoldering
timbers and captured the post without firing a shot. Although the
triumphant Forbes came to the forks later and died shortly after his
return to Philadelphia, he left a lasting legacy on the region. He
named the subsequent post that dominated the site Fort Pitt after
Secretary of State William Pitt, and the new settlement Pittsburgh

Fort Ligonier museum displays a range of rare artifacts from the Seven Years' War period. (*Capitol Museum Services*)

(pronounced Pitts-boro), a winking homage to his home capital of Edinburgh, Scotland.

WHAT TO SEE: To put it simply, Fort Ligonier remains the best Seven Years' War museum in the country. Its collection is vast, and its people are some of the most knowledgeable in the business. Thanks to generous private and public funding, Fort Ligonier can do a great many things that other small-market museums can only dream of, including investing its funds into world-class historic artifacts and shunning a lot of the generic tropes that so many other museums fall victim to. Among the highlights of its collection are George Washington's personal dueling pistols, presented to him as a gift from the Marquis de Lafayette. Also in the museum are a collection of guns, armor, and relics that span the breadth of the Seven Years' War. From jackets with bullet holes to elephant armor from India and statues from Africa, one truly gets a sense of the size and scale of this ultimate global conflict. On a personal note, I have been there many times and still manage to find something new and intriguing each time I return.

Alongside the world-class museum collection is the greatest asset of all: Fort Ligonier itself. While it's not technically Fort Ligonier, the current structure is a copy of the original, designed and constructed by carpenters trained in eighteenth-century construction. Guests are encouraged to wander throughout the post and take note of the hewn logs and sharpened stockade that so embodied practical military defense of the frontier. In its two hundred square feet with four bastions and three gates, guests can tour all the essentials of a colonial military fortification. Explore the mess, commissary, officers' quarters, powder magazine, hospitals, sawmill, bake ovens, and forge—in short, the full frontier experience in a single afternoon. If you are nearby in October, attend Fort Ligonier Days for the total eighteenth-century experience. Arts, crafts, historical reenactments, and a festival make it an annual tradition not to be missed.

PART TWO

THE AMERICAN REVOLUTIONARY ERA (1775–1783)

With the signing of the Treaty of Paris in 1763, the British Empire rejoiced in its global victory over France. While the governments of the warring sides negotiated and haggled over tiny Caribbean islands, the French signed over their North American empire with little hesitation. For the victorious British citizens of the American colonies, the year was a time of great joy; their French neighbors had been neutralized, and the continent appeared to be theirs for the taking. There was never a time of greater national pride in British North America than in the months following the surrender of New France, and it appeared that the English ethos of self-government would reign supreme in the New World. Gone was the threat of autocratic rule under a French king and religious domination under a Roman Catholic pope. In short, Americans had never felt more proudly British than in the year 1763.

But the pomp and circumstance were not all they seemed. After nearly a decade of war, the imperial debt had skyrocketed from £74 million to approximately £124 million. British North America had nearly tripled in size with the negotiated peace of 1763, but the imperial system was strained by its inability to protect and defend the new lands it had recently acquired. Even more pressing, the allied Indian warriors who had fought alongside the forces of New France had never signed a surrender and made no peace; in 1763, their war against British settlement was still raging in the west. For the American colonists who fought so valiantly to defend the British way of life, the defeat of the French became a revealing experience in the aftermath of the war.

To manage the empire's economic hardships, British policymakers elected to attack the debt using a two-fold approach: revenue increases and austerity. After consideration of a number of factors, it was decided that the New World would bear most of the burden. In the minds of the British politicians, the Americans did most of the fighting in the Seven Years' War and therefore cost the most. They also collectively paid some of the lowest taxes in the empire, and they stood to gain the most in the settlement and sale of former French lands. All of these reasons placed the majority of the cost-cutting measures squarely on America's shoulders. The new taxes came quickly, and mostly as a shock to the colonists. They believed they should have received a grand gesture of thanks for their efforts to win the war but instead received new taxes in the form of the Sugar and Stamp Acts. Along the frontier, the Indian warriors of North America waged a brutal war known as Pontiac's Rebellion, and instead of being protected, British settlers were left open to attack as a means of cutting royal expenditures.

The colonists of British North America had an intense attachment to English values and considered themselves the freest people on earth, and many believed these new financial measures to be the price of that freedom. But for others, the calamitous aftermath of the Seven Years' War presented them with a more difficult question: if they were truly valued as British citizens, why were their rights being violated so openly?

8

The Battle of Bushy Run

(AUGUST 5–6, 1763)

BACKGROUND: At the close of the Seven Years' War in 1763, the British Empire acquired all of France's colonial holdings in North America. It was a great victory for the Crown, but administering a space that was triple the size of its former Atlantic colonies proved to be untenable. While the forces of New France had to leave the continent altogether, the allied Indian warriors who fought beside them would not depart, and unlike King Louis, they made no peace agreement. Thus, in the wake of the largest war in world history, combat between British settlers and dozens of Indian nations continued to rage. As the war with France, known in North America as the French and Indian War, came to a close, it appeared that a whole new conflict was beginning against the continent's native peoples. In truth, for the warriors involved it was simply a continuation of the previous conflict. In time, this would become known as Pontiac's Rebellion after the Ottawa chief of the Great Lakes region, but this struggle actually had many leaders from across the frontier.

Primarily led by Pontiac in the Great Lakes and a Mingo sachem named Guyasuta in the Ohio Country, the warrior populace had a thoughtful strategy to expel white settlers from its homelands. Instead of trying to remove all peoples through extended conflict, these warrior chiefs instead focused on attacking key points of British power across the frontier. Their primary targets were Fort Detroit, a former French post in modern Michigan, and the newly completed Fort Pitt at the Forks of the Ohio. While they could not attack and capture these forts outright, they understood that they did not need to. Instead they elected to surround the forts, cut them off from supplies and reinforcements, and simply wait them out. Known in military parlance as a siege, this tactic was very time consuming but highly effective. For all of summer 1763, Fort Pitt was choked off from the rest of the British colonies by Guyasuta's warriors, and the fortification appeared to be on the verge of collapse.

BATTLE: While the major cities of the Eastern Seaboard celebrated their great victory over the forces of New France and reveled in the fact that North America's destiny would be an English one, attitudes were very different along the frontier. For these settlers, the French and Indian War had felt like one successive raid after another, and the fear of marauding Ohioans proved to be an existential disruption to the very soul of the region. By summer 1763, these feelings had greatly intensified. Since the Treaty of Easton in 1758, when the Ohioan tribes agreed to halt raids during the Seven Years' War, the Ohio Country was much more subdued. The completion of Fort Pitt at the Forks of the Ohio as well as the subsequent conquest of the former French posts Machault, Le Boeuf, and Presque Isle added to this calm. At the close of the Great War for Empire, though, the Ohioans went on the warpath once more, and fear gripped the region again. Beginning with attacks in the Great Lakes, North America's Indian nations rose up in rebellion against the British and began destroying forts across the frontier. Like a terrible hurricane, the destruction spread from Fort Detroit and its satellite posts into the Ohio Country. Before long, the Forks of the Ohio appeared to be in the crosshairs.

Trepidation gripped the tiny settlement of Pittsburgh when a bloody hatchet was found buried in the ground just a few hundred yards from Fort Pitt; full-blown panic struck when, on May 29, 1763, approximately five hundred Ohioan warriors attacked the settlement. The man in charge of Fort Pitt was Simeon Ecuyer, chief second to Lieutenant Colonel Henry Bouquet, and the Swiss officer immediately sent word to Fort Ligonier some fifty miles east that they were under attack. Ecuyer's swift decision was critical, as the Ohioans surrounded the location and settled in for an extended siege. Throughout the remainder of the summer, Ecuyer sheltered the men, women, and children of Pittsburgh inside the fort's earthen walls. The siege was devastating; when adventurous settlers would exit the fort to gather vegetables or livestock, an Ohioan sniper would open fire. They were running out of food and medicine, smallpox was beginning to spread, and the warriors outside seemed determined to bring Fort Pitt to its knees. To Ecuyer's dismay, word soon arrived that the three forts to the north—Machault, Le Boeuf, and Presque Isle—were all destroyed. Summer 1763 was a claustrophobic terror like the Ohio Country had never seen.

Fearing the loss of one of his most vital posts, the commander in chief of British forces in North America, General Jeffrey Amherst, called on Bouquet, who was at Carlisle, to liberate Fort Pitt. Amherst was far away in New York and had no idea if Pittsburgh had survived the attack. Knowing that Bouquet was intimately familiar with the site, he tasked him with marching seven hundred men into the Ohio Country to break the siege. Bouquet accepted with no hesitation. With the 42nd Highland Regiment, also known as the vaunted "Black Watch"; Montgomerie's 77th Highland Regiment; and the 60th "Royal American" Regiment (which was actually a diverse collection of foreign soldiers), Bouquet set out from Carlisle to save the besieged post, enlisting the help of twenty provincial rangers to serve as guides and scouts. They arrived unmolested at Fort Ligonier on August 4.

When Bouquet's men left Fort Ligonier on August 5, they had no idea that their expedition had been long anticipated by the Ohioans besieging Fort Pitt. Weeks earlier, the warriors had intercepted a letter destined for Simeon Ecuyer laying out Bouquet's plan. With that valuable intelligence in hand, the Ohioans were eager to ambush Bouquet along the Forbes Road. Onlookers at Fort Pitt noted in their letters that the day of August 5 had grown suspiciously quiet, unaware that the majority of the Ohioans had run to meet the unsuspecting rescue force. Bouquet's men marched at a brisk pace, as the commanding officer hoped to reach the unofficial halfway point between Forts Pitt and Ligonier, known as Bushy Run Station, that day. There they would rest, recuperate, and prepare for a potential showdown at the Forks of the Ohio. Little did they know that the showdown would find them first.

As Bouquet's men trekked through the forest, at approximately 1:00 PM, the front of the column came under fire. The stillness of the midday was splintered by the crack of musket fire, and the Highlanders scrambled to form a defensive position. As the colonel attempted to rally his men, the gunfire from the Ohioans continued to pour on, and Bouquet's force was dangerously caught in a valley between two hills. The warriors knew the ground well and waited until the redcoats were trapped in a terrible kill zone to begin their attack. As the fighting continued throughout the afternoon, Bouquet's Highlanders managed to form a defensive perimeter and slowly extricate themselves from the gully. They finally managed to regroup around the column's supply train atop a piece of high ground known as Edge Hill. With the sun beginning to set and no true means of defense available, Bouquet ordered his men to stack up enormous bags of flour destined for Fort Pitt in the shape of a circle. This would become known as the Flour Bag fort.

During the night of August 5, the fighting came to a virtual standstill. There was little sense to fighting in the dark as no one, British or Indian, could see well enough to hit a target. Throughout the night, however, Bouquet developed a scheme to potentially save his column; he wrote to General Amherst that he did not expect to survive the battle. Using his knowledge of Indian warfare from previous

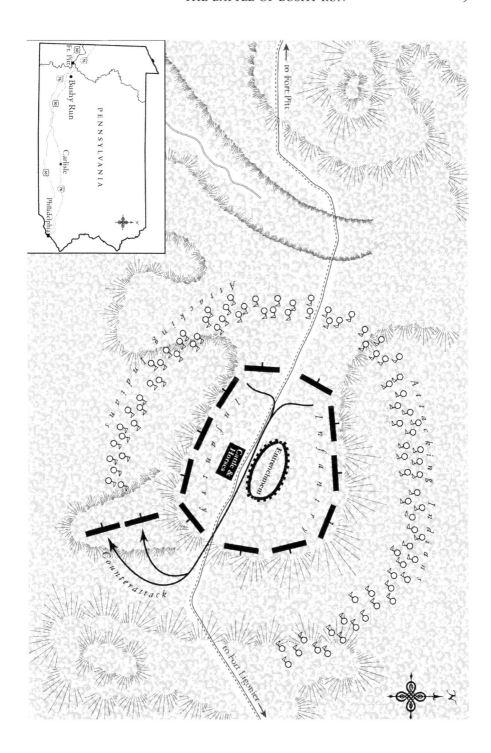

The Highlanders fought ferociously on the second day of the battle. (*Harper's Weekly*)

campaigns, Bouquet believed that the Ohioans would pursue a retreating enemy at all costs. At dawn, the gunfire began anew, and Bouquet put his plan into action. By telling a portion of his men to retreat off the back of Edge Hill behind the Flour Bag fort, Bouquet hoped to draw enough warriors in pursuit that he could capitalize on their overly aggressive tactics. His men withdrew, and the Ohioans followed over the blind hill, unaware they were falling into a trap of their own. When the warriors broached the crest of the hill they fell into the waiting bayonets of the desperate Highlanders. Caught off guard, many Ohioans were killed on the spot, and the rest scattered into the forests. The redcoats opened fire as their shocked enemy fled, and Colonel Henry Bouquet had engineered one of the unlikeliest victories in the history of the American frontier. Wasting little time, Bouquet's column advanced triumphantly to rescue Fort Pitt.

LEGACY: The Battle of Bushy Run was a critical moment in the history of the Ohio Country. Bouquet's victory represented the only time a British force ever defeated an exclusively Indian force on the field of battle in the history of British North America. With the success, Bouquet's men were able to march to Fort Pitt and liberate it. More than simply saving the locus of British power in the region, the Battle of Bushy Run effectively neutralized any hope of continuing the Indian insurgency in the Ohio Country. Guyasuta's warriors were exhausted from a decade of war, and the fall harvest was upon them. Rather than fighting to the end, most of the Ohioans elected to return to their families to prepare for the long winter. While not all of the warriors gave up, only the most ideologically extreme remained tied to the cause, and most traveled to strike the more primitive settlements of the far west.

For Bouquet, the victory at Bushy Run was the biggest feather in his cap. He had already overseen the construction of forts along Brigadier General John Forbes's legendary protected advance in 1758 and held command of Fort Pitt in 1763. Though he was absent for the siege, his liberation of the site only boosted his reputation. Perhaps most importantly of all pertaining to family life on the frontier, Bouquet spent 1764 traveling deeper into the Ohio Country to negotiate the release of dozens of prisoners taken captive during the Seven Years' War. Because of his efforts after ten long years of war, they finally were able to return home.

WHAT TO SEE: Bushy Run Battlefield rests outside of Harrison City, Pennsylvania, and offers the true battlefield experience for guests. Along with its interpretative museum, the site presents the battle in a clear and understandable way, using numbered signposts as guides. Considering the chaotic nature of the event, the site is easily navigable now. The battle took place in thick, heavy forest, so the scene can be hard to visualize today because the battlefield appears like a well-manicured meadow. Despite the missing trees, one can still note the rolling ground and flowing creek that played major roles in the 1763

These concrete flour sacks today mark the location of Edge Hill and the makeshift fortification constructed to protect the wounded. (*Mark A. Wilson*)

engagement. Atop the high ground known as Edge Hill, a copy of Bouquet's flour-bag fort offers guests a location to orient themselves on the battlefield. Bushy Run Battlefield was originally operated by the Commonwealth of Pennsylvania but was abandoned and is now operated by dedicated local history advocates. Still, clues remain that aid in the interpretation of the site. When the property was first acquired, noted architects planted trees to trace the path of critical moments in the battle. Today they appear random and have grown considerably, but these arboreal behemoths can still be used to trace the original progression of the battle.

As with other Seven Years' War sites, major questions remain as to the exact location of the Battle of Bushy Run. Using the best avail-

The monument at the Bushy Run battlefield. (*Kelly Ruoff/Pennsylvania Historical and Museum Commission*)

able information at the time, early historians believed that the property was the undeniable site of the 1763 battle, but some doubt remains. If the accepted location is not exact, it's very close, and park administrators have undertaken an effort to acquire surrounding plots of land just to be sure; today it spans over two hundred acres. In the mid-twentieth century, locals told stories of visiting the creek that runs through the site and picking up centuries-old musket balls following heavy rains. While these careless acts certainly damaged this site over the years and caused the loss of innumerable artifacts, professional historians and archaeologists have come to understand that these types of stories are quite common, and all part of the challenge of preserving a battlefield.

9

The Massacre of the Conestogas

(DECEMBER 27, 1763)

BACKGROUND: With Pontiac's Rebellion still reverberating through the Ohio Country, settlers along the Appalachian Mountains grew restless. They believed that their natural rights as British citizens were being infringed on and blamed Indian raids on a passive government in Philadelphia that was unable to protect them. In many ways this animosity was a direct result of the Seven Years' War, when ethnic tensions within the colony began to boil over: the Scots-Irish Presbyterians of the west openly feuded with the English, Quaker elites of Philadelphia. These tensions had been present for years in the Peaceable Kingdom, but the coming of war and threat of Ohioan raids only served to expose them further. By fall 1763, the frontiersmen had grown fiercely critical of their colonial legislature and seemed determined to take their defense into their own hands.

The political dispute erupted into violence on December 14, 1763. John Elder, a Presbyterian minister known as "the Fighting Parson," used his bully pulpit to preach a message of violence and retribution to his congregation. Quoting scripture as justification, Elder roused the men of Paxtang, Pennsylvania, into a furor over recent Indian raids and framed a retaliatory strike in biblical terms. Angered, alienated, and frustrated, a group of men picked up weapons and marched to the nearest Indian community they could find to vent their outrage. Unsanctioned by any government, the so-called Paxton Boys attacked a nearby village of peaceful, Christian Conestogas without cause or accountability. Despite the fact that the Conestogas lived and dressed as their white neighbors and were entirely nonviolent, the mob burned their village and murdered its residents in cold blood.

BATTLE: The Conestogas had been given a tract of land decades earlier by William Penn that became known as Conestoga Manor. Formerly part of the Susquehannock tribe, the Conestogas were established along the Susquehanna River by the colony as a model of sorts to demonstrate the ability of Indians to "civilize" into an eighteenth-century European culture. They had served as ideal citizens and became staples of the community; they farmed, manufactured, traded, and educated their children in a way that was completely foreign to their ancestors with the hopes of being accepted into the greater framework of colonial Pennsylvania. They did not participate in Pontiac's Rebellion and were as appalled as any at the level of horrid bloodshed that had resulted. Despite these glaring facts, the Paxton Boys destroyed the Conestogas' village and murdered many of the tribal community. It was the definition of an unruly mob, and they would not be satiated until every Conestoga was dead.

With the news of the attack spreading through the colonies, immediate steps were taken to protect the Conestogas who were lucky enough to be absent the day their village was attacked. Using the jailhouse in Lancaster as a safe haven, fourteen remaining men, women, and children were locked inside for their own protection. All the while they remained under the watch of Lancaster sheriff John Hay, there was an armed guard on duty to prevent anyone from accosting the people inside. These efforts kept the Conestogas safe until De-

Following their earlier attack against local American Indians, the Paxton Boys massacred the survivors in the heart of Lancaster during broad daylight. (*New York Public Library*)

cember 27, two days after the Christmas celebration. That day the town of Lancaster was conspicuously quiet; the streets were empty, and the jailhouse defending the Conestogas was left unguarded. With nothing separating the surviving Indians from the revenge-fueled animosities of the frontier, the Paxton Boys rode into town.

Despite the fact that there was a pronounced military presence in Lancaster, no one came to the aid of the helpless Conestogas. The Paxton Boys entered the jailhouse, dragged the families out of their chambers, and murdered all of them. In broad daylight, they brutalized their victims with tomahawks and scalping knives. William Henry, a Lancaster resident, later wrote:

> I ran into the prison yard, and there, O what a horrid sight presented itself to my view! Near the back door of the prison, lay an old Indian and his women, particularly well known and esteemed by the people of the town, on account of his placid and friendly conduct. His name was Will Sock; across him and his Native women lay two children, of about the age of three years, whose heads were split with the toma-

hawk, and their scalps all taken off. Towards the middle of the gaol yard, along the west side of the wall, lay a stout Indian, whom I particularly noticed to have been shot in the breast, his legs were chopped with the tomahawk, his hands cut off, and finally a rifle ball discharged in his mouth; so that his head was blown to atoms, and the brains were splashed against, and yet hanging to the wall, for three or four feet around. This man's hands and feet had also been chopped off with a tomahawk. In this manner lay the whole of them, men, women and children, spread about the prison yard: shot-scalped-hacked-and cut to pieces.[1]

Although there were enough people who could have saved the Conestogas, none did. Questions remain regarding precisely who was involved in the massacre and how many participated. But other lingering problems are still unresolved. Why was there no guard on duty on December 27? Why were the streets virtually empty of people? Lancaster was North America's largest inland city and an unrivaled commercial hub. Foot traffic flowed through the city day and night, and Lancaster earned a reputation as a place to buy a wide variety of hand-crafted, finished goods from the frontier. Rumors circulated that the Paxton Boys had stated their intentions earlier that week and Lancaster's residents simply took cover for fear of being caught in the middle. Whether the city was aware of the murderous plot or not, the rangers clearly presented an air of intimidation to the citizenry of the frontier.

With blood on their hands, the Paxton Boys soon found themselves at the head of a political revolution. Fed up with eastern elites for their perceived inability to defend the backcountry from Indian attacks, they turned their violent brand of influence toward the capital city of Philadelphia. As they marched, panic swept through the towns and villages of the east, and excitement grew among the settlements of the west. By the time the rangers reached Germantown

---

1. William Henry, quoted in Jeremy Engels, "Equipped for Murder: The Paxton Boys and the Spirit of Killing All Indians in Pennsylvania, 1763–1764," *Rhetoric and Public Affairs* 8, no. 3 (2005): 355–356.

(then a separate community from Philadelphia), their numbers had reached over two hundred strong. While most did not participate in the massacre of the Conestogas, all were sympathetic with the overall message and ideology of the movement. For the moment it seemed that open combat was the only way to settle the affair. As Benjamin Franklin later wrote, "It grieves me to hear that our Frontier People are yet greater Barbarians than the Indians, and continue to murder them in time of Peace."[2]

Franklin, who was critical of the Paxtons, was instrumental in saving Philadelphia. After a long standoff, he and other representatives from within the city brokered an agreement with the frontiersmen to petition the government through official channels and to abandon their hyperaggressive advance on the capital.

LEGACY: Winter 1763 to 1764 stands as a dark and terrible chapter in the history of colonial America. While imperial forces brought war to the American frontier, the trickle-down effects of the conflicts left a cultural disaster in its wake. The Conestogas were all killed in the streets of Lancaster, but none of the Paxton Boys were ever brought to justice. The murders were seen as an atrocity in Philadelphia but were hardly a concern in the tumultuous west. Many of the participants in the massacre went on to hold prominent positions within their own communities and participate in later rebellions along the frontier. In the wake of the uprising, Pennsylvania found itself embroiled in a heated debate over the role of Indians in the colony. With open debate becoming something of a modern pastime, Philadelphia's newspaper and pamphlet industry flourished, giving new voices to those who had been previously left out of the colony's collective public consciousness.

Perhaps the greatest legacy of the affair was its role in the larger history of colonial Pennsylvania. William Penn had established the

---

2. Benjamin Franklin to Sir William Johnson, September 12, 1766, in Benjamin Franklin, *The Papers of Benjamin Franklin,* vol. 13, January 1, 1766–December 31, 1766, ed. Leonard W. Labaree (New Haven, CT, and London: Yale University Press, 1969), 416.

colony a century earlier as a Holy Experiment of Quakerism, a Peaceable Kingdom where all peoples were welcomed to live as they wished. The harsh realities were very different, and the colony designed to be a melting pot soon turned into a compartmentalized land of ethnic enclaves. When the Seven Years' War came, those divisions were widened by the threat of violence, and by 1763, Pennsylvania was on the verge of disintegration along ethnic lines. By the time the Paxton Boys' wrath befell the Conestogas, it appeared as though Penn's Peaceable Kingdom was lost forever.

WHAT TO SEE: Two centuries later, one can easily follow in the footsteps of the Paxton Boys. Beginning in Harrisburg, locate the Paxtang Presbyterian Church on Sharon Street. This is the location of "the Fighting Parson" John Elder's original congregation, and the rallying point of the rangers before their murderous march. After walking the grounds, take a short car ride southeast to Manor Township in Lancaster County. Travel to the junction of Safe Harbor Road and Indian Marker Road until the large stone marker memorializing the original site of "Conestoga Indian Town" is visible. Placed alongside a vast meadow, this marker was dedicated by the Pennsylvania Historical Commission and the Lancaster County Historical Society in 1924 to commemorate the location of the Paxton Boys' initial assault on the Conestoga village. The remoteness of the area and the sameness of the landscape make this location a place of peaceful reflection honoring the innocent dead.

To visit the site of the final massacre, journey east to Lancaster's Fulton Theater on North Prince Street. A historic marker is placed on the upper floor of the main lobby listing the names of the people murdered on-site. After returning to the street, walk to the back of the building to North Water Street and visit the heavy, black iron door embedded into the original stone foundation of the Lancaster Prison. Built in the eighteenth century, this stone structure has been incorporated into the modern Fulton Theater's construction. Although the prison was built a few years after the attack, the Conesto-

The *Battlefield Pennsylvania* set in the Green Room of the Fulton Theater where the Conestogas were murdered. (*Author*)

gas were brutally killed in the area just on the opposite side of where the black door currently sits; it was an open yard in 1763. As we filmed *Battlefield Pennsylvania* on-site, we sat in the "Green Room" of the Fulton Theater where actors prepared for their roles on the stage above our heads. As a point of reference, North Water Street was just outside, and the filming location is deep in the cavernous basement of the massive entertainment venue. To end the afternoon on a more upbeat note, walk due west to the original city square and stop by the Lancaster City Visitors Center for daily, guided walking tours.

10

The Black Boys Rebellion

(MARCH–JUNE 1765)

BACKGROUND: In the wake of the Seven Years' War, the Pennsylvania frontier remained unsettled. Pontiac's Rebellion was an existential threat to the settlers of the region, and domestic uprisings like the Paxton Boys' murder of the Conestogas set the entire colony on edge. With the passage of the Proclamation of 1763, settlement of the newly won Ohio Country was put on hold by official proclamation of the king; this did little to stop the spread of settlers into the region. As new peoples moved farther west, so moved goods of all varieties, and fortunes were made trading with Indians in the distant backcountry. This created a new host of issues that plagued Pennsylvania, and many looked to the colonial government to arbitrate the disputes. Frontier families were concerned that by trading with the Ohioans, eastern investors were putting the colony at risk. Who was arming these raiding parties? While the merchant class of Philadelphia was getting rich by trading firearms and powder to the Ohioans, the people of the backcountry were being killed by those very same weapons. If east-west tensions were intense before, this new facet of the debate sent them into a fever pitch.

As a means of calming the colony, administrators froze and out-
lawed any trade with the Indian peoples of the west. The frontiers
were jubilant, but wealthy investors in Philadelphia were outraged.
This new development made them feel aggrieved, like the frontiersmen months earlier, and they clamored that their natural rights as
Englishmen were being infringed upon. Special interests flooded the
capital city, and in March 1765, licenses were once again dispensed
certifying participation in the Indian trade. The frontiers exploded
in protest. Already feeling as though the colonial government catered
to the money interests of the east, the frontiersmen felt frustrated
and disenfranchised. As pack caravans traveled west filled with all
manner of goods destined for the Ohio Country, settler families
nearby were determined to stop them at all costs.

BATTLE: In March 1765, the Philadelphia firm of Baynton, Wharton, and Morgan restarted its lucrative trade with the Ohio Indians.
One of its initial shipments was a large wagon train of supplies destined for Fort Pitt, with instructions that a specific amount of goods
would travel deeper into the frontier after stopping at the Forks of
the Ohio. The settlers of the Conococheague River valley were immediately suspicious of this arrangement and believed that the supply
train also contained contraband weapons and powder that would be
traded to eager Indian warriors. Taking matters into their own hands,
a party of local settlers stopped the wagons and demanded that they
be inspected before continuing their westward journey. The wagon
drivers refused and pushed on. Some days later, the train was stopped
again, this time more forcefully, and the driver allowed the men of
the Conococheague to inspect their stock; some stated that scalping
knives were found, and others that there were in fact no illegal items.
Regardless, on they traveled.

The buzz surrounding Baynton, Wharton, and Morgan's business
dealings made it a hated institution on the frontier, and some refused
to believe that it was not trading illegal goods with the natives. One
of the most vocal opponents was French and Indian War veteran

The Black Boys dressed as Indians and attacked a wagon train loaded with goods to trade with Indians in the Ohio Country as it crossed the Conococheague River valley. (*Library of Congress*)

James Smith, a longtime Indian fighter and former captive in the Ohio Country. Smith and his followers soon rallied into a sizable force and swore to stop the supply train before it reached Fort Pitt. Smith and his men painted their bodies with black soot in the traditional way of an Ohioan warrior going into battle and ambushed the train at a place called Sideling Hill. Smith's men killed a number of horses and destroyed the goods inside; survivors mounted the remaining horses and fled. The symbolism of their Indian appearance was deeply meaningful, and their intention was clear.

The wagon drivers managed to escape the ambush and traveled swiftly to the nearest military post, Fort Loudoun. There, Lieutenant Charles Grant commanded a force of Highlanders from the 42nd Regiment, the fabled Black Watch. The Scotsmen having fought the Ohioans at Bushy Run two years earlier, it appeared their time on the frontier would not end quietly. Grant ordered his men to march to Sideling Hill and salvage whatever goods remained, and if possible apprehend the people responsible for the wanton destruction. Marching under a sergeant named McGlashan, the Black Watch trekked to Sideling Hill with little idea of what lay ahead. En route they stumbled upon two of Smith's men still covered in soot and arrested them on the spot. As they reached Sideling Hill, they encountered more of these so-called Black Boys and captured them as well.

With the prisoners now safely held in Fort Loudoun, Lieutenant Grant's post was becoming a symbolic focus of what many frontiersmen believed to be unjust treatment that denied them their rights as Englishmen. Whispers of unrest continued to course through the frontier, and James Smith once again maintained that he could handle the problem on his own. A few days after the initial arrests, the Black Boys returned to surround Fort Loudoun and demanded that Grant release the men and all firearms confiscated in the initial arrests. If he failed to comply, Smith threatened to open fire on the fort and remove them by force. The demands were seditious, but the undermanned Highlanders were hesitant to open fire on their own citizens. After a tense standoff, Grant released the prisoners but kept all the weapons he had taken from them.

The guns became a symbol of the Black Boys struggles, and a standoff developed in the weeks that passed. Guns were a rare commodity in the backcountry, despite the high level of violence that occurred there. One day Smith's men unexpectedly raided a group of horses near Fort Loudoun; they killed the beasts and abused their riders. Grant immediately sent a party of Highlanders to pursue the rebels, and a firefight began at a nearby home called the Widow Barr's Place. One of Smith's men was shot through the leg and became a living martyr for the cause. In another instance, on May 28, Grant was captured by a band of rebels while riding near the fort and was released on the condition he give back the confiscated guns. He promised to do so but promptly went back on his word once inside Fort Loudoun's protective walls. In the aftermath of this affair, an advertisement was published in a local newspaper by advocates of the Black Boys, and it made some controversial claims. It read:

> These are to give notice to all our Loyal Volunteers, to those that has not yet enlisted, you are to come to our Town and come to our Tavern

and fill your Bellys with Liquor and your Mouth full of swearing and you will have your pass, but if not your back must be whipt and your mouth be gagged; you need not be discouraged at our last disappointment, for our Justice did not get the Goods in their hands as they expected, or we should all have a large Bounty. But our Justice has wrote to the Governor, and everything clear on our side and we will have Grant, the Officer of Loudon, Whip'd or Hang'd, and then we will have orders for the Goods, so we need not stop; what we have a mind and will do for the Governor will pardon our crimes, and the Clergy will give us absolution, and the Country will stand by us."[1]

It was a scandalous note, and it claimed that Governor John Penn supported their cause. That was news to the governor, and he immediately withdrew any support or sympathy he had toward the people of the frontier. Finally that summer, the Black Boys besieged Fort Loudoun a final time, and a full-scale engagement broke out. The men of the 42nd Regiment fired their muskets from behind the walls of the post, and the rebels returned fire in singular bursts. No one was killed or even wounded in the affair, and the matter fizzled out when Grant's men ran out of ammunition. They ultimately surrendered the post, returned the coveted muskets, and abandoned the site. The Black Watch was reassigned to Fort Bedford, from where it peacefully finished out its North American service. Smith went on to become a legendary figure in the Conococheague valley and wrote extensively about his experiences until his death in 1813.

LEGACY: When the Black Boys opened fire on royal forces inside Fort Loudon a full decade before the skirmish at Lexington Green, it represented a flash point in the history of North America. Many have taken this to represent the true "first shots" of the American Revolution. They weren't. The campaign to label the Black Boys Rebellion as a part of the American Revolution began in the middle of the twentieth century and has been utilized as a marketing tool, but basic

1. Advertisement, *Minutes of the Provincial Council, Colonial Records of Pennsylvania, Vol. 9* (Harrisburg: Theo. Fenn, 1852), 271.

facts quickly put that claim to rest. James Smith was a rebel to be sure, but he was not a separatist in 1765. This event was not part of the revolution per se but was certainly an early indicator that the Crown faced serious problems on its western frontiers. The Black Boys were fiercely independent, but the source of their unrest came from a sense that their rights as Englishmen were being infringed upon by their government. They did not seek to break free from that government, only to be treated with the same rights as others in the empire. In 1765, the call for independence and separation was still a decade away and would have seemed absurd at the time; this was a matter of enforcing existing laws, not conspiring against them.

In this regard, the Black Boys Rebellion was closely tied to the Paxtang Rangers march on Philadelphia and the Regulator Movement in the Carolinas. If there is a greater legacy that historians can point to it is that the backcountry residents of colonial America developed a sense of independence in the face of perceived prejudice from their wealthier, urban counterparts of the east. As a much older man, James Smith echoed these very sentiments, writing, "The King's troops and our party had now got entirely out of the channel of the civil law, and many unjustifiable things were done by both parties. This convinced me more than ever I had been before, of the absolute necessity of civil law, in order to govern mankind."[2]

WHAT TO SEE: You cannot travel through time, but standing at Fort Loudoun in Franklin County is about as close as one can get to 1765. Just off of historic Route 30 sits a faithful copy of Fort Loudoun, askew from its original location two centuries ago. From inside the post, one can marvel at the immensity of the Allegheny Mountains as they jut up abruptly all around the site. With Mount Parnell looming overhead, walk the property and locate the Conococheague Creek that has been the lifeblood of the region since the eighteenth century.

2. Samuel G. Drake, *Indian Captivities: A Collection of the Most Remarkable Narratives of Persons Taken Captive by North American Indians* (Boston: Antiquarian Bookstore and Institute, 1839), 271.

The reconstructed Fort Loudoun rests in the shadow of Mt. Parnell, part of the towering Appalachian Mountains. The original fort was built hastily at this site in 1756 to combat the threat of Shingas's Lenape (Delaware) raiders. (*Fort Loudoun Historical Society*)

Note while visiting the site that Fort Loudoun had a long history before the Black Boys Rebellion. Archaeologists have discovered evidence of thousands of years of habitation on the site by prehistoric peoples. Long before Europeans ever touched the Cumberland Valley, it was teeming with Paleoamerican families. Fort Loudoun was built in 1756 in response to the raid on Penn's Creek just before Armstrong's Kittanning Raid, and it was later the place of a great native gathering with Colonel Henry Bouquet during the Forbes Campaign. A century later, General James Ewell Brown Stuart rode through the location with his Confederate cavalry during the Civil War. Venture over to the museum to see its impressive collection of artifacts that were collected during an archaeological survey completed on-site, and stop into the hearth room to see where *Battlefield Pennsylvania* taped our episode. It is an impressive site with deep history, and the solitude grants visitors a tiny taste of life on the Pennsylvania frontier in the colonial period.

State archeologists discovered the location of Fort Loudoun's long lost well, and even found its original bucket preserved at the bottom. Today the 250-year-old artifact can be found at the state museum in Harrisburg. (*Fort Loudoun Historical Society*)

Other remnants of the rebellion remain in more furtive locations. Along Route 75 approximately a mile and a half south of Fort Loudon is an unassuming stone house known as the Widow Barr's Place. It was here that British regulars had a firefight with James Smith's rebels, and members of the 42nd Highland Regiment took cover inside. A rebel named James Brown was shot in the thigh, and it was the only engagement that drew blood during the whole affair.

11

The Battle of Brandywine

(SEPTEMBER 11, 1777)

BACKGROUND: By summer 1777, the American Revolution was in its second year. For policymakers in Britain, the revolution represented a challenge to royal authority. If it were allowed to fester, it could spread to other colonies; for them, the faster the patriot movement was crushed, the better. The British mishandled the war in its early stages when it was isolated to Boston, and after months of fighting they switched strategies and decided to occupy New York City. New York was the largest natural harbor in the Atlantic world and gave the forces of King George a reliable entrepôt to send troops and supplies into the combat theaters of the New World. Under General William Howe, the redcoats were determined to capture General George Washington's Continental army, for if there were no army, the revolution was nothing more than a political movement.

Defeating Washington proved to be difficult, but on a few occasions, Howe came close. After nearly ending the war at Long Island only to have the patriot army escape from his grasp under the cover of darkness, Howe chased Washington into New Jersey and across the Delaware River into Pennsylvania. In one of the Virginian's most daring maneuvers, he led his beleaguered Continentals across that same river on Christmas 1776 and captured the occupied city of Trenton, followed days later by Princeton. As the cold winter of 1776 gave way to spring 1777, the British once again recalibrated their efforts and devised a new strategy for ending the war. This time, Howe placed his sights solely on capturing the capital city of Philadelphia and the seditious Continental Congress that resided there.

BATTLE: At the end of August 1777, Howe moved almost seventeen thousand troops on 260 vessels out of New York City, along the Atlantic Coast, and into Chesapeake Bay. His target was Philadelphia, and he believed that a land-based campaign through Maryland and Pennsylvania would deliver him the capital. After landing at Head-of-Elk, Maryland, Howe planned to march his army through the countryside, fully aware that George Washington's' Continental army would await him somewhere nearby. Howe understood that the Brandywine and Schuylkill Rivers were the only natural obstacles he faced in the region; it was at these river crossings that he expected to finally engage the American rebels in open combat. For the British officer, a head-to-head confrontation with the patriot army was an ideal scenario. Each time Howe and Washington had met in 1776, Howe got the better of the exchange. He believed that his army was larger, far better supplied, and infinitely more disciplined. To the redcoats, the wily Washington used guile to escape total defeat at Long Island, and if they could force him to fight in a traditional engagement, they could end the war outright in fall 1777.

Washington understood what was at stake when Howe's army disembarked in Maryland. If his patriots failed to stop the British march northeast, there would be nothing to stop Howe from capturing the capital city. If it fell, then the civilian government of the American colonies would be captured and dismantled. In short, the dangers had never been higher. After small skirmishes with Howe during the early days of his march, Washington calculated that the British would need to pass over the Brandywine River at or near a famed crossing

In September 1777, George Washington, left, and his Continentals were all that stood between the British army and Philadelphia. (*Library of Congress*) Sir William Howe, right, first landed at Head of Elk, Maryland, and proceeded to a fateful meeting with the patriots along Brandywine Creek. (*New York Public Library*)

known as Chadds Ford. Chadds Ford was a staple of the Brandywine River valley and was the primary crossing on the road connecting Baltimore and Philadelphia. Washington decided that here, along these banks, his army would make its great stand. Notables at his side were Major Generals Anthony Wayne and Nathanael Greene and Brigadier General John Armstrong (of Kittanning fame).

On the night of September 10, Howe's seventeen thousand soldiers made headquarters at the small village of Kennett Square, some seven miles west of Chadds Ford. There, by candlelight, Howe met with his commanders to plan their great assault on the Continental army. It was decided that Hessian commander Wilhelm von Knyphausen would unleash a frontal assault on Washington with approximately seven thousand troops. The remainder of Howe's army would attempt one of the greatest tactical feats of the war with Lord Charles Cornwallis leading nine thousand troops directly north and east in a massive flanking maneuver to crush the patriots' right side in a surprise attack. In his mind, Howe had climbed the ranks of the British military over a long career while Washington was nothing

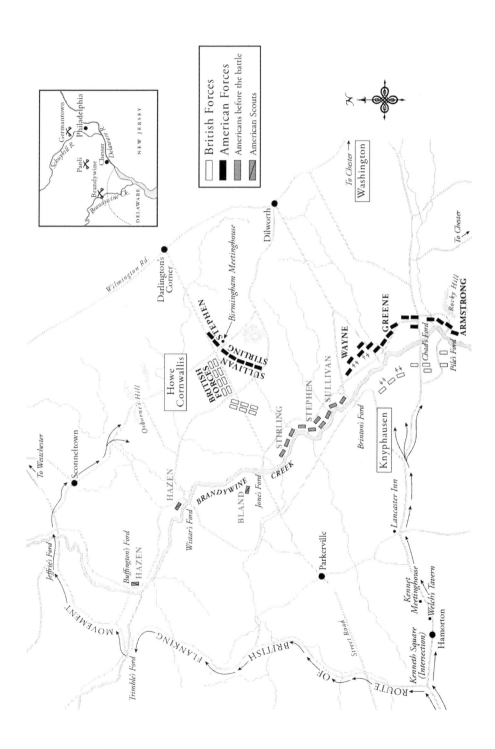

Continental soldiers facing a British advance during the Battle of Brandywine, drawn by F. C. Yohn, 1898. (*Library of Congress*)

more than a provincial colonel bestowed the title commander in chief by a rebel Congress in Philadelphia. In short, Howe believed that Washington lacked the training and experience to deserve the title general, and he hoped to use this maneuver to prove his own superiority once and for all.

At 5:30 AM on September 11, Knyphausen's Hessians began their march toward the Brandywine. Arriving later that morning at the Kennett Meeting House, a Quaker congregation, the Germans and Americans engaged in a fierce battle. The fighting continued for nearly four miles, all the way to the banks of the creek, with the two sides pushing one another back and forth in a fiery clash. At the same time that Knyphausen began his march, Cornwallis pushed north with his nine-thousand-man force in a march that took them the whole day. By the time they turned south after crossing the Brandywine at a northern point known as Trimble's Ford, patriot spies had been alerted to their presence and immediately rushed south to warn their unsuspecting commanders.

From his vantage point on the eastern bank of the Brandywine, Washington watched as his Continentals tangled with the Hessians

The Birmingham Friends Meetinghouse witnessed the most explosive fighting of the entire battle when Howe's flankers crashed into the patriot right side. (*Library of Congress*)

at the center of his army. He realized he had a great numbers advantage over the enemy but knew that once he ordered the bulk of his army to cross at Chadds Ford, he would be committed to fighting at that narrow spot for the remainder of the battle. The men before him were only a third of Howe's army, but a forceful push could potentially be enough to win the day. Washington had gambled in the past with mixed results, but on September 11 he rolled the proverbial dice yet again and ordered Major General Greene to cross the Brandywine and engage the Hessians.

Washington's decision to launch an assault across the river was a terrible mistake. Just as his men began to cross, a great commotion stirred on the far right of his army; the men engaged in Howe's great flanking maneuver had arrived, and they were determined to collapse his right flank. In a flash of panic, Washington ordered his men to return to their positions on the eastern bank of the Brandywine and fend off this new attack. Amazingly, most of his men were able to abandon the charge and regroup in time to save the right side of the Continental army. For the next several hours, the two armies tangled north of Chadds Ford near the Birmingham Meeting House, another Quaker establishment, until Washington decided he was badly outgunned. He ordered a full retreat and hoped he could generate enough space between his army and Howe's to establish a new defensive line farther east to spare Philadelphia. In one of the most unheralded but vitally important engagements during the Battle of Brandywine, Brigadier General George Weedon covered the rear of Washington's retreating army and halted any hope of pursuit by the redcoats. When it seemed that all was lost in the largest single battle of the American Revolution, Washington managed to salvage a small glimmer of hope as the sun set on September 11, 1777.

LEGACY: The Battle of Brandywine was a military disaster for George Washington's Continental army. His forces were the only thing standing between the capital city of Philadelphia and the charging army of Sir William Howe, and he failed. Brandywine was the largest battle of the war, and Washington failed to make an adequate stance to save the home of the Continental Congress, as the British occupied America's capital. Facing arrest and possible execution for treason, the congressional delegates were forced to flee just two weeks later and remain outside the city for nine months. During their flight, they met in Lancaster for one day and spent the remainder of their time in York. While in York, they drafted the Articles of Confederation and brokered critical diplomatic treaties with the empire of France. Even today, Lancaster and York rightfully boast about having been the former capitals of the United States, and their importance is irrefutable.

Washington's military failure along the banks of the Brandywine came with some silver linings, but their true value was likely unrecognizable at the time. Despite being beaten back, Washington was able to abort his forward assault across the river in time to avoid being crushed by Howe's now-famous flanking maneuver. Even more, he executed one of the cleanest, most effective retreats in the history of North American combat. Considering the utter defeat he had suffered, his orderly withdrawal allowed his men to safely escape Howe's army and, most vitally, extend the war five more years.

Dawn at Brandywine battlefield, from Birmingham Hill. (*Photograph by Meredith Barnes.* © *Molly Picture Studio*)

WHAT TO SEE: Brandywine was the largest engagement of the American Revolution, and the battlefield now encompasses a large swath of Chester County. Begin your survey on US Route 1 approximately one mile east of Kennett Square. There you will find a blue Pennsylvania Historical and Museum Commission marker indicating this was the location where General Howe formed his plan to split his army and capture the Continental army. If you are adventurous, you may drive north to Camp Linden Road just south of Marshallton to see one of the redcoats' major river crossings, known as Trimble's Ford. Continue into Marshallton to see the ruins of Martin's Tavern, where patriot scout Squire Cheyney first spotted Howe's large flanking force and rushed to warn General Washington about the oncoming attack. Drive southeast to Birmingham and explore the town and surrounding countryside. Here one can find the legendary Birmingham Meeting House and many other locations and markers associated with that fateful day, September 11, 1777.

Continue southwest along Creek Road with Brandywine Creek to your right; soon you will be at the heart of where the battle took

The John Chads House, left, and the Benjamin Ring House, right, served as George Washington's headquarters at the time of the battle. (*Wikimedia Commons*)

place at Chadds Ford. At the site are some important stops to make note of. First is the ford itself, a longtime river crossing that was vital to the economic health of the region. Behind you will be the John Chads House, which was witness to the battle and may have been damaged by British artillery. Proceed to the Benjamin Ring House farther east along US Route 1. This was General George Washington's headquarters and a must-see attraction. Finally, drive north to the intersection of Brintons Bridge Road and Dilworthtown Road to see where the Battle of Brandywine finally ended.

12

The Battle of Paoli

(SEPTEMBER 20, 1777)

BACKGROUND: In the wake of the loss at Brandywine, George Washington struggled to maintain his primary objective. He had to keep General Howe from reaching Philadelphia at all costs, and the unique geography of Pennsylvania afforded him one more chance. Just as Howe had to first cross the Brandywine River, he faced a second watery obstacle in the form of the Schuylkill. Although the Schuylkill ran very close to the American capital, local operatives informed the commander in chief that the only viable crossing point was a small ford more than fifteen miles northwest of the city known as Matson's Ford. This gave Washington a second chance to make a stand akin to the one at Brandywine. Using the river to its advantage, Washington's Continental army crossed to the eastern bank to set up a defensive position. For the patriot officer and future president, this strategy seemed most practicable; both Philadelphia and their primary supply depot at Reading lay east of the river. With the right conditions, he could protect both from the British army.

Soon Washington's natural inclination toward risk and opportunity changed his mind. The British had moved little since their victory at Brandywine, and they were slowed by a lack of wagons and supplies. If Washington stayed east of the Schuylkill, he would be waiting for Howe to build strength and fight a much stronger army; instead he chose to take advantage of the redcoats' weakened state. Using the elements to his advantage, Washington tangled with Howe again at an engagement known as the Battle of the Clouds on September 16, just five days after Brandywine. As the fighting began, though, a massive rainstorm turned the battlefield into a flooded mess. The rain lasted for hours, fog covered both armies, and as wagons and troops sank into deep mud, Washington reluctantly called for a retreat. It was an abortive affair, and the sullen Washington once again removed his troops across the Schuylkill, leaving Philadelphia open for the taking.

BATTLE: George Washington's Continental army limped across the Schuylkill, and the British were jubilant. With the abortive Battle of the Clouds behind him, Howe saw that the patriots were going to cede Philadelphia in an attempt to extend the war by saving their army. Like many imperial commanders before and many more after, Howe believed that by capturing the capital city of an enemy territory, he could effectively end the war. For Washington's part, he needed to do something—anything–to at least slow the British march if he could not stop it outright. For this reason, he called on one of his most trusted generals, "Mad" Anthony Wayne. Wayne was thirty-two and a Pennsylvania native. He had fought in Canada with Benedict Arnold and at Fort Ticonderoga, as well most recently alongside Washington at Brandywine. He knew the area intimately and had spent his boyhood living and working in the very communities now threatened; for the commander in chief, Wayne was an ideal candidate to offer a final defense of the region.

Inasmuch as the British had been halted at Brandywine because of logistical difficulties moving supplies and wagons, Washington believed that to be Howe's most vulnerable point. By exacerbating these problems, the Virginian hoped he could give the Continental Congress enough time to slip out of Philadelphia before imperial forces arrived to apprehend them. General Wayne was ordered to remain on the western bank of the Schuylkill River while Washington led the remainder of his forces to the opposite shore. Using stealth and his close, personal knowledge of the area as a weapon, Wayne was to lead the 1st, 2nd, 4th, 5th, 7th, 8th, 10th and 11th Pennsylvania Regiments, as well as Hartley's Regiment, some dragoons, and an attached artillery company against the supply train of Howe's army. These men, totaling one thousand five hundred, were to make

"Mad" Anthony Wayne's primary objective was to harass the rear guard of Howe's army and interrupt his supply train. (*Library of Congress*)

the British commander's march a logistical headache by attacking his wagons and entangling it in a frustrating quagmire.

If invisibility was Wayne's primary objective, he failed. On the evening of September 19, Howe received intelligence from local spies that a patriot army was encamped nearby. From his position at Tredyffrin some six miles north, Howe dispatched Major General Charles Grey to launch a surprise raid on the patriots. Grey marched with one thousand two hundred men; among the British troops were the 2nd Light Infantry, the 44th Regiment, and yet again the 42nd Regiment, the Black Watch. Grey's furtive attack began at 10:00 PM on September 20 in the dark of night. Fearing that his men would be detected early, Grey ordered his troops to remove the flint from their muskets; it was an unorthodox decision, but it would ensure that no guns would fire accidentally to reveal his attack.

Wayne's army was encamped between three busy taverns, the White Horse, the Admiral Warren, and the General Paoli. Although the word "tavern" may have a different meaning today, they were critically important to understanding how news and information spread

The Battle of Paoli was a hectic, nighttime engagement. This painting was commissioned by a British officer in 1782 to commemorate the battle. (*Valley Forge Historical Society*)

in the eighteenth century. Along with imbibing and carousing, taverns were places of public debate, politicking, and discussion. It was likely that some of Wayne's men, and some of the British, as well as Loyalist spies had all been drinking and conversing in these taverns together. In that instance, spying can be quite easy when all one needs to do is keep quiet and listen intently to the ramblings of loose-tongued infantrymen. However the Loyalists discovered Wayne's plan, General Grey was well on his way to spoiling it. Using the Moores Hall Road as their primary marching route, Grey's men found a local blacksmith who resided near the Admiral Warren tavern and forced him to guide them to their destination. Thus far, the patriots were totally unaware of the force bearing down on them from the north.

Upon reaching an intersection, the British came into contact with a patriot picket who was guarding the outskirts of the campsite. It was the middle of the night, and most of Wayne's men were asleep, but the firefight that began between Grey's vanguard and the rebel picket became a blaring alarm for the Continentals. As the patriots were roused from their sleep and struggled to prepare for battle,

Grey's 2nd Light Infantry burst through the forest and overran the camp. The battle scene was chaotic, and the only light came from the dying fires of Wayne's encampment. With the initial shock of the battle delivered by the 2nd Light Infantry, the 44th Regiment and the Black Watch also took to the field. The Continentals were caught woefully off guard and had little option but to flee for their lives. As they had been sleeping in a farming community turned war zone, many retreating patriots had to avoid pasture fences while they ran.

A short distance away, a small force of Maryland militiamen arrived near the White Horse Tavern, but they too were routed by the British and offered little resistance. In total the British suffered fewer than ten casualties, but they inflicted over two hundred on Wayne's unsuspecting patriot force. In addition, the British took seventy-one prisoners. It was a complete victory, and General Howe's army marched onward to Philadelphia undeterred.

The capital was lost.

LEGACY: "Massacre" was a loaded term in the eighteenth century, and its implication was clear. Typically reserved for an attack by Indians on settlers, the notion of the massacre came with an unmistakable political message that a savage band of marauders had attacked an innocent or honorable party. It was fraught with feelings of dishonor, disgrace, and desecration, all of which proved to be useful propaganda during a time of war. Just as the Boston Massacre, describing the events of March 1770, was known as the Incident on King Street in Britain, the main difference between two designations was often which side of the political aisle a person was on. In the wake of the defeat at Paoli, patriots cried "massacre," while royalists maintained that no such thing took place.

William Hutchinson, a militiaman from Pennsylvania, recalled the death of one of his comrades in terrifying detail, stating "more than a dozen soldiers had with fixed bayonets formed a cordon round him, and that everyone of them in sport had indulged their brutal ferocity by stabbing him in different parts of his body and limbs . . . examining him there was found . . . 46 distinct bayonet wounds."[1] Lieu-tenant Colonel Adam Hubley of the 10th Pennsylvania Regiment witnessed British soldiers "cut & hack some of our poor Men to pieces after they had fallen in their hands and scarcely shew the least Mercy to any."[2] The British commander Grey refuted the claims out-right, noting that they captured seventy-one rebels, a great feat con-sidering that patriot sources claimed the redcoats took no prisoners. Even if atrocities did occur, Loyalists maintained that the patriots were in fact traitors, and they felt little sympathy for the dead regard-less of what happened.

The truth lies in the eye of the beholder, but the patriot and British sides certainly capitalized on the charges of inhumanity; for the remainder of the war, the men of the 2nd Light Infantry bran-dished symbolically dyed red feathers in their caps to intimidate their enemies, and patriots shouted "Remember Paoli!" when they fought. As part of the fallout from the event, General Wayne came under heavy scrutiny for allowing his men to be caught so badly off guard. He demanded a court-martial, and the thirteen-member panel de-clared he was not to be blamed for the disaster. As for Major General Grey, he would be known as "No Flint" Grey for his actions at Paoli. (Grey was the 1st Earl Grey; his son Charles, 2nd Earl Grey, is be-lieved to be the namesake of the famous tea variety that bears his name.)

WHAT TO SEE: The Paoli Battlefield is a busy place and preserves the legacy of the event very well. Although the eighteenth century is hard to visualize from the site, the interpretation is strong and easy to fol-low. The battlefield itself is owned by the borough of Malvern, Penn-sylvania, and encompasses forty acres. It is surrounded by all the amenities of a local public park, including athletic fields and play-grounds, and it may surprise you as you approach. As you drive

1. Account of William Hutchinson, in Thomas J. McGuire, *Battle of Paoli* (Mechanicsburg, PA: Stackpole Books, 2000), 130.
2. Ibid. Account of Adam Hubley, 314.

through the beautiful homes and farms of suburban Philadelphia, you will first see a large stone obelisk that graces a special portion of the battlefield. Erected in 1817, this obelisk marks the mass grave of fifty-three men who died during the engagement and is the second-oldest war memorial in America. To preserve the marker, it remains behind protective shielding, but the stone wall that surrounds the perimeter of the grave is a sobering reminder of what actually occurred on-site.

This marker indicates a mass grave on the battlefield. Today it is encased in a protective casing for preservation. (*Wikimedia Commons*)

The battlefield itself is neatly kept with well-placed signage that readily shows the primary features of the fighting. Adorned by period cannons found hidden in a Chester County forge, the field is a large meadow that was General Wayne's encampment site on September 19, 1777. Markers on-site identify the six pickets engaged in the battle, as well as the approach of Grey's men and the retreat of Wayne's patriots. Signage also locates important reference points such as the Great Valley Presbyterian Church, Warren Tavern, and Paoli Tavern. Sites such as the Paoli Battlefield can feel artificial because of the clean cuts of the meadows and its neat organization in a modern neighborhood, but the presence of the honored dead make this park an essential pilgrimage for those interested in paying their respects.

13

The Battle of Germantown

(OCTOBER 4, 1777)

BACKGROUND: After soundly defeating General George Washington's Continental army at Brandywine, the Clouds, and Paoli, Sir William Howe entered Philadelphia as both conqueror and liberator. As the American colonies were hotly divided on the issue of independence, a large percentage of Pennsylvania's inhabitants remained loyal to the Crown. When Howe's army arrived in the city, the Tories cheered with joy and the patriots fled for their lives. As Philadelphia was the capital of the patriot rebellion, Howe hoped to capture, arrest, and imprison the seditious Continental Congress that had been meeting at the State House, today known as Independence Hall. Fortunately for the congressional delegates, they were well aware of Howe's designs for the city, and all had fled by September 26.

Despite having full possession of the city, Howe was uneasy with his occupation. He did not control the Delaware River, and therefore could not acquire vital supplies for his men. To avoid placing his army of redcoats in a dangerous situation, Howe ordered approximately three thousand men to remain in Philadelphia and moved the remainder of his army north to the community of Germantown.

As the British commander arranged his men into a defensible position, the watchful Continental army took notice. For General Washington, Germantown presented itself as one final chance to save the
capital.

BATTLE: From his position sixteen miles north, Washington devised
a scheme to duplicate his victory at Trenton. He directed four of his
most trusted officers to use four main roads to slink toward the
British position at Germantown and deliver a sudden, unexpected
blow. For the mission to be successful, the officers needed to maintain
a steady pace and place special emphasis on beginning their attacks
simultaneously. They failed in stunning fashion. A number of factors
worked against the patriots from the outset, but the greatest was
Mother Nature. Throughout the Philadelphia Campaign, the
weather of eastern Pennsylvania had been a perpetual uncertainty,
and the blackness of the night coupled with a heavy fog worked
against Washington's army on the evening of October 3. Utilizing
the southern roadways as planned, Continental regulars under Generals Nathanael Greene and John Sullivan marched at the center of
Washington's army, while militiamen under Generals John Armstrong (of Kittanning fame) and William Smallwood were positioned
on the left and right, respectively.

The defining and lasting memory of the participants involved in
the Battle of Germantown was the fog; relentless and smothering, it
virtually blinded them. At approximately 5:00 AM, the vanguard of
Sullivan's column encountered the outer pickets of Howe's line, and
a firefight ensued. Howe was immediately aroused from his sleep and
inspected the action, but the low visibility left the experienced officer
confused. Believing the enemy to be a mere scouting party, he urged
his men into the bulk of the patriot force; he was soon shoved back
by the unexpected boom of artillery. In the confusion, 120 men of
the 40th Regiment of Foot were separated from the main body of
Howe's army and took shelter in a large stone mansion nearby known
as Cliveden. For the men of the 40th Regiment, it was their Rock of

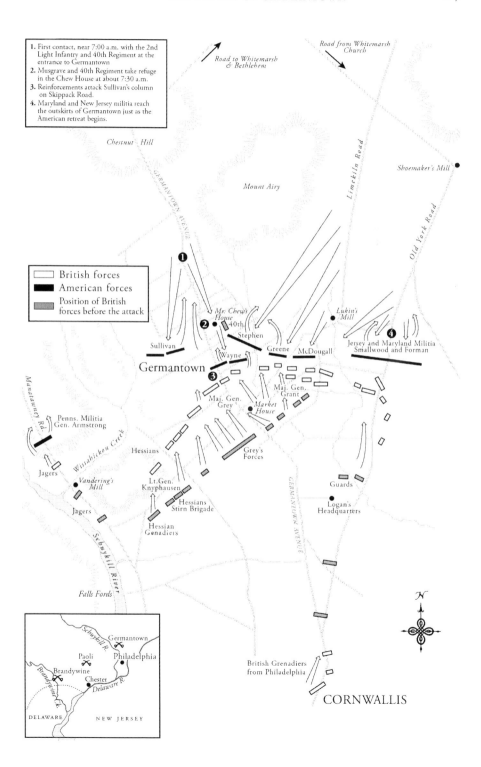

1. First contact, near 7:00 a.m. with the 2nd Light Infantry and 40th Regiment at the entrance to Germantown
2. Musgrave and 40th Regiment take refuge in the Chew House at about 7:30 a.m.
3. Reinforcements attack Sullivan's column on Skippack Road.
4. Maryland and New Jersey militia reach the outskirts of Germantown just as the American retreat begins.

Road to Whitemarsh & Bethlehem

Road from Whitemarsh Church

Chestnut Hill

GERMANTOWN AVENUE

Mount Airy

Limekiln Road

Shoemaker's Mill

Old York Road

British forces
American forces
Position of British forces before the attack

❶

❷ Mr. Chew's House
40th
Stephen

Lukin's Mill

❹
Jersey and Maryland Militia
Smallwood and Forman

Sullivan

Wayne

Greene

McDougall

Germantown

❸

Maj. Gen. Grey

Market House

Maj. Gen. Grant

Manatawney Rd.

Penns. Militia
Gen. Armstrong

Wissahickon Creek

Hessians

Grey's Forces

Jagers

Vandering's Mill

Lt. Gen. Knyphausen

Hessians Stirn Brigade

Guards

GERMANTOWN AVENUE

Logan's Headquarters

Jagers

Hessian Grenadiers

Schuylkill River

Falls Fords

N

Schuylkill R.
Germantown
Paoli
Philadelphia
Brandywine Ck.
Brandywine
Chester
Delaware R.

British Grenadiers from Philadelphia

CORNWALLIS

DELAWARE   NEW JERSEY

"The Attack on Chew House" by Howard Pyle, *Scribners Magazine*, 1898. The attack was led by General William Maxwell's brigade. (*New York Historical Society*)

Gibraltar. From inside this mansion, the redcoats fended off multiple attacks and cannonades from the Continentals, and the sturdy walls of the country manor succeeded in freezing the rebel assault. From that moment, the stately mansion became a place of legendary status; future chief justice of the United States John Marshall was wounded during the attack.

The remainder of the battle was a military disaster for the patriots. While Sullivan's column remained steadfast and punched deeper into enemy territory, Greene's men were terribly delayed. Fighting in support of Sullivan's column, a brigade under the command of General Anthony Wayne was halted when it heard the blasting of cannon fire from the rear; it was the attack on Cliveden. Sensing trouble behind him, Wayne immediately retreated, only to crash headlong into one of Greene's brigades arriving late to the scene. Its commander, General Adam Stephen, had disobeyed orders and veered from his original course via a separate roadway. With dense fog blanketing the entire battlefield despite the midmorning sun, Wayne's and Stephen's

wn as the Benjamin Chew House, was the scene of an intense firefight
ect link to the battle today. (*Library of Congress*)

hew House. This was the house soldiers of the British
ent of Foot used to fend off the attack of their patriot
ing today as a museum, Cliveden offers interpretations
th-century cooking, colonial living, enslavement, and, of
Battle of Germantown. Although Cliveden has grown
ars, including a two-story addition, the expansion was de-
blaced in the back of the home to retain its revolutionary
e. Continue next to the Concord School and Upper Bury-
nd. Built in 1775, this school was unique for its time; the
rying Ground holds the remains of over fifty Revolutionary
rans.

taste of the greater history of the area, visit Stenton, the for-
ne of William Penn's secretary, James Logan, and the head-

Continental brigades made contact and immediately began firing on
one another. It was a scene of total confusion and rising panic.

The element of surprise on which General Washington so depended had expired, and the British were gaining momentum.
Rather than making his final stand at Germantown, the Virginian
ordered his men to retreat as he had done so many times in the previous weeks. Armstrong's and Smallwood's militia were pulled back,
followed by Sullivan's column. At this time the attack on the mansion
house of Cliveden was also abandoned, and though he was hotly engaged with General Charles Cornwallis, Greene's regulars also withdrew. Again showing his technical prowess even in the most desperate
of times, Washington salvaged his army from its failed attack on Germantown in an orderly and efficient retreat.

With Philadelphia occupied by an enemy army and the Continental Congress exiled to the Pennsylvania backcountry, George
Washington was running out of options. While he was in a far worse
position, Sir William Howe had growing concerns of his own in the
American capital. When Howe first marched into the city, he was
greeted with throngs of cheering Loyalists, and those who supported
the patriot rebellion either fled or lay low in the wake of the British
occupation. For Howe, the capture of Philadelphia was a great boost
to his personal morale; for much of winter and spring 1777, he had
debated openly with his superiors in England regarding what his next
move should be. Administrators in the Court of St. James's hoped
he would march in support of General John Burgoyne's Saratoga
Campaign, but Howe remain fixated on ending the revolution by
capturing its primary field army under Washington along with the
capital city. In the previous three weeks, he had nearly destroyed the
Continental army at Brandywine, and with the fall of Philadelphia
it seemed as though his instincts were fully validated. But the victory
over the American capital was not yet secure, and Howe understood
how precarious his situation was. Ten miles south of Philadelphia,
the rebels maintained two forts on either side of the expansive
Delaware River. Called Forts Mercer and Mifflin, these posts virtually

choked off the entire river and denied Howe's redcoats critical supplies needed to hold the city. Until the Royal Navy fully controlled the Delaware, Howe's occupation of Philadelphia was tenuous at best.

To place his army in a most advantageous position, Howe split his forces; he left approximately three thousand four hundred men in Philadelphia and moved nine thousand northeast to the village of Germantown. Spreading out in a long line stretched east to west, Howe took up residence in the already historic Stenton, the former home of William Penn's secretary, James Logan. His right flank was defended by a force of Queen's Rangers, his left by Hessian Jaegers, and the center by Generals James Grant and Wilhelm von Knyphausen. Both Grant and Knyphausen had proven to be reliable seconds to Howe by 1777, the former being most memorable for his disastrous attack on Fort Duquesne in 1758.

While the arrangement was not ideal, Howe had very little concern about an attack from his patriot foes. After the previous weeks' victories, it was believed that the Continentals were far too damaged to attempt any assault on the rested redcoats. For Washington, though, the war had been anything but conventional, and the royalist position at Germantown presented him a unique opportunity. History had taught the American commander that engaging Howe in a conventional manner often resulted in defeat, but a calculated and unexpected attack would pay dividends. He had used this line of thinking a year earlier when he passed his forces across the icy Delaware to strike the New Jersey encampments of Trenton and Princeton; just as with Germantown, most believed that such a crossing was far too unlikely to be considered a viable threat. Facing a long winter of occupation and doubt, the commander in chief understood that if Philadelphia was going to be liberated, he would need to act immediately.

LEGACY: Germantown was yet another example of Washington's reach exceeding his grasp. Much like Trenton a year earlier, his attack

on Germantow
between his Co
ecute as Washing
heavy fog and the
Trenton had alread
its enemy with well
revealed that fortui
well. Germantown h
ton's men paid the pri
disobedience among th
ton's army saw 152 kill
For Howe, the totals we
It was a tremendous vict
failed to finish off the wou
would continue into 1778.

The defeat at Germantov
arena of the revolution. After
phia, it regrouped for a day in
Susquehanna River in York.
many prominent politicians b
mand. Men like John Adams a
criticized him openly, and a fie
mander in chief ensued. Many be
quate military leader, and General
made him a popular possible replac
army at Valley Forge to protect the
the capital, the movement to replace
the brokering of a new treaty of allia
the rebel coffers with new money, Wa
Forge in summer 1778 at the helm of

WHAT TO SEE: Long before Germantowr
was a neighboring immigrant communit
tour of the battle site should begin at Cl

Cliveden, also kno
and is the most di

Benjamin C
40th Regim
enemy. Ser
on eighteen
course, the
over the ye
liberately
appearan
ing Grou
Upper B
War vete
For a
mer ho

quarters of Sir William Howe during the Battle of Germantown. Finish your tour of the community at the Germantown Mennonite Meeting House; inside is the table where the first formal protest against African slavery was signed in 1688. By far, though, the best way to experience all that Germantown has to offer is the Revolutionary Germantown Festival. Held each October since 1927, the festival comprises live music, period food, detailed reenactments of the battle, and guided tours.

14

The Siege of Fort Mifflin

(SEPTEMBER 26–NOVEMBER 16, 1777)

BACKGROUND: On September 26, 1777, Sir William Howe's British army arrived in Philadelphia. In the days before, the various delegates of the Continental Congress fled for their lives for, if captured, they would have been arrested as traitors. While Independence Hall was cleared, many Philadelphia residents welcomed the British as returning heroes and were anxious to see law and order reestablished. The American Revolution was a messy, partisan affair, and the occupation of the American capital served as a high-water mark of the uncertainty that defined the era. With Washington's Continental army encamped in the countryside of Pennsylvania, Howe believed that Philadelphia, as well as New York, had now been reclaimed in the name of the Crown.

Capturing the largest city in North America had been far from easy; battles at Brandywine, the Clouds, and Paoli cleared a path to the city. But keeping Philadelphia was one of Howe's greatest challenges. Unlike New York, which could receive dozens of ships at a time, Philadelphia was not a coastal city. The British relied entirely on their ability to constantly resupply their armies with their massive

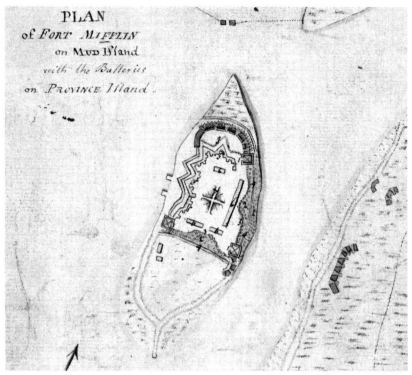

Plan of Fort Mifflin. A shining example of eighteenth-century military engineering, Fort Mifflin served the United States military for nearly 200 years. (*Library of Congress*)

navy and tremendous resources, but if those transatlantic vessels could not reach the troops in the field, they were rendered ineffective. For those precious goods and reinforcements to reach the capital, they first needed to travel up the Delaware Bay, and most critically into the Delaware River itself. Despite controlling the city, Howe did not control the mouth of this strategic waterway. Situated approximately ten miles south of the capital on Mud Island was Fort Mifflin, an impressive patriot stronghold housing five hundred soldiers. Armed and ready, Fort Mifflin's heavy guns effectively neutralized river travel to and from the city. Howe took Philadelphia in fall 1777, but without capturing Fort Mifflin he had virtually no chance of keeping it.

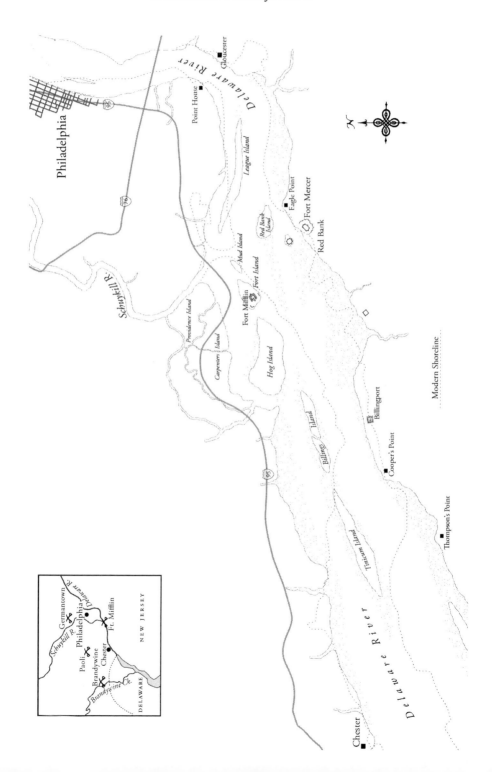

Philadelphia

Delaware River

Gloucester

Point House

League Island

Schuylkill R.

Eagle Point

Fort Mercer

Red Bank Island

Red Bank

Mud Island

Fort Island

Fort Mifflin

Providence Island

Carpenters Island

Hog Island

Modern Shoreline

Billingport

Billings Island

Cooper's Point

Thompson's Point

Tinicum Island

Delaware River

Chester

Schuylkill R.

Germantown

Delaware R.

Philadelphia

Ft. Mifflin

NEW JERSEY

Paoli

Chester

Brandywine

Brandywine Ck.

DELAWARE

BATTLE: In 1771, Captain John Montresor began building the structure that would eventually be known as Fort Mifflin. At the time the post was called the Mud Island Fort, as it sat on a river island in the Delaware River. Montresor never finished construction on the fort and went on to serve the Crown as the American rebellion exploded in 1775. Now, with the British occupying Philadelphia and the patriots having completed the remaining structure of the fort in 1777, it was poetic justice that Captain Montresor was again called to Mud Island—this time to capture the fort he had labored so hard to design. Taking Fort Mifflin was crucial to opening a channel for supplies to reach the British soldiers occupying Philadelphia, but capturing it was no small feat. On the opposite bank of the Delaware River sat a sister fortification to Mifflin known as Fort Mercer. With a position on each side of the river, the patriots could make the Delaware a dangerous place for oncoming British ships. That, however, was only the enemy one could see, as the Continentals also filled the shallow channel of the Delaware River with sharpened wooden pikes that would shred the hulls of unsuspecting vessels unlucky enough to sail over the tops of them. It was a formidable defense, and Howe knew it had to be broken for his occupation to succeed. It would be a long, slow affair, but one of the utmost importance.

The command situation for the Continentals was complicated. General Washington assigned Colonel Samuel Smith to reinforce Fort Mifflin shortly before Howe reached Philadelphia, but he later assigned the Prussian commander Henry Leonard D'Arendt to replace Smith. When D'Arendt became too sick to command, Smith once again took charge. Amid the confusion of determining who was in charge, the patriots needed to prepare for the oncoming British attack; it was a chaotic affair. When Captain Montresor arrived with his redcoats to begin preparations for an extended siege, the patriot leader Smith ordered the dikes around the Delaware to be destroyed. It was October 10. This flooded out premium land for Montresor to place artillery batteries, and he was forced to construct them in two feet of water. While the British were building these attack posi-

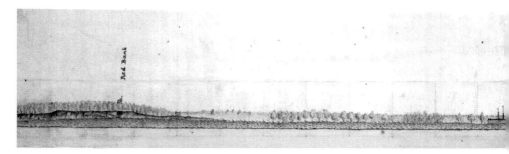

"View of Mud Island before its reduction, 16th Novr., 1777. . . taken from the dyke in front of the six gun battery on Carpenter's Island." Fort Mifflin as it appeared to the British attackers. (*Library of Congress*)

tions, Smith ordered an attack on the workers and captured fifty-six prisoners.

Across the river on October 22, action boiled over at Fort Mercer when a Hessian force commanded by Colonel Carl von Donop attacked the patriot position. After demanding that the fort surrender on two occasions, the German officer ordered his men to charge the stronghold. With German victory seemingly assured, the 1st Rhode Island Regiment waited until the Hessians were directly upon them and unleashed a ferocious fire. The regiment, famous for being made up entirely of African American soldiers, obliterated the Germans, killing 90, capturing 69, and wounding 227. With supplies running dangerously low and the fighting at Fort Mercer in mind, the garrison inside Fort Mifflin prepared for a British attack. The following day, five warships from the Royal Navy appeared to bombard the position. Though it was a show of strength, for the British it was the beginning of a disaster. The HMS *Merlin* and HMS *Augusta* ran aground shortly after arriving near Mud Island, and the men inside Fort Mifflin focused their artillery fire on the crippled vessels. The *Augusta* exploded spectacularly, causing windows to rattle in Philadelphia ten miles upriver. Sensing defeat, the crew of the *Merlin* burned their vessel before retreating. With the weather becoming colder and time running out for the British in Philadelphia, Howe ordered a land-based assault on Fort Mifflin to be led by Lieutenant Colonel George Osborn.

For much of the last month, the British and Continentals had traded heavy artillery fire, and the command of Fort Mifflin was constantly in flux. On November 10, Captain Samuel Treat was killed by an artillery round that landed inside the fort, and later that same day Colonel Smith was hit directly in the hip; by a miraculous measure he survived the blast, but barely. He was quickly ushered across the river to New Jersey, and Major Simeon Thayer took command of the beleaguered post. In support of the upcoming infantry attack, the British also called on the HMS *Vigilant* to sail alongside Mud Island and blast the patriot fort. In the main part of the Delaware, the *HMS Roebuck*, *Pearl*, and *Isis* fired in support, and the situation inside Fort Mifflin grew bleak. Sensing the end was upon him, Major Thayer lowered the American flag to raise a flag of distress. When the official colors dropped, the British in the Delaware cheered, believing it to be a full surrender. Thayer ordered a sergeant to raise the American flag again, and the man given the duty was abruptly cut in half by a British cannonball.

Although the main attack meant to overrun Fort Mifflin was to be a land-based assault, the artillery bombardment from the British navy was devastatingly effective. From his position in the city, Howe hesitated to order Osborn to charge the fort; he hoped that a suddenly rising tide would simply wash out the garrison and the patriots would surrender on their own. The surrender of the fort came in short order. On the night of November 15, Major Thayer ordered the three hundred men inside the post to scrape together whatever usable materials they could, load them onto barges, and quietly ferry

"Action off Mud Fort in the River Delaware," by William Elliot, 1787. The mighty British navy tangled with patriots along the Delaware River ten miles south of Philadelphia. (*New York Public Library*)

them across the river to New Jersey. He left a small contingent of soldiers behind with orders to burn as much of Fort Mifflin as possible, and after firing the barracks, they too abandoned the post. At sunrise on November 16, the *Vigilant* dispatched a force of marines to lower the American flag still flying over Fort Mifflin.

LEGACY: When Fort Mifflin was abandoned in mid-November, Sir William Howe had full command of Philadelphia and a means to resupply his men. So long as Fort Mifflin stood, Howe's grasp on the American capital was tenuous at best. But with its fall it became clear that the general could hold on to the city for nearly as long as he liked. It was a snowy day when British marines came ashore to officially take the fort, and save for a lone deserter inside, the massive post was empty. Casualty figures are difficult to calculate because of the extended nature of the siege, but best estimates show that the British fared far better than their patriot counterparts. The survivor inside claimed that the Continentals had lost fifty men, and that anywhere from seventy to eighty were injured; modern estimates place the casualties around 250. British casualties are listed at fifty-two killed and almost seventy wounded. It was not a glorious affair, but one of starvation and loss; the Siege of Fort Mifflin remains a truly grim reminder of how terrible warfare can be.

The scene upon entry by the redcoats was shocking, even by the standard of a partisan rebellion. Blood was splashed throughout the fort, and bodies lay strewn about. When Fort Mercer fell four days later on the New Jersey side of the Delaware River, any hope of stopping the mighty British navy from thoroughly dominating the water was lost. Charles Cornwallis once again proved his mettle by orchestrating the capture of the eastern post, and British supply ships sailed into the city within days. Perhaps one of the greatest legacies of Fort Mifflin is the literature it produced, including a detailed journal kept by Private Joseph Plumb Martin. His journal was first published in 1830 and has been continuously in print ever since. In its pages he writes about everything from drills to diet to experiences in combat, and to this day, it remains one of the single greatest windows into what the American Revolutionary era was like for the average soldier.

WHAT TO SEE: Given its importance and immaculate condition, Fort Mifflin should be an essential stopover for any visitor to the City of Brotherly Love. Located ten miles south of downtown Philadelphia just off one of the runways of Philadelphia International Airport, Fort Mifflin stands as a testament to American military power and ingenuity. Along with its important role in the American Revolution, Fort Mifflin was used continuously through World War II. The history rests in layers on the site, ranging from the eighteenth to the twentieth centuries, and in-house interpretation gives visitors a taste of each era of American military history. When it was constructed in the eighteenth century, Fort Mifflin stood on Mud Island, but today it rests on the shore of the Delaware River. Many guests speculate as to why and how the fortification was moved, and the answer is simple—it wasn't. The changing course of the river over the last 250 years has left Fort Mifflin onshore. When visiting the fort, be sure to stand on the bastions and take in the stunning view of the

Fort Mifflin today. The white portion of the south and east walls around the fort are the only remnants of John Montresor's original construction. Buildings in the background are, from left to right, the artillery shed, commandant's house (with cupola), officers quarters, soldiers barracks, and arsenal. (*National Park Service*)

Delaware River, as well as the wide angle that artillerymen would have had to strike passing British ships. Also make note of the powder magazine and the soldiers' barracks on-site. The very dedicated can buy a copy of Private Martin's diary, *A Narrative of a Revolutionary Soldier*, and read the entries written inside Fort Mifflin during the 1777 siege.

Fort Mifflin is proof that history has a funny way of reminding you that it's there. In 2006, a caretaker was mowing grass inside the fort when he suddenly sank into a collapsing shaft. After pulling himself from the hole, investigators uncovered what became known as Casemate 11. It was used as a jail cell in the Civil War, and investigators were stunned to see names inscribed into its walls as graffiti written by the cell's inhabitants. Among them was William H. Howe, a Confederate soldier who was famously captured in Pennsylvania and imprisoned on-site in 1864. Howe was hanged and was an infamous character in Philadelphia. The discovery of Casemate 11 and Howe's signature inside is a startling reminder that the past is real, and Fort Mifflin highlights that point like no other historic site in the commonwealth.

15

The Battle of Wyoming

(JULY 3, 1778)

BACKGROUND: The American Revolution was a brutal partisan war on the western frontiers. Far from the traditional battles between the Continentals and the redcoats along the Eastern Seaboard, the war in the west was made up of sudden, extremely violent raids pitting village against village and neighbor against neighbor. Following the Saratoga Campaign of 1777, which saw the British army suffer a surprising defeat along the Hudson River, imperial administrators along the frontier recalibrated their efforts to tame the western regions of the American colonies. Using Fort Niagara on Lake Ontario as a base, imperial agents courted the warriors of the Iroquois Confederacy to join their cause. While the Iroquois had been neutral for the first two years of the conflict, American ambitions for westward expansion drew a clear line for the Haudenosaunee, or the People of the Longhouse. The British offered them favorable terms of trade and alliance, but the Americans seemed committed to consuming their ancestral hunting grounds and forever altering the Iroquois way of life.

For these political, social, and economic reasons, all but two of the six nations that made up the Iroquois Confederacy sided with the Crown. In support of the war effort, Loyalist rangers collaborated with Iroquoian leaders like Guyasuta, Joseph Brant, Cornplanter, and Sayenqueraghta to cause mayhem along the North American backcountry regions of the Ohio, Mohawk, and Wyoming valleys. Giving special consideration to areas with strong patriot sympathies, the Anglo-Iroquois alliance transformed the western theater of the war into one of terror and bloodshed.

BATTLE: The Wyoming Valley was one of richness and prosperity and had long been considered a model for the westward growth possible in North America. Like the backcountry, it was once a wild and difficult place, but the Wyoming Valley stood as a potential model for the settler families willing to brave the elements and trek into the frontiers. Along with the region's large population, the American Revolution also revealed it to be heavily influenced by the patriot politics that fomented rebellion against the British Empire. As an agricultural hub, the Wyoming Valley provided reliably rich harvests year after year, and by 1778, it had become the breadbasket of George Washington's Continental army. The valley was only loosely protected by a series of small forts, including Forty Fort and Forts Durkee, Wilkes-Barre, Pittston, Ogden, and Jenkins. For all these reasons, the valley drew the attention of British operatives along the frontier, and the area was considered vulnerable to attack should the need arise.

The infrastructure of the British military machine was vast, and as such it required a broad collection of individuals to serve as administrators. While they all operated in different theaters of combat and played different roles, the hierarchy was designed to work collectively in pursuit of the common imperial mission. Along the frontiers of North America, these positions of authority often fell to Loyalist commanders with intimate knowledge of the region and the people who lived there. In the case of the Niagara frontier, there were few men more qualified than Lieutenant Colonel John Butler. Born in Connecticut but raised in the politically divided Mohawk River

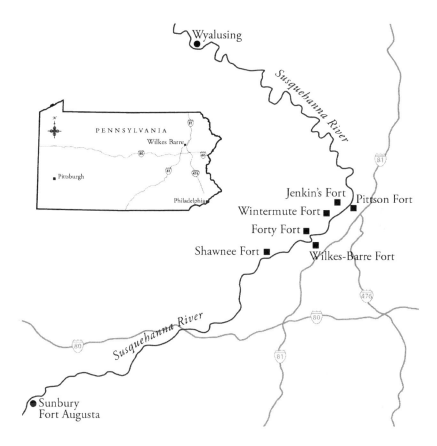

valley of New York, Butler was an instrumental figure in Britain's efforts to sway the warriors of the Iroquois Confederacy to its side. Based out of the castle-like fortification known as Fort Niagara along Lake Ontario, Butler was a hands-on commander who often participated in the raids and campaigns he devised. It was this quality that garnered him the respect of the Iroquois sachems and warriors and that also brought him to the Wyoming Valley in 1778.

The fighting style of the American Indian was jarring to Europeans who had never experienced it before, but it was well suited to the task of winning a partisan war. In many ways, the American Revolution was a civil war in the western backcountry, and the Iroquois' guerrilla-style raids were effective at causing chaos and disrupting important channels of communication and supplies. Given the agricultural importance of the Wyoming Valley, it was a natural target for Colonel John Butler's irregular militia group known as Butler's Rangers and their Anglo-Iroquois warriors. On July 1, Butler arrived in the valley with approximately one thousand men and began to march on the fortifications that defended the region. With little trouble, the rangers and warriors captured Forts Jenkins and Wintermoot just north of modern-day Wilkes-Barre. Sensing victory, the Loyalists and Iroquois ventured to Forty Fort the following day. Forty Fort was not unlike other posts in the region, but it was of particular political importance before the beginning of the war. According to its colonial charter, Connecticut claimed the region; but so did Pennsylvania, and this dispute added another wrinkle to the unique politics of the region.

Forty Fort was garrisoned primarily by 386 Connecticut soldiers known more commonly as "Yankees" and commanded by Colonel Zebulon Butler, who was also from Connecticut. On July 2, the invading Loyalists arrived outside of Forty Fort to demand its surrender; inside, a fiery debate ignited. As Zebulon Butler was a colonel in the Continental army, he did not have the leeway in decision making that an unaffiliated militia officer might have. He believed that the most prudent course of action would be to await support from George Washington's forces to the south; but as they had just begun a campaign through New Jersey, they were unlikely to arrive in time. From inside of Forty Fort, the younger, more excitable troops under the Yankee Butler's command began to clamor for a fight, and their insubordination became so great that they ridiculed the colonel as a coward. Giving in to the pressure, Zebulon Butler elected to fight back against the joint Loyalist-Indian force and ordered his men to march to Fort Wintermoot and confront the enemy.

As the Yankees marched toward the Loyalist position, Indian spies alerted Lieutenant Colonel Butler as to their approach. Sensing great opportunity, he ordered Fort Wintermoot to be set on fire, with hopes of misleading the patriots into believing he had abandoned the post. He promptly ordered his men to hide in the trees in preparation for an ambush. Upon their arrival, Zebulon Butler's Yankees saw the blaze but were not fooled. According to one participant, the patriots shouted, "Come out, ye villainous Tories! Come out, if ye dare, and show your heads, if ye durst, to the brave Continental Sons of Liberty!"[1] At 3:00 PM, the Loyalists rangers and Iroquois warriors did just that, and the Battle of Wyoming began. After the Yankees shouted their challenge, John Butler instructed his Loyalists to stay low to the ground and not strike until ordered to do so. The patriot commander waited for a response, but none came. Knowing full well that the Tories were in the forests, he ordered his men to fire one probing volley of their muskets. Still, the woods remained silent, so Zebulon Butler ordered two more volleys. As his men fired, they came within one hundred yards of the hidden enemy, and after the third volley, the Iroquois warriors struck. Running out of the trees brandishing tomahawks and shouting their infamous war whoops, the Iroquois charged the unsuspecting Yankee line. In a flash, the patriot line crumbled, and the native fighters became emboldened. Soon the Yankees turned and ran in a full-scale retreat, but the warriors did not give up their pursuit. Loyalists guns maintained a steady fire in support of the Indian assault, and the men of the Wyoming Valley were overrun.

While the Battle of Wyoming ended with the Yankee retreat, the Wyoming Massacre was only just beginning. Zebulon Butler's troops fled for their lives, but many were run down and killed in brutal fashion by the pursuing warriors. Some leaped into the Susquehanna River with hopes of escaping, but they were chased down and murdered as well. By the end of the fighting, approximately sixty of the nearly four hundred Yankees who challenged the Loyalist-Iroquois force survived the battle. For a long time afterward, the carcasses of their companions floated down the Susquehanna. The events of July 3, 1778, revealed the true nature of the American Revolution on the

---

1. Richard McGinnis, in Glenn F. Williams, *Year of the Hangman: George Washington's Campaign against the Iroquois* (Yardley, PA: Westholme 2005), 128.

The British described the Battle of Wyoming as a great victory, while the patriots saw it as nothing less than a massacre. Alonzo Chappel, 1858. (*New York Public Library*)

western frontier as well as the horrible price paid by the people who lived there. Colonel John Butler claimed that his raiding party had collected almost 230 scalps and burned one thousand homes.

LEGACY: The Battle of Wyoming and the massacre that followed had immediate and long-term consequences for the Anglo-Iroquois forces involved. Only a day later, another raiding party captured nearby Fort Pittston in modern Luzerne County, and the royalists held the position until the negotiated peace that ended the war in 1783. The devastation was total, and in the wake of the raids, the Wyoming Valley was nearly emptied of its inhabitants. In a panic sometimes called "the Big Runaway," hundreds of settlers fled the region of northeastern Pennsylvania out of fear of another attack similar to that of July 3, 1778. As was part of Britain's overall goal, small posts like Fort Augusta in the Susquehanna River valley were soon overrun by fleeing refugee families and rendered militarily obsolete.

By far the greater consequence of the joint raids, however, was the punishment that befell the Iroquois as a result. In 1779, Commander in Chief George Washington set out to entirely dismantle the ancient lands of the Haudenosaunee. Launching three separate campaigns, he hoped to raze Iroquoia to eliminate the threat it posed to the frontier. From Easton, Pennsylvania, Major General John Sullivan marched north to the Susquehanna River and into central New York, while Brigadier General James Clinton marched west into the Mohawk River valley. In support, a third column under Colonel Daniel Brodhead trekked north via the Allegheny River valley, and each was told to launch total war on the Iroquois villages they encountered. In what was likely Washington's most successful military operation when comparing objectives and tangible results, the Sullivan-Clinton-Brodhead campaigns were incredible achievements. Dozens of Iroquois villages were burned, and countless acres of crops were destroyed. As the raid came just before the harvest, thousands of Iroquois families were doomed to starve in the coming winter 1779–1780. When that winter arrived, it was one of the harshest on record, and thousands of Iroquois refugees flooded the British Fort Niagara as a result. Washington's war on Iroquoia was so successful that virtually all of its ancient villages were destroyed, and only a scant few would ever be inhabited again.

WHAT TO SEE: The most immediate place for visitors to begin their tour of the Battle of Wyoming is in the borough of Wyoming, Luzerne County. At the intersection of Route 11 (Wyoming Avenue) and Susquehanna Avenue sits the Wyoming Monument, an obelisk flanked by two nineteenth-century cannons. These are not Revolutionary War guns, however, as they are clearly marked as 6.4-inch cannons dated to 1863. As far as monuments go, the Wyoming obelisk is impressive in its details. On each side of the monument is a plaque highlighting a separate feature of the battle. On one side is a general description of the event and the dedication details of the obelisk. The remaining three sides provide detailed lists for field officers slain in battle, civilians and soldiers slain in battle, and survivors of the battle.

The story of the obelisk is fasci-
nating, and worth noting while
preparing for a visit. After the fighting subsided in July 1778, families
were unable to return to their home-
steads until October. For over three
months, the mutilated bodies of
their loved ones lay exposed to the
elements, unmoved from where they
died. After the settlers returned
home, they gathered their family
members' remains and interred
them in a mass grave. Fifty-four
years later, in 1832, a public ceremony was held with some elderly
survivors in attendance, and the
bodies were exhumed from the
grave. In 1833, all of the remains
were reinterred in a large, communal
vault under the current site of the

The Wyoming Monument is a solitary
memorial to the battle and the many
lives lost in the aftermath. (*Wikimedia
Commons*)

Wyoming Monument. When you approach the obelisk, be mindful
of this fact, for it is literally a grave marker as well as an interpretive
memorial. The monument was struck by lightning in 2008 and badly
damaged, but after some repairs in 2010 led by the Wyoming Commemorative Association, it stands again in perfect condition. The
Wyoming Monument was rededicated on Independence Day 2011.

16

The Burning of Hannastown

(JULY 13, 1782)

BACKGROUND: The Ohioan frontier was a dangerous place, but by no means was it desolate. With Fort Pitt acting as the headquarters of the Continental army's Western Department, the emerging village of Pittsburgh was an unofficial capital of the American west. It was a small smattering of cabins and gardens, and without the massive fort at its heart, it would have been nearly impossible to sustain. Interestingly enough, Pittsburgh was not even the largest settlement of the backcountry, for thirty miles east along the Forbes Road was the bustling village of Hannastown. Established in 1773 by Robert Hanna as a stopover on the main highway west, Hannastown was fifteen years younger than Pittsburgh but already surpassed it in population by the time of the Revolutionary War. It was constructed on a rolling meadow and made up of tiny, hand-hewn log cabins built primarily by Scots-Irish Presbyterians, and it was a place of major political importance.

In the years leading up to the war, the Ohio Country had been claimed by rival colonial interests, and a bloodless type of civil war began. Virginia, using Pittsburgh as its administrative base of operations, claimed the entire region and even went so far as to organize it into counties. In response, Pennsylvania strengthened its claim by establishing a courthouse and, by extension, its own political authority, at Hannastown; it was promptly named the seat of the newly organized Westmoreland County. The dichotomy of power on the frontier between Pittsburgh and Hannastown made for a tense situation. Agents of Virginia arrested Pennsylvania officials for illegally operating out of their jurisdiction and imprisoned them at Fort Pitt. In response, Pennsylvanians apprehended and sentenced Virginians at Hannastown. Colonial America was a complicated entity with messy politics, but all was set aside at the beginning of the War for Independence.

BATTLE: By 1782, Hannastown already had a deep connection with the American Revolution. In 1775, delegates from across Westmoreland County met in the town to write what became known as the Hannastown Resolves. This document admonished Parliament for its alleged abuses to the American colonies and openly defied royal authority; written a full year before the Declaration of Independence, this document served as rallying point for the rebels of the backcountry. It was no surprise that in the wake of the resolves, frontiersmen from around Hannastown were some of the first to volunteer in the Continental army. In May 1775, the sheriff of Westmoreland County, John Proctor, organized a volunteer force to fight the redcoats and defend the frontier from their Indian allies. It became known as the Independent Battalion of Westmoreland County Pennsylvania, or IBWCP for short. They went on to serve in a number of battles as part of George Washington's Continental army as well as in many campaigns in the west.

As part of their greater war effort, royal forces utilized the assistance of Indian nations in the same fashion that the French had during the Seven Years' War. While the regular armies of Sir William Howe and John Burgoyne tangled with the Continentals in the east, British agents relied on allied Indian warriors to raid and destroy the colonial frontier. In the previous war, regular French troops marched with the natives during some of these raids, but in the revolution, the British greatly improved on that strategy. Lieutenant Colonel John Butler was born and raised in America, and at the outset of the war was loyal to the Crown. Because of his natural leadership abilities, he garnered the support of many like-minded frontiersmen and formed an irregular militia group called Butler's Rangers. They were partisans, and they often fought alongside Iroquoian allies to raid known patriot settlements. By 1782, Butler's Rangers were intimately associated with all of the brutality and depredations associated with Indian warfare. They were regular participants in some of the biggest battles of the frontier, and Butler's Rangers played prominent roles at the Battle of Wyoming and a similar attack on Cherry Valley in New York. From the Niagara frontier to Virginia, from the Ohio Country to the Illinois Country, Butler and his allied warriors kept patriot America on edge.

In 1781, just two months before Washington's great victory at Yorktown, the men of Hannastown participated in a major offensive into the Ohio Country under the command of Colonel Archibald Lochry. As part of the assault on Fort Detroit planned by the famed commander George Rogers Clark, Lochry's expedition took most of the able-bodied men out of Westmoreland County and left its settlements largely undefended. On August 24, Lochry's men were ambushed by British-allied Indians under sachem Joseph Brant at the mouth of the Great Miami River in modern Indiana; all were either captured or killed. Many were executed even after surrendering, and Lochry was killed and mutilated. The event, which quickly became known as Lochry's Defeat or the Lochry Massacre, placed Westmoreland County in a tenuous position.

As the world reeled from news of Washington's defeat of Charles Cornwallis at Yorktown, many along the Eastern Seaboard became hopeful for a treaty with Britain and the creation of a new United States of America. The frontier, however, shared in no such jubilation, and for the settlers and Indians there, Yorktown did not represent the end to anything. In summer 1782, Butler's Rangers planned yet another raid into the Ohio Country, this time against Fort Pitt, and recruited many Ohioan warriors to join them. Spies were everywhere on the frontier, and when commanders at the patriot post heard of the oncoming attack, they greatly reinforced Pittsburgh. Butler and his rangers used Fort Niagara on Lake Ontario as a headquarters and planned on rallying their allies at Lake Chautauqua. With the news of Pittsburgh reinforcement, the militiamen abandoned their campaign, but their Indian allies were determined to carry it out. Attacking Fort Pitt seemed to be foolish, but not Hannastown. The settlement was still recovering from Lochry's Defeat, and warriors led by the Mingo-Seneca Guyasuta and Sayengaraghta moved to destroy it. Using canoes, the war party moved south on the Allegheny River, and although the details are not entirely clear, they appear to have abandoned their boats near the remnants of Kittanning and continued either on horseback or on foot. While this has never been verified by an Indian source, residents of Pittsburgh witnessed empty canoes floating down the Allegheny a few days later and assumed they had been left by the war party.

Moving from the north, the Indian raiders were first spotted at the farm of Michale Huffnagle approximately one and a half miles north of Hannastown. The men of the farm immediately ran for the town to warn it of the approaching danger. With word of the raid coming, the citizens of Hannastown rushed into the meager stockade (known as Fort Reed) and closed the heavy wooden doors in preparation for the raid. Sixty people took cover inside the post, twenty being men with only seventeen guns. The inadequacy of the situation was a stunning testament to the horrible losses at Lochry's Defeat a year earlier. The warriors were intimately familiar with the region and, to disguise their approach, did not utter a whoop or war cry until they entered the town. Numbering approximately one hundred, Guyasuta and Sayenqueraghta's warriors began to ravage Hannastown. They sought the total destruction of the settlement, and they killed cattle and livestock first to ensure that it would not recover.

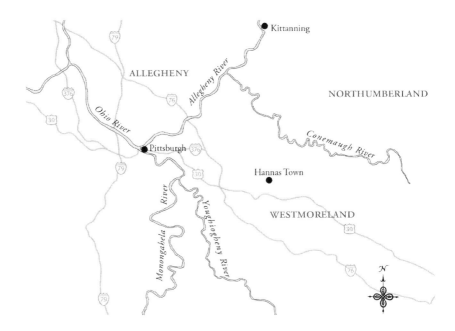

From inside the stockade, the citizens could only watch in horror as the warriors began to fire the cabins and burn most of the village to the ground.

The lone casualty from the burning of Hannastown was sixteen-year-old Margaret Shaw, who was struck by a bullet while inside Fort Reed. The citizens were relieved to see the war party eventually leave the area, but their town could not be saved with the exception of a few scattered buildings. The following day it was discovered that other settlements in the area were raided and razed, including Miller's Station two miles south at the time a wedding party was taking place. The warriors stormed the celebration without warning, and many of the guests fled for the trees. Those who resisted were killed, and fifteen men, women, and children were taken captive. Westmoreland County was devastated by the raid, and Hannastown never recovered.

LEGACY: Hannastown was destroyed by Guyasuta and Sayenqueraghta, and it was never rebuilt. The burning of Hannastown was the most destructive and complete Indian victory of the American Revolution, and it drastically reordered the political makeup of the Ohio Country. Prior to the outbreak of war, Pittsburgh (representing Virginia) and Hannastown (representing Pennsylvania) were embroiled in a territorial dispute over which colony controlled the region, but the debate ended when Hannastown burned. Because Virginia's claims were largely reinforced by its military presence at Fort Pitt, renamed Fort Dunmore by Governor John Murray, 4th Earl of Dunmore, the southern colony lost most of its clout when the Continental army established its headquarters at Pittsburgh. Despite Hannastown being mostly reduced to ashes, court sessions were still held there in whatever structures remained until being officially moved to Greensburg after the war. The site remained abandoned into the nineteenth century, when it became farmland. Had Hannastown not been attacked in 1782, the urban geography of modern Pennsylvania could be very different, as the town was likely to have continued to grow. If nothing else, Hannastown is evidence that the backcountry was just as dedicated to the patriot cause as any major city of the east. Its destruction stands as a clear statement that although Washington and the British ended combat operations at Yorktown in 1781, the war was far from over on the frontier.

WHAT TO SEE: The reconstructed site called Historic Hanna's Town sits today in the heart of Westmoreland County farm country. It is an unassuming place at first glance, but after a brief survey of the site, one cannot help but marvel at what is preserved there. Hannastown was a sprawling settlement that was dependent on the Forbes Road, but after it was destroyed by British-allied Indian warriors in 1782, it never fully recovered. Standing at the flagpole at the top of the hill, one gains a sweeping view of the meadow that Hannastown once occupied. The property boundaries are there, as well as the original tree line; all that is missing are the cabins and people themselves. With a little imagination, guests can visualize the bustling community of settlers cooking their meals and bringing in their harvests, entirely unaware of the calamity about to befall them.

Historic Hanna's Town features several reconstructed buildings. From 1773 until its destruction in 1782, Hannastown was Pittsburgh's rival in size and population on the Pennsylvania frontier. (*Westmoreland County Historical Society*)

Historic Hanna's Town has some wonderful interpretations of the town's vital history on display. Hannastown had the first courthouse west of the Allegheny Mountains, and the reconstructed village has myriad court documents just waiting to be studied by an enterprising historian. For a better view of daily colonial life, guests can tour a faithful re-creation of Robert Hanna's Tavern, and see archaeological artifacts that have been pulled from the ground. The collection includes expected things like utensils, tools, balls, and buttons as well as the unexpected; Chinese porcelain was found on-site, revealing that this tiny backcountry outpost was far more connected to the larger imperial world than most realized at the time. Other points of interest include the rebuilt stockade that saved the city's residents on July 13, 1782, rebuilt log homes typical of the period, and a preserved Conestoga wagon of the type that opened the west for migrating families. Historic Hanna's Town closes for the winter, and the city truly comes to life in the fall. The smell of burning campfires and a backdrop of changing leaves presents a scene that truly brings out the site's best. For an additional connection, visit the Fort Pitt Museum. On display there is the original flag of John Proctor's Independent Battalion of Westmoreland County, Pennsylvania, with its legendary motto, "Don't Tread on Me."

PART THREE

THE REPUBLIC'S FIRST TESTS (1794–1844)

In 1783, the world turned upside down when the Peace of Paris was signed between the United Kingdom of Great Britain and the new United States of America. From the outset of the American Revolution, many traditional Old World powers scoffed at the idea of democratic self-government. Born in the salons of Paris, the notion of a free republic of the people, by the people, and for the people was believed by some to be only a dream. But a world away, the patriot movement put the thoughts and ideas of the great Enlightenment thinkers into action and gave rise to the world's first modern republic. The Americans had won their freedom, but major questions remained regarding the future of the young nation. The patriots who won the American Revolution took up arms for the promise of a country of their choosing, but what if that vision was not shared by all who fought? Was a Connecticut Yankee's idea of a perfect America the same as that of a Virginia slave owner? If not, how could the warring parties ever reconcile? All were legitimate concerns, and how they were addressed would determine if the dream of self-government would prosper or fail.

The United States faced serious problems in its earliest years. It was buried in debt, racked with plummeting wages, and handcuffed by an ill-conceived legal document called the Articles of Confederation, and many of its most severe issues appeared as though they could topple the republic before it truly had a chance to begin. After an abortive tax revolt in Massachusetts known as Shays's Rebellion, the nation's leaders were pressed into action to create a broader, more practical legal framework. When the US Constitution became effective in 1789, a new set of principles and promises was canonized into law for all the world to see. The 1790s were fraught with challenges ranging from domestic rebellions to an Indian war to partisan squabbles, but through the leadership of the first president, George Washington, the nation persevered.

In 1800, the United States cleared one of its greatest hurdles when Thomas Jefferson was elected president, and the decade-long rule of the Federalist Party came to an end. Many questioned whether the

Federalists would step aside for the states' rights-oriented Democratic-Republican Party. President John Adams did step aside, and the two-hundred-year tradition of the peaceful transition of power began. The Constitution, it seemed, had just passed its most extraordinary challenge yet. As the eighteenth century gave way to the nineteenth, the American people were tested in unexpected ways; declarations of war against foreign powers, the suppression of Indian uprisings, the sectional challenges of slavery, and the difficult realities of a pluralistic society all spread fear and uncertainty across the growing country. The Constitution did not always provide a specific solution to the problems of the day, but it did offer a clear path forward. Bolstered by a balanced government, limits on individual power, protections of free speech and the presence of a rigid judiciary, order was restored time and again.

That is not to say that peace always prevailed; many times in American history it appeared as though the entire system might collapse under the weight of public outcry and reactionary politics. Rioters stormed America's streets, demagogues distorted everyday situations for temporary political gain, and countless lives were lost. Each time, though, the public turned its faith toward the legal tradition established by the Constitution, and despite its being pushed to its limits, the levees of democracy held strong. Despite its beginnings as the Peaceable Kingdom, Pennsylvania was not immune to violent and painful surges, and when they occurred, the nation took notice.

17

The Whiskey Rebellion

(JULY 1794)

BACKGROUND: In many ways, winning independence and establishing the world's first modern republic was the easy part—keeping it would be much more difficult. After the ratification of the US Constitution in September 1787, the American nation established a new order over the former thirteen colonies. For the first president, George Washington, the protection and maintenance of this new standard became paramount. He understood that he was not a king or an autocrat but merely a placeholder. As the first president, however, he was far more important than he realized, as his actions would become the standard for all future executives to come. Washington's administration lasted two terms, and his challenges were many. Problems—including interstate disputes, an Indian war, and a looming national debt—made for many sleepless nights, and many of these dilemmas were beginning to intersect in western Pennsylvania.

To solve the young nation's financial problems, Washington turned to Alexander Hamilton of New York. Hamilton was a faithful officer during the revolution and an ardent believer in using the broad powers of the federal government to achieve his desired goals.

As secretary of the Treasury, Hamilton faced down many critical issues, but America's outstanding debts from the revolution were among the most crucial. To pay down these sums, Hamilton devised an excise tax on whiskey as a means of generating more revenue. As the tax was placed exclusively on domestic goods, many along the frontier believed it to be a direct assault on their rights as Americans. With an abundance of rye, corn, wheat, and barley, western Pennsylvanians felt unjustly squeezed by this new regulation, and whispers of rebellion began to spread across the southwest counties of the state.

BATTLE: In 1790, Hamilton was in a difficult position. He needed to pay off the debts of the revolution, specifically to the bondholders who financed the war. As he had already raised import duties to their maximum, he turned to taxing the domestic product of whiskey to increase revenues. Because western Pennsylvania was the largest grain producer in the country, most of its farmers distilled their crops into spirits to sell to the thirsty markets of the east. When word of the tax crossed the mountains, it was received with myriad righteously indignant complaints: some said it unfairly favored the major whiskey distillers of the east and placed undue burden on the small-time operations of the west; to others it was an unjust tax levied on the poor to pay off the rich bondholders, a reverse Robin Hood scheme. Meanwhile, the backcountry was beset by other problems: the Spanish blocked trade on the Mississippi River, and the developing Ohioan rebellion known as the Northwest Indian War left settlers on constant edge. There was a feeling in the 1790s that the federal government all but ignored the travails of the west. The politically minded citizens of western Pennsylvania began meeting to express their distaste for the tax.

The unrest on the frontier was not violent yet, but it was an increasingly volatile situation. The frontier was an extremely isolated place, so many farmers completed business transactions using trade goods rather than hard currency. When Hamilton's tax was levied, it had to be paid in specie, but without a large supply of coinage in cir-

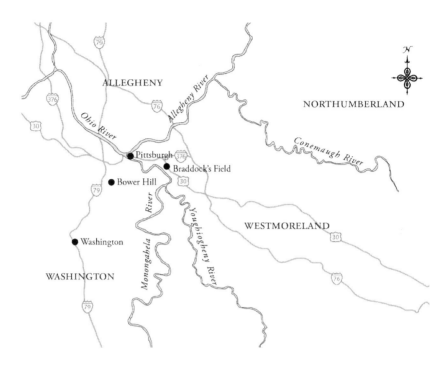

culation, many in the west simply could not pay. As a result, dozens
of farmers received summonses to appear in court to explain their
delinquency; but the courts were in distant Philadelphia, not Pittsburgh. All of these factors swirled together by 1794 to cause a maelstrom of unrest along the Pennsylvania frontier. Just as had happened
in the revolution, mobs burned tax offices and raised liberty poles;
in many cases the Whiskey Rebellion truly felt like an extension of
the partisan demonstrations seen in the 1770s. Key figures like
Fayette County congressman Albert Gallatin and Pittsburgh lawyer
Hugh Henry Brackenridge backed the rankled populist movement
early on, but as the protests devolved into violent revolt, most legitimate political players recanted their support.

In summer 1794, the situation exploded into violence. In May, a
federal district attorney issued subpoenas for several dozen farmers
in the Ohio Country. By July they were being issued by US marshal
David Lenox, and most were issued without any problems to speak
of. That all changed on July 15, when Lenox was joined by John

Neville, who was a federal tax inspector and Revolutionary War general. As the two men issued subpoenas in Allegheny County, they both felt a palpable tension in the air. As they approached the homestead of Oliver Miller, a local farmer, they suddenly heard gunshots. There is no indication that the muskets were aimed at the men, and the firing was most likely warning shots, but the point was made. Lenox retreated to the safety of Pittsburgh while Neville fled to his nearby estate, Bower Hill.

Bower Hill was a statement of federal power on the frontier, but to the rebels it was a symbol of government corruption and extravagance. Consisting of a large mansion house and several outbuildings, it was the largest home in the area and was maintained by enslaved men and women. On July 16, a party of approximately thirty rebels surrounded the mansion, and while the details remain unclear, a shot was fired from inside that killed Oliver Miller. From over 150 yards away it was probably the result of more luck than skill, but for the westerners it was a bridge too far. They fled and returned the next day in an enormous mob led by a Revolutionary War veteran, Major James McFarlane. Some estimated the crowd to have been from three hundred to six hundred strong. Women and children were allowed to leave the house, and they fled toward Chartiers Creek to Woodville Plantation, the home of Neville's son, Pressley. At that point a battle ensued. Ten soldiers garrisoned at Fort Fayette in Pittsburgh had reinforced the position, and after an hour-long firefight, a truce was called. As the rebels dropped their weapons and prepared to discuss terms, someone inside the mansion house shot and killed the commander, McFarlane, and chaos ensued. By the end of the night, prisoners were taken by the rebels, and Bower Hill was incinerated.

On August 1, over seven thousand rebels met on Braddock's Field, site of the 1755 Battle of the Monongahela, and declared their intentions to march on Pittsburgh and destroy the city. For President Washington, this was the breaking point. After careful analysis of his constitutional duties, he decided it was within his rights and responsibility to suppress the insurrection in the west. If that meant that he

The suppression of the Whiskey Rebellion was the first and only time that a sitting president led the army as commander-in-chief in United States history. A circa 1795 painting shows Washington reviewing troops massed to quell the rebellion. (*Metropolitan Museum of Art*)

would need to open fire on American citizens, he was prepared to do so. On August 4, Washington declared western Pennsylvania to be in a state of rebellion, and he called out the state militias to suppress it. With few volunteers eager to go west, a draft was instituted, causing great frictions across the young nation. The army was untrained and undersupplied, and its tendency to rob farmers of their crops as it marched made it very unpopular in local communities. Washington led the thirteen-thousand-man force, pejoratively known as "the Watermelon Army," as far as Bedford, Pennsylvania. From there, Revolutionary War hero Henry "Lighthorse Harry" Lee and Alexander Hamilton took it the last one hundred miles to Pittsburgh. Upon the arrival of the armed forces, the rebels dispersed, and after the ringleaders of the affair were arrested, the Whiskey Rebellion was effectively over. Some of the highest-profile figures involved, such as David Bradford, escaped deeper into the frontier, but others were detained. In an act of great foresight, President Washington pardoned the remaining ringleaders six months later. For the first commander in chief, America was ready to move forward into the nineteenth century.

LEGACY: The Whiskey Rebellion was a watershed moment in the history of the young American republic. For the first time in the constitutional era, the direct sovereignty of the United States was challenged. After a careful reading of the law, Washington decided that the insurrection needed to be suppressed immediately, for if it were allowed to fester, it would certainly spread to other states. When Washington mounted his horse and traveled west to stamp out the uprising, it was the first and only time a sitting president led a military force himself as commander in chief, even though he traveled only as far as Bedford. The fact that the rebellion dissolved peacefully was a great relief to the sixty-two-year-old Virginian.

The bloodless end to the Whiskey Rebellion may seem anticlimactic, but the restoration of law and order was a critical hurdle for the United States to clear. Until the Civil War began in 1861, the Whiskey Rebellion was the single largest domestic uprising in American history. Many historians today consider the event two different ways. For some it is the first true test of our constitutional republic; for others it serves as an epilogue to the American Revolution. Both interpretations have merit, and they are not mutually exclusive, but the fundamental concerns of this event are clear: the people of the frontier were eager to participate in the war against Britain when they believed their rights were violated. The events of 1794 proved that they would not hesitate to rise up again even if it meant resisting their own government. The independent streak of the frontiersmen had plagued French and British administrators, and now it plagued American ones. It was that quest for self-governance that carried the American nation into the distant west over the next hundred years.

WHAT TO SEE: The Whiskey Rebellion was a regional phenomenon, and the sites one can visit make for a long but worthwhile road trip. Most of the uprising occurred around Pittsburgh, where travelers can visit a number of important sites. In Allegheny County, the rebels held their famous rally at Braddock's Field in modern-day Braddock. While the site is currently under a massive steel mill, historical mark-

Historic Woodville Plantation, in Bridgeville, Pennsylvania, is open to the public and re-mains the most tangible connection to the Whiskey Rebellion. The plantation is a short distance from the original location of Bower Hill. (*Woodville Plantation*)

ers exist throughout the community. For a more hands-on experi-ence, drive southwest to the Woodville Plantation. The former home of Pressley Neville, Woodville remains in its original condition from the days of the rebellion. With a great deal of interpretation on-site and full house tours available, one can walk through a home of the 1790s with a direct tie to the event. A short drive up Kane Boulevard reveals the original site of the enormous confrontation at John Neville's Bower Hill Plantation; the home is gone, but the vistas over Chartiers Creek and of Woodville below are unchanged. A short drive to South Park takes visitors to the Oliver Miller Homestead, a stone home associated with some of the opening shots of the general insurrection.

Next, weary travelers will be on the road driving south on Inter-state 79 to Washington County. Another hotspot of the rebellion, Washington County has two sites of note: Mingo Creek Presbyterian Church and David Bradford's former home. The church, a staging ground for the rebel movement early on, stands preserved just outside of Finleyville. The Bradford House, located in downtown Washington, was the home of one of the prominent ringleaders of the insurrection and remains preserved for public tours. Continuing south on I-79, visitors can find Albert Gallatin's Friendship Hill, a National Park and former home of America's longest-serving Treasury secretary. Gallatin supported the rebellion in its infancy, and while he gave the movement legitimacy, he disavowed the violence that followed.

Continue east on the Pennsylvania Turnpike, taking note of the Bonnet Tavern just off the main road; rebels met here to raise a liberty pole. Finish your tour at Bedford Village, where President Washington stayed during the campaign to suppress the insurrection, and visit the Espy House to explore his headquarters. For a more complete list of the twenty-plus historical markers associated with the Whiskey Rebellion, visit the website of the Pennsylvania Historical and Museum Commission.

18

The US Brig *Niagara* and the Battle of Lake Erie

(SEPTEMBER 10, 1813)

BACKGROUND: In 1812, America was struggling to find its place in the world. It was neither an economic nor military superpower, and in an age of empires, it was barely able to control its own states. Under President James Madison, the young nation watched tepidly as Great Britain and Napoleonic France, the two strongest nations on earth, did battle to decide the fate of Europe. That struggle seemed to entangle the whole civilized world, but America's geographic placement in the Western Hemisphere offered enough distance that the Madison administration could mostly watch from afar. There were instances, though, when Americans suffered because of their proximity to the world war. As the British relied heavily on what was far and away the world's greatest navy to fend off Napoleon, they often engaged in an ancient practice known as impressment. This meant it was standard practice to capture an American merchant vessel and force its crew to serve in the British navy. It may seem outrageous, but on the high seas, America's sailing men had little choice but to join or die.

In the confusion of the war, Britain and France paid little attention to the American states, and this emboldened Madison. With British Canada just opposite the St. Lawrence River, he devised a scheme to invade the colony and annex it into the United States while Britain was distracted fighting Napoleon. After all, the entire population of Canada hovered around one hundred thousand, and its border was undefended. On June 18, 1812, Congress declared war for the first time, and "Mr. Madison's War," as it came to be known, began.

BATTLE: Despite winning their independence in 1783, the American states had yet to fully rid the British military from its newly acquired territories. While the original thirteen colonies were never in doubt, the Crown maintained a number of its garrisons that were fortified in the vast Northwest Territory. Until the Americans were in a position to force them out, British administrators in Canada defiantly kept their men stationed along the US frontier. By the outset of the War of 1812, the British had abandoned many of these vital posts, but they soon refocused their energies on recapturing many of them. Among the most critical was Detroit, as it commanded a vital supply line in the heart of the Great Lakes. Just as the French had done in the Seven Years' War and the British in the revolution, the Americans were committed to retaining their control over this strategic location.

When the British moved to recapture Detroit under Major General Isaac Brock in 1812, they retained a major naval advantage that the Americans simply could not compete with. For the previous two hundred years, the British had been recognized as having the finest and most formidable navy on earth, and while they used it to rule the high seas, they could easily take control of the Great Lakes as well. By the time Fort Detroit was attacked, the mighty British navy had made its appearance in Lake Erie; as for the Americans, they only had one ship to speak of, the brig *Adams*. When Detroit fell to the British, the *Adams* was also captured and promptly reassigned to the Royal Navy. For the fledgling Americans, it became clear that to make any serious attempt at reclaiming Detroit they would need to be competitive in the Great Lakes. They needed ships and sailors, but in 1812 they had neither. It was decided that Erie's Presque Isle Bay was an ideal location to construct warships; it was a natural harbor that could shelter the vessels from extreme weather conditions and offer easy access to Lake Erie and the British fleet on it. In March 1813, Rhode Island commodore Oliver Hazard Perry arrived at Erie to see the task completed. Perry was an experienced seaman who had fought piracy in the Caribbean and Mediterranean. Lake Erie would be the greatest challenge of his life.

By the beginning of August, Perry had completed his warships at Presque Isle, but his men were exhausted and falling ill. While no one would have mistaken them for the Spanish Armada, he had managed to build and recruit nine ships into service, including two brigs, the *Lawrence* and the *Niagara*. The former would serve as his flagship, but the latter would mark his place in history. Perry's men were raw and untrained, but he moved on Detroit with no hesitation. When he arrived at Put-in-Bay near Sandusky, Ohio, he positioned his ships in such a way that he effectively blockaded his enemy's supply line. The blockade lasted five weeks, and the British commander, Robert Hariot Barclay, was slowly watching his men wither away. They had no food, no supplies, and no apparent hope of help arriving. In early September, Barclay decided the only way to survive the blockade and maintain control over Detroit was to charge Perry's fleet. It was, in the words of one historian, the starving fighting the sick.[1]

At 11:45 AM on September 10, the British and Americans began their duel in Lake Erie. Perry hoped to fire on Barclay's men from aboard the *Lawrence,* but he was unable to close the distance in a timely manner. Instead the *Detroit,* formerly the American *Adams,* pounded Perry's flagship with its much more accurate long-range guns. By the time the *Lawrence* came within its own firing range an

1. Walter Rybka, in David Frew, *Perry's Lake Erie Fleet: After the Glory* (Charleston, SC: History Press, 2012), 74.

"Perry's victory on Lake Erie, Sept. 10th 1813," drawn by J. J. Barralet, engraved by B. Tanner, and published in 1814. (*Library of Congress*)

hour later, the neophyte crew had overloaded the guns with too much powder and shot, rendering them ineffective. While Perry was being hammered by Barclay's gunners, Perry's second brig, *Niagara,* stayed far behind the rest of his ships. The *Niagara* was led by Master Commandant Jesse Elliot, and speculation and confusion swirled around the ship's apparent lack of interest in engaging, considering that conditions were present to allow it to join the fight. Perry's flagship was steadily demolished by the heavy cannon fire of his British enemies. After 80 percent of his men were killed or wounded and all but one gun rendered useless, Perry had no choice but to abandon ship. He quickly boarded a small row boat and paddled approximately half a mile to the *Niagara* and took command.

When Perry transferred his flag, disaster struck for the British. Two of their primary fighting vessels, the *Detroit* and *Queen Charlotte,* collided. They became entangled and were unable to separate themselves, and many onboard were badly wounded; Commander Barclay and his first lieutenant were among the casualties. Despite the controversy surrounding Elliot's initial hesitance to engage, the *Niagara* remained basically unscathed during the battle. Sensing opportunity amidst the chaos, Perry ordered his ships forward and unleashed heavy fire on the two entangled ships. While the British believed victory was assured when the *Lawrence* was disabled, the

Battle of Lake Erie now took a sudden and drastic turn in favor of the Americans. By 3:00 PM, the British vessels could take no more and had no choice but to surrender to Perry's jubilant men. As a symbolic gesture, the commodore requested that the capitulation be signed aboard the disabled deck of the *Lawrence*. After engineering one of the unlikeliest victories in the history of North American combat, Perry wrote a note to General William Henry Harrison, commander of the Army of the Northwest. It famously read:

> Dear Gen'l:
>   We have met the enemy, and they are ours, two ships, two brigs, one schooner and one sloop.
> Yours with great respect and esteem.
> O. H. Perry.[2]

LEGACY: It has been said that most nations fight wars to defend a national identity, but in the War of 1812, the United States fought to create one. The war is one of the least understood events in US history, and few Americans have any idea why it happened or what resulted. While these points are still debated today, there is no question that Perry's victory on Lake Erie was a critical point in the war effort that had a dramatic effect in other theaters of combat. When Perry wrested the Great Lakes from the British, it allowed American forces in Michigan, Ohio, and New York to succeed. With no threat of retaliation from the water, Detroit was captured within days of Perry's victory, and the wilderness of the Ohio Country was no longer threatened by a British invasion from Lake Erie. Perry's defeat of Barclay was minor in the greater history of naval conflict but loomed large in the overall picture of the War of 1812. After his victory, Perry was quick to note that he had several free black men in his crew, and much to the chagrin of the slave-holding states and President Madison, he declared, "I have yet to learn that the Colour of the skin, or

---

2. Oliver Hazard Perry to James Madison, in Stephen Howarth, *To Shining Sea: A History of the United States Navy, 1775–1998* (Norman: University of Oklahoma Press, 1999), 112.

cut and trimmings of the coat, can effect a man's qualifications or usefulness."[3]

The War of 1812 ended as strangely as it began. After Napoleon was defeated, the refocused British quickly moved to defeat the Americans in 1814. The city of Washington was burned by the British, and Baltimore was nearly captured. Another invasion force tried to cross the St. Lawrence River at Plattsburgh, but American soldiers repelled the attempt. With no clear goals in mind for the British and

Oliver Hazard Perry in an 1814 portrait commemorating his victory. (*Library of Congress*)

no hope of capturing Canada for the Americans, agents of the king asked President Madison if he was willing to negotiate a truce. In the Treaty of Ghent, signed on Christmas Eve 1814, the United States and Great Britain agreed to end the conflict under the terms of status quo ante bellum; in short, they simply pretended like it never happened. In a most bizarre twist because of the poor communication of the age, word of the peace didn't reach America until after the British tried to capture New Orleans. Major General Andrew Jackson saved the city, making him a national hero. The Battle of New Orleans was the most important battle of the war, and it happened three weeks after it had already ended.

WHAT TO SEE: The Erie Maritime Museum in Erie, Pennsylvania, is a sailor's dream. While much of its collection focuses on the Battle of Lake Erie, it also offers an incredible number of artifacts relating to Erie's history as a hub of maritime trade. Other exhibits include a detailed study of lighthouses and lifesaving history, the General Electric steam generator and its effect on the industry, countless meticu-

3. Oliver Hazard Perry, in Alexander Sliddell Mackenzie, *Commodore Oliver Hazard Perry: Famous American Naval Hero* (New York: MacLellan, 1907), 142.

A replica of the US Brig *Niagara* still sails the Great Lakes in honor of Perry's victory. (*Wikimedia Commons*)

lously crafted model ships, and an exhibit about the USS *Michigan*, the first iron-hulled ship in the US Navy.

The museum has a stunning collection of artifacts from the period of the War of 1812. Hats, buckles, uniforms, and coats are on display that are so well-preserved they look like they were worn yesterday. The most impressive and exhilarating piece of the collection is what awaits guests outside. A full-scale, functional rebuild of Oliver Hazard Perry's brig *Niagara* bobs gently in the waters of Lake Erie, just waiting to be boarded and explored. The ship is massive and is an incredibly valuable resource for anyone interested in knowing more about the period. Depending on the weather and time of year, the Erie Maritime Museum takes guests out onto the lake for a sailing expedition to see the *Niagara* in action. Extremely dedicated guests can even spend a week "at sea" living like a sailor of the nineteenth century and fully participating as a member of the *Niagara*'s crew. It's a once-in-a-lifetime opportunity not available anywhere else, but like the real thing, it's not for the faint of heart.

19

The Philadelphia Nativist Riots

(MAY–JULY 1844)

BACKGROUND: Pennsylvania has always been defined by its embrace of immigrants. When William Penn founded the colony in the 1680s, he called it a Holy Experiment of Quakerism. Because Quakers believe that all people contain the light of God within themselves, Penn dedicated his life to creating a society where all residents were treated equally in the eyes of the law. This Peaceable Kingdom was one of the proprietor's greatest legacies, and he not only talked the talk, he walked the walk. Religious dissidents from all across Europe made their home in Pennsylvania, and Penn demanded that fair land deals were granted to the neighboring Indians. For all of his good intentions though, Penn's colony was not always what it seemed. Instead of blending together in harmony, the Finns, Swedes, Dutch, Scots-Irish, and English immigrants separated themselves into enclaves in the colony; while they all shared Pennsylvania, they treated one another with suspicion and maintained a safe distance.

By the 1830s, Philadelphia was a hotbed of ethnic and religious tensions. Irish immigrants flooded America's shores in the nineteenth century, and one of the greatest pull factors was their search for jobs that had been replaced by the industrial machinery of the British Isles. When they arrived, they brought the Old World with them, including their traditions, lifestyles, and religion. As most were dedicated Roman Catholics, the newly arrived immigrants immediately found themselves at odds with second- and third-generation American-Irish who had been faithful Protestants. Tensions were always hot, but after Protestants openly celebrated the anniversary of the Battle of the Boyne (a famous Protestant victory in Ireland) to antagonize Catholics in 1831, a massive brawl ensued. By the nineteenth century, William Penn was long gone and so was his City of Brotherly Love.

BATTLE: As Philadelphia was Pennsylvania's great melting pot of the nineteenth century, its public institutions were often battlegrounds in microcosm over some of the most contentious issues of the day. For Irish Protestants, the control that was exercised over institutions like schools and public works facilities became a platform for suppressing the "foreign" view and traditions of Catholics from their ancestral homeland. The school system was one of the Protestants' primary mechanisms of control, and administrators took proactive steps to minimize the Roman Catholic Church's newfound presence in their communities. One of the most contentious policies came in the form of the daily scripture reading and accompanying hymns that schoolchildren were required to sing. Instead of accommodating the Catholic children by allowing them to read from the Roman version of the text, officials instead demanded that only the Protestant King James version of the Bible be used in schools. Catholic students sang and read from the text, mostly unaware that their efforts were complicit in pushing their parents and family out of the public forum. In response to this perceived injustice, Catholic bishop Francis Patrick Kenrick began to air his grievances to community leaders; this ignited a political firestorm that nearly tore Philadelphia apart.

In response to Bishop Kenrick's complaints, local political party bosses capitalized on the unrest brewing in Philadelphia's Catholic neighborhoods. Framing the debate as a Roman attempt to wash away the deep Protestant roots of American Christianity, politicians fingered the bishop's effort as proof of a greater conspiracy. In the early 1840s, America was at a crossroads. Those who valued immigration saw hundreds of thousands of Irish newcomers settling into their cities seeking a better life, and those who opposed it saw the same migrants as nothing less than an invasion force. With nativist parties popping up across the East Coast, Philadelphia was swept up in the political wave more than most cities. Protestant ministers and preachers banded together to form political action groups like the American Protestant Association to Defend America from Romanism, and church services began to appear more like political rallies than religious ceremonies. Finally, the *Daily Sun* newspaper fully committed itself to anti-Catholicism, and Philadelphia nativists were given a platform to share their ideals. The American flag was used as their most prominent symbol, and they waved it angrily at recently arrived Irish families as a passive-aggressive threat.

The tension was palpable across the Philadelphia area, but nowhere more so than in the city of Kensington. There had long been a sense of unease in this mixed community, but when Catholic school director Hugh Clark recommended that schools suspend all Bible reading until an amicable solution could be found, nativist outrage exploded. Using the suggestion as a flash point, anti-immigrant politicians staged a massive demonstration in the Catholic section of Kensington on May 3, 1844. The location, Independence Square, was selected to be deliberately provocative because of its direct ties to the founding of America, and the Catholic Philadelphians took the bait. They chased the nativists out of their communities, but they returned in force three days later. On May 6, nativists restarted their rally at the Nanny Goat Market, and the angered Catholics again attacked. A chaotic brawl ensued, and before long, nativists were being shot at from nearby windows. A young man named George Shiffler was killed. Shiffler became an icon of the nativist movement and further justified the cause.

After a lull in the madness, fighting between the two mobs reignited on May 8. That day, nativists came with torches and burned a number of Catholic households, including school director Clark's home. As the riot expanded, the Protestants destroyed a Catholic seminary, and in their boldest statement of all, they burned two of the largest Catholic churches in Philadelphia. St. Michael's Parish and St. Augustine's Parish were the lifeblood of the Roman Catholic community in Philadelphia; that evening, both were burned

The killing of George Shiffler became a rallying point and propaganda call for anti-Catholic demonstrators. (*Library of Congress*)

to the ground. As the historic steeple of St. Augustine's collapsed into the blaze, the nativists shouted pro-American slogans at their Catholic neighbors. With the city burning, the Pennsylvania Militia was called out to break up the fighting; only when it was joined by US Army and Navy forces as well as city law enforcement did the combatants disperse.

For nearly eight weeks, an uneasy peace gripped the city. As Catholics sifted through the ashes of their former churches, nativists were emboldened by their success. To the Protestants, the demolition of St. Michael's and St. Augustine's were unfortunate but essential to keeping the regular order of their city in place. Emboldened, nativists planned another march through the Southwark area on July 4 as a celebration of Independence Day. As the only Catholic parish in that section of town, St. Philip Neri was a vulnerable target should the marchers turn violent. In preparation for hostilities, the church's pastor, Reverend John Patrick Dunn, made a formal request to the state that the church be used as an informal arsenal in the event it came under attack. The Fourth of July parade came and went with no problems, but the mood quickly soured. When the marchers re-

The Philadelphia Nativist Riots was a watershed moment in American immigration history. Note St. Philip Neri Roman Catholic Church in the background. (*Library of Congress*)

turned outside of St. Philip Neri Parish on July 5, they witnessed some muskets being transferred from the building to a secure location, and the peaceful parade turned hostile. Through the evening, the nativists surrounded the church and demanded the weapons be removed. Just after midnight, Major Robert Patterson of the state militia ordered the streets to be cleared of the protestors. Patterson was a relative unknown in 1844, but he would serve as a major general in the Civil War and deliver an early defeat to Thomas Jonathan "Stonewall" Jackson at Hoke's Run in 1861.

The next day, July 7, was catastrophic. The nativist crowd returned to St. Philip Neri's to confront the militia and demand it vacate the church. Tensions boiled over when the crowd began pelting the militiamen with bricks and bottles, and the soldiers opened fire; two protestors died, and countless more were wounded. At approximately 9:00 PM, the rioters counterattacked with a vengeance and surprised the militia by wheeling a cannon onto Queen Street and firing it at the soldiers. While the details are unclear, sources indicate that the nativists took the gun from a ship in the Delaware River. Wherever it came from, the mysterious artillery piece leveled the playing field in dramatic fashion. The fighting lasted all night and would have appeared as a disorganized melee. A local alderman from Southwark was able to negotiate with the militiamen to leave the area, and the chaos finally ended. In the end, the riots saw four Pennsylvania militiamen and at least ten nativists killed. In the ensuing days, hundreds of militiamen from across the state arrived to occupy the city and tamp down the violence once and for all.

LEGACY: Nativist riots happened in nearly every major coastal city in the 1840s. New York and Boston had their shares of violence, but most were over quickly. Philadelphia's riots were days long, and in that way they were unique. Politics was at the heart of the violence between the Catholic and Protestant Irish; in the 1840s, every Philadelphian had an opinion about the riots that tore apart the city. In the abstract, nearly every Philadelphian believed that fighting and violence were morally and ethically wrong, but when pressed, their true political feelings emerged. Case in point: elections were held in fall 1844, and nativist parties won sweeping victories at all levels of government. That year saw record-breaking voter turnout, and Philadelphia overwhelmingly elected a nativist congressman to represent them in Washington, DC.

Locally, Philadelphia changed a great deal in the wake of the riots. One year after the violence, a law was passed increasing the size of the city's police force to prevent another incident. According to the law, there needed to he at least one police officer for every 150 residents within his jurisdiction, and the force grew so large that in 1850, a new police district was created to cover the whole Philadelphia region. Four years later, all of Philadelphia County was consolidated into a single county government, a feat that many thought would have been impossible given the divided nature of its citizens. While the existence of new police district was not singularly responsible for the consolidation, it laid an important foundation, proving that a unified Philadelphia County could function despite its deep historical divisions.

WHAT TO SEE: An exploration of the nativist riots of 1844 leads to a tour of early Catholic Philadelphia. As most of the major events were focused around churches, visiting these sites can feel like a holy experience. Any tour should begin in Philadelphia's Kensington neighborhood. It was here that the nativists held their first rally and where fighting first broke out at the Nanny Goat Market and the Sisters of Charity Convent was attacked. Next, walk to historic Cadwallader Street, where rioters attacked and burned the Hibernia Hose House along with thirty homes. The violence and destruction escalated dramatically from this point, and prominent churches became a major part of the story.

St. Philip Neri Roman Catholic Church was the site of a large battle with cannons between rioters and state militia. (*St. Philip Neri*)

Walk to the corner of Second and Jefferson Streets to see the reconstructed St. Michael's Catholic Church, which was destroyed on May 8. Next, walk to the rebuilt St. Augustine's Catholic Church at Fourth and New Streets; this building is identified by a Pennsylvania Historical and Museum Commission marker. St. Augustine's was one of the most prominent churches destroyed by the rioters and was rebuilt three years later in its current majestic form. Finally, return to St. Philip Neri Parish on Queen Street to witness the narrow city blocks where rioters and the Pennsylvania Militia battled in July 1844.

For our filming of *Battlefield Pennsylvania,* our crew set up in Mario Lanza Park directly across the street from St. Philip Neri Parish. Note the tight quarters and limited line of sight that the area provides, and imagine the chaos of the fighting there. As within most of the city limits, guests will be using street parking, but a long walk across this historic part of the former American capital reveals a bustling neighborhood on the upswing, still very tied to its deep and rich history.

PART FOUR

THE CIVIL WAR ERA (1861–1865)

Since the earliest days of the American republic, the divide between North and South had been growing, and by the eve of the Civil War, the differences were irreconcilable. During the Constitutional Convention, the sectional conflicts emerged early and passionately, and in many ways the document itself was a compromise between Northern and Southern interests. During the long summer of debates, Southern slave-holding states demanded concessions and protections for their economic system, which was almost entirely based on human bondage. Landmark concessions such as the Three-Fifths Compromise and the Electoral College owe their roots to appeasement of the planter class's interests in the American South.

The Civil War had been brewing for generations in the United States, and with the benefit of hindsight, historians have been able to accurately trace its origins from the beginning of the republic until the secession winter of 1860–1861. In 1790, sectional divisions were already present when Treasury Secretary Alexander Hamilton and Secretary of State Thomas Jefferson brokered a deal to move the capital from New York City to Virginia. Although it would become a separate district known as Washington, DC, the presence of the American capital in the Old Dominion was a tremendous symbolic victory for the Southern way of life. As the nation grew, the sectional animus swelled until it virtually consumed American politics in the nineteenth century. Anytime a territory applied for statehood, tensions between Northern and Southern politicians flared up in familiar ways. In 1850, when California voted to enter as a free state, the anger was so intense that America nearly descended into civil war; only a last-minute compromise regarding land recently acquired from Mexico calmed the outrage.

The decade of the 1850s was one of most tense and divisive in history, and the institution of slavery dominated the headlines. In the wake of critically important events like the Dred Scott Decision and the partisan war known as Bleeding Kansas, extreme positions became increasingly mainstream. Northern radicals who preached for the total abolition of slavery were brought from the fringes of American politics to the forefront; in the South, proslavery radicals known as Fire Eaters began calling for the annexation of Cuba to act as an entrepôt for reopening the African slave trade. As US senator Albert Gallatin Brown of Mississippi stated, "I want Cuba . . . I want Tamaulipas, Potosi, and one or two other Mexican States; I want them all for the same reason—for the planting and spreading of slavery."[1] The most shocking position to gain support, though, was total secession, and Southerners displayed an increasing appetite for separating from the Union and ending the American experiment of self-government.

In 1860, Abraham Lincoln was elected president, and reaction was swift across the South. Fearing that Lincoln would threaten the institution of slavery, on which the entire economy of the South was based, states began to declare their secession from the republic. Calling itself the Confederate States of America, the new government of the South represented the largest domestic rebellion in American history. The secession shocked Northerners and was a stunning testament to the value that enslaving human beings held in the economic and cultural ethos of the Southern states. When discussing the new government and causes of the secession, Confederate vice president Alexander Stephens stated plainly, "Its foundations are laid, its cornerstone rests, upon the great truth that the negro is not equal to the white man; that slavery . . . is his natural and normal condition."[2] The causes of the Civil War can be thought of as a solar system; there existed economic, cultural, social, and territorial differences between North and South, but they all rotated around the great star that was slavery. On January 25, 1861, delegate G. T. Yelverton offered these sentiments at the Alabama Secession Convention: "The question of Slavery is the rock upon which the Old Government split. It is the cause of Secession."[3]

1. "Speech at Hazlehurst," Albert Gallatin Brown, *Speeches, Messages, and Other Writings of the Hon. Albert Gallatin Brown* (New Orleans: Maginiss, 1859), 595.

2. "Cornerstone Speech," in Christopher Cameron, *The Abolitionist Movement: Documents Decoded* (Santa Barbara, CA: ABC-CLIO, 2014), 221.

3. G. T. Yelverton, in James O. Horton and Amanda Kleintop, *Race, Slavery and the Civil War* (Richmond: Virginia Sesquicentennial of the American Civil War Commission, 2011), 103.

On April 12, Confederate forces opened fire on Fort Sumter in Charleston Harbor, and three days later President Lincoln famously called for seventy-five thousand military volunteers to suppress the Southern rebellion. The Civil War remains the most critical period in the nation's history. The war lasted four years and claimed over seven hundred thousand lives, and Pennsylvania played a central role in the conflict.

20

The Allegheny Arsenal Explosion

(SEPTEMBER 17, 1862)

BACKGROUND: In fall 1860, the American republic was hopelessly divided along sectional lines. In the North, industry ruled the day, and thousands of migrants came to the United States to pursue freedom by selling their labor in its factories and foundries. In the South, the economy was based almost entirely on agriculture, and cash crops like cotton, tobacco, and rice bloomed into great riches for the citizens. At the heart of the matter was Southern Americans' deep attachment to enslaving their fellow humans and the perceived threat that the Republican presidential candidate, Abraham Lincoln, posed to that institution. In the months after Lincoln's election in November 1860, Southern states gradually seceded from the Union, and though both sides spoke of a peaceful resolution, war seemed inevitable.

If war was to come, Pittsburgh would play a vital role. Since its earlier days, the region was known for its manufacturing prowess; a steady supply of immigrants, an abundance of locally mined coal, and three rivers running in alternate directions made it perfectly suited for an industrial boom. In 1814, the federal government hoped to capitalize on these circumstances by creating the Allegheny Arsenal east of the city in modern-day Lawrenceville. Designed by Benjamin Logan, the arsenal spanned thirty acres and employed over one thousand one hundred workers. By the time the Civil War began in spring 1861, Pittsburgh was producing guns, ammunition, and ordnance in record amounts.

BATTLE: Serving as a bulwark of employment for the Lawrenceville neighborhood for almost fifty years by 1862, the Allegheny Arsenal employed people from all walks of life. In many cases residents spent almost their entire lives working in the arsenal, as it regularly employed children as young as ten. By the time of the Civil War, the majority of those who worked in the arsenal were young women, supplanting the men of the area who were serving in combat throughout the South. Most were first or second generation Americans, mainly from Ireland, and worked for wages dramatically less than their male counterparts. Regardless, they faithfully came to work in support of the Arsenal of the Union and took great pride in their work. While the crosstown Fort Pitt Foundry manufactured heavy guns, rifles, and ammunition, it fell to the Allegheny Arsenal to create cartridges and leather harnesses. The women packed rolled paper tubes with live gunpowder, dropped in a bullet, and folded off the ends before shipping them to the Union armies in the field. At full capacity, the Allegheny Arsenal could produce over forty thousand cartridges per day.

As vital as the manufacturing facility was to the community, its commander, Colonel John Symington, was far from beloved. Symington made enemies in the community early on; in December 1860, he fulfilled an order given by Secretary of War John B. Floyd to send one hundred 20-pound guns to New Orleans despite resounding threats of secession across the South. Floyd, who went on to be a Confederate general, was believed to have put in the order to flood the Confederacy with weapons and ammunition in the event that secession actually occurred. Louisiana split from the Union just

A Civil War-era photograph of the Allegheny Arsenal. Mortars are in the foreground, with horse stables at right. (*Heinz History Center*)

one month later and took the Allegheny Arsenal's cannons with it. Since the news broke regarding the sale, Symington had been a loathed character in Pittsburgh. Matters worsened when his daughter married a Confederate general, and his own son fought for the rebels.

The arsenal was a sprawling place, and individual buildings were designated for specific work. Along with the officer's quarters at the northern end of the site, there was also the shop, several powder magazines, and soldiers' barracks on-site. Near the center of the campus was a laboratory outbuilding constructed in 1859; the events of September 16 would place great scrutiny on this unassuming structure. While Colonel Symington was in command of the entire location, he was seemingly unhappy with the assignment. In August of that year, he requested an official retirement from the United States Military Retirement Board but was rejected, and he begrudgingly continued his yeoman's work in Lawrenceville. For months leading up to summer 1862, there had been concerns about the safety of the arsenal. As young women stuffed cartridge after cartridge, gunpowder was carelessly dropped across the grounds. To avoid any untoward sparks, the workers were forced to wear moccasins made of leather, careful to contain no metal that could cause a spark.

The afternoon of September 16 was a payday, and the young workers of the arsenal had just returned from their 1:00 PM lunch break. At approximately 2:00 PM, wagon driver Joseph Frick arrived on-site carrying ten barrels of gunpowder, an ordinary delivery he had made many times before. Frick would have almost certainly felt safe running the task; the barrels themselves were carefully fabricated from organic materials to contain no metal, rendering them entirely innocuous. Historians speculate that as his wagon arrived, a spark flickered from his iron-rimmed right front wheel as it screeched to a halt on the arsenal's stone road. When the spark landed, it ignited the loose powder on the road and traveled quickly to the porch of the 1859 laboratory building, where three 100-pound powder barrels exploded. Frick was thrown aside but survived; however, a worker named Robert Smith died in the blast.

After the initial explosion, workers began to approach the blast site. Curiosity soon melted into panic, however, when the worst-case scenario was realized. One worker, Mary McCandless McGraw, re-called, "At 2 o'clock another girl and I were the only persons in Room 13. The other girls were in another building getting their pay and in the yard. Suddenly there was a terrific roar. The earth seemed to split apart." The first explosion caused a fire to break out along the build-ing, and it took five minutes for the blaze to finally contact more gunpowder, five full barrels. When these powder kegs caught fire at 2:05 PM, the entire building exploded with a violent rage. As they worked at their regular duties, the young women of Lawrenceville had no chance to save themselves. The explosion was so great that it rocked the entire city, and sixty-nine people at the arsenal perished immediately. A general panic swept through the town, and family members rushed toward the arsenal with little doubt as to what dis-aster had befallen their small community.

The scene was horrifying. Loved ones collapsed at the calamity before them. Victims were unrecognizable. Charred body parts were strewn across the grounds, and as the wreckage from the laboratory building was cleared, only the wire frames of the victims' hoop skirts were recovered intact. According to one local newspaper account "there was not a particle of clothing left on a majority of the victims, and mangled and disjointed as they were it was impossible to identify them. The very stockings were torn from their feet, rings from their fingers, and in some instances nothing but a headless trunk remained. Nevertheless, many were identified by their hair, by a scrap of the dress they wore, but the greatest number never can be fully recognized."[1] Some women were pulled from the fire alive but few survived their wounds, and nine others died in the following weeks. The final count saw seventy-eight young people killed in the tragedy: six boys and seventy-two young women. When the smoke cleared, the arsenal continued its important work just days later, but the community of Lawrenceville and the city of Pittsburgh were never the same.

LEGACY: The Allegheny Arsenal explosion was the most devastating industrial accident in Pittsburgh's history, and more critically, it stands as the worst loss of civilian life of the entire Civil War. The tragedy shocked the nation and was poised to become a seminal moment that could have prompted changes in women's rights in the workplace, equal pay, and safe working conditions; but the backlash never came. Americans were stunned by the disaster at the Allegheny Arsenal but only temporarily, as a far greater tragedy took place in the public consciousness just one day later. On September 18, 1862, George B. McClellan's Army of the Potomac squared off with Robert E. Lee's Army of Northern Virginia outside Sharpsburg, Maryland, at the Battle of Antietam. The fighting lasted all day on a field that offered little to no shelter or maneuverability. The bloodshed was historic, and the death toll was catastrophic. Still worse, despite Lee's retreat south into Virginia, there was little evidence that either Union

1. "Frightful Calamity Near Pittsburg—Eighty Persons Killed," *Clarence and Richmond Examiner*, January 13, 1863.

or Confederate forces had actually won anything along Antietam Creek. Union forces suffered 12,140 casualties and Confederates 10,316; in total, 3,650 Americans died. Antietam was the bloodiest day in American history until then—and it still holds that terrible title today.

For an America quickly growing accustomed to tragedy, the Allegheny Arsenal explosion was sadly one of many tragedies experienced during the Civil War. After the smoke had cleared in Lawrenceville and the dead were interred, the federal government hosted an inquest into the events of that day and determined that no one was at fault. Much to the dismay of the families who lost loved ones that day, no one was held accountable for the blast that claimed seventy-eight innocent lives. Colonel John Symington was exonerated of any wrongdoing but was reviled by the Lawrenceville community for the remainder of his tenure at the Allegheny Arsenal.

WHAT TO SEE: Arsenal Park, which stands at the heart of Pittsburgh's Lawrenceville neighborhood, was the former grounds of the sprawling Allegheny Arsenal. Today the park offers subtle clues about the events of 1862; they are easy to spot with a quick walk through the green space. The entire park still retains the original plot shape of the arsenal grounds, and a large stone building still stands in the southeast corner that was part of the original structure designed in 1814. It bears a large plaque that reads "US April 1814" and is adorned with a sculpture of cannons and balls. Around the edges of the park are a number of monuments placed over the 150 years to commemorate the explosion. Note the difference in the appearance and emotion of these markers according to the date; some were made quite early, and their intentions evolve from memorization of the dead to interpretation of the location itself. Staying in Lawrenceville, walk northeast to the Allegheny Cemetery to see the communal grave where thirty-nine of the seventy-eight victims of the explosion were buried. Their gravestone is a large monument with each of their names carefully inscribed.

This maintenance shed is all that remains of the mighty Allegheny Arsenal. The heavy gun at the site, lower right, remain a testament to the forgotten arsenal, but cannon balls and shells have been uncovered by construction crews in the area as late as 2017. (*Wikimedia Commons/Author*)

The Allegheny Arsenal was an enormous enterprise, and it still finds ways to surprise historians in the twenty-first century. In 2016, as construction crews were digging in Lawrenceville, operations came to a halt when a cache of dozens of unfired cannon balls were unearthed by digging equipment. In most cases when a historical discovery is made, a team of archaeologists is called in to investigate, but this time the first call immediately went to the local bomb squad. Fortunately, the cannon balls and shot were not live, as many did not have their fuses in place, but it was a stark reminder of the terrible events of September 1862. To complete a tour of the Allegheny Arsenal site, visit the Senator John Heinz History Center in downtown Pittsburgh to see its exhibit on the explosion. On display are many of the materials manufactured at the arsenal as well as at the Fort Pitt Foundry, Pittsburgh's other ordnance facility. The history center displays lifelike models of women who worked in the arsenal and shows them completing the monotonous routines their job entailed; their clothing is period correct down to their spark-proof moccasins. Make a special point to see the history center's recent scale model of Thomas Jackson Rodman's ninety-ton, 20-inch caliber cannon made in Pittsburgh; with shot the size of a beach ball and a range of almost five miles, this formidable gun protected Fort Hamilton at New York City's Verrazano Narrows.

21

The Raid on Hanover Junction

(JUNE 27, 1863)

BACKGROUND: In June 1863, Robert E. Lee's Army of Northern Virginia began to move north into Pennsylvania. Nearly the entire Civil War had been fought on Southern soil; Virginia's farms lay fallow, its cities were destroyed, and the war had taken on a terrible, interminable feeling. Lee had a brilliant tactical mind and understood the partisan conflict at its core. To truly turn the tide of the war, he had to make the American public vote for change in the 1864 election, and the best way to do that was to win a major battle on Northern soil. He felt that it would shock the Northern consciousness and reveal to it the horrors of the war that Southerners had seen for three years. Like a great fan, the Army of Northern Virginia spread itself across south central Pennsylvania and feasted on the endless acres of corn, wheat, apples, and livestock.

Major General Jubal Early led his division into York County to attack one of the major lifelines of the Union: railroads. Railroads were vital arteries to President Abraham Lincoln's war effort, and Pennsylvania contained many vital intersections from across the

Northeast, including the Northern Central Railway. To sever those lines would mean a total disruption of supplies, troops, and foodstuffs; all were critical to sustaining Union troops across the South. While Early set his sights on the town of York, he dispatched cavalry units under the command of Lieutenant Colonels Elijah White and William French, both Virginians, to raid and wreak havoc along the rail lines of York County. By the end of June 1863, there was no doubt that the war had arrived full steam in Pennsylvania's heartland.

BATTLE: On June 26, a component of Major General Early's Division of the II Corps of the Army of Northern Virginia arrived at the small town of Gettysburg, Pennsylvania. After running the 26th Pennsylvania Militia from the town, the Confederates set their sights on much bigger targets to the north. The first battle of Gettysburg was over, and not a Southerner was killed. Of course, this was not *the* Battle of Gettysburg that would begin five days later, but the fact that Confederates had already captured the town and proceeded to abandon it reveals just how far ranging the rebels' invasion of Pennsylvania was. No solider marching that summer could have anticipated that the largest battle in the history of the Western Hemisphere was less than a week away in that same sleepy town.

Pennsylvania was a great conquest for Robert E. Lee's army, but it was hemmed in by the natural boundary of the Susquehanna River. For the Southerners, the prime targets of the Keystone State were all across the vast river; Harrisburg was the single most important railroad junction in the North, but it was safely shielded from Confederate attack by a waterway more than a mile across. For Lee, crossing this river meant opening an entirely new realm of possibilities to attack, and endless ways to strike fear into the hearts of Northern voters. There were only a few crossings along the Susquehanna River, and Lee sent Early's division out to capture them. While it is often lost in the greater narrative of the Civil War and the Gettysburg Campaign, Jubal Early's march to the Susquehanna was a critical component of the rebel army's Northern invasion.

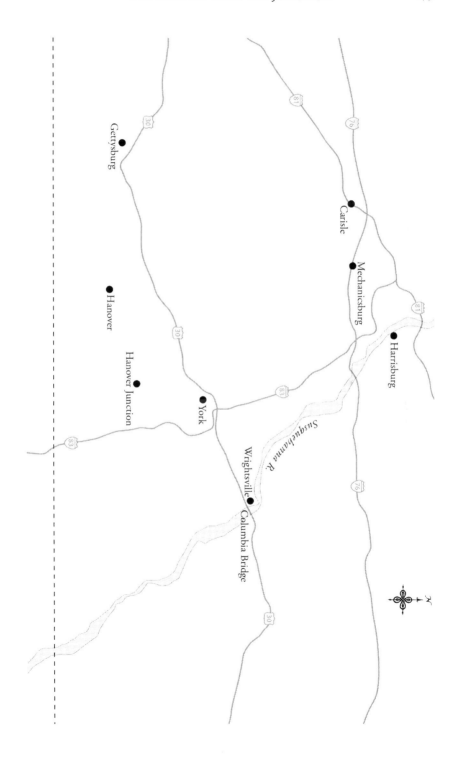

The hotel, left, and railroad station, right, at Hanover Junction, August 1863. Several days before the Battle of Gettysburg, a Confederate cavalry raid cut telegraph wires here and burned nearby railroad bridges. The station was left unharmed. (*Library of Congress*)

As Early's division coursed toward York, he called on two of his most trusted cavalry commanders to raid the Pennsylvania countryside. The 35th Battalion Virginia Cavalry, led by Lieutenant Colonel Elijah Viers White, had a reputation for being especially effective in this regard. Known as "White's Comanches," they had already earned their stripes fighting alongside Thomas "Stonewall" Jackson in his Valley Campaign a year earlier. Starting out, the rebels raided small towns, pillaging and plundering their way across the countryside. At McSherrystown, White's Comanches raided a dry-goods store and walked away with clothing, boots, and ten gallons of alcohol. Finding the railroad trace of the Hanover Branch Railroad, they followed the tracks, destroying telegraph lines and demolishing bridges. Their strategic aim was to cause chaos, and their tactics mirrored in kind.

Fifteen miles east of McSherrystown sat Hanover Junction, a valuable intersection of the Northern Central Railway and the Hanover Branch Railroad. It was a heavily trafficked junction and was defended by the 20th Pennsylvania Volunteer Militia; at only 225 men

The railroad bridge over the Codorus Creek near Hanover Junction burned by the Confederates. (*Library of Congress*)

strong, it was an armed force hastily called together by Governor Andrew Curtain. They lacked training, experience, and strong leadership, but they were Pennsylvania's only defense against the invading rebels. At approximately 1:00 PM, the telegraph station inside Hanover Junction stopped receiving updates from the west. The operator understood that the only logical explanation of this was that someone must have cut the lines, effectively isolating the tiny outpost. Hanover Junction was typical of many train stations of its day. The first floor was a collection of various essential operations, including ticket sales, office space, and a waiting area for passengers. The top floor had rooms available for rent, but the traffic increased so much that the Scott Hotel was built nearby. Pennsylvania forces under Lieutenant Colonel William H. Sickles had received intelligence that railroad tracks and bridges were expected to be destroyed by the marauding Confederates, and on the afternoon of June 27, the reports were proven correct. In the days leading up to the battle, White's men split up to inflict more damage to the Union infrastruc-

ture and agreed to reconnect on Saturday at Hanover Junction following the existing railway traces. The day had come, and so had the
Confederates.

At midday, train engineer George Small was operating The
Susquehanna, a locomotive headed north on the Northern Central
Railway. As he approached Hanover Junction, he was shocked to see
White's men speeding on horseback along the intersecting Hanover
Branch line in an apparent attempt to cut off his train. Small abandoned the engine as the Confederates began blasting it with gunfire.
The scene was almost fictional in its melodrama but signaled to the
Pennsylvania volunteers that White's forces had arrived. From atop
an adjacent hill, the militiamen watched as the rebels flooded into
the junction valley below. They began collecting wood in large piles
and igniting it on the station's turntable to disable the instrument
for future use. They poured oil onto a railcar, set it on fire, and
pushed it onto a nearby bridge with hopes of destroying both. As
Hanover Junction was decimated, the bewildered Pennsylvanians
turned and fled the scene; if they had any stomach for war, it disap-
peared in the billowing black smoke of the ruined train station.

While cowardice abounded, there was one bright spot of courage
at Hanover Junction. As the outside of the facility was being destroyed, sixteen-year-old apprentice John Shearer managed to send
out a series of desperate telegraph messages to all points east and
south, including Baltimore and Washington, DC. For his efforts,
young Shearer was captured, held at gunpoint, and robbed by the
rebels. He was then forced to sit on a fence rail and watch as the cavalry continued to pillage and plunder what remained of Hanover
Junction. In another twist of good fortune, White sent one of his
men to destroy Shearer's telegraph machine, which he did, but the
uneducated cavalryman failed to damage the telegraph battery. After
White's men fled the scene, the young apprentice was released and
immediately saw that the vital battery was unharmed. Once the
clipped lines were repaired, it seemed that Hanover Junction was
sending out messages again in just a few days.

LEGACY: Hanover Junction was disabled by Elijah White's Virginians, but only temporarily. The Military Railroad Department was an essential part of the Union bureaucracy, and its focused attention had the railroad junction up and running less than a week after the raid. The destruction of the bridges and crossings by the Virginia cavalry was a continual nuisance for the North, but the damage was minimal and easily repaired. In total, nineteen bridges were destroyed between Hanover Junction and the major railway hub of Harrisburg during June and July 1863; in many ways, Early's cavalry was a temporary disruption to the Northern Central Railway. Perhaps equally valuable was White and French's constant snipping of Union telegraph wires. Though telegraph lines were easier to repair than torn-up railroad track, the cutting of the wires reduced communication between Washington and Union field commanders to highly inefficient handwritten notes.

For Lincoln and the rest of the Union high command, the raid on Hanover Junction was a clear indicator that the federal militia were no match for Lee's Confederate army. Although the rebels paled in comparison to the regular soldiers of Europe's great armies, the inept and untrained Pennsylvania volunteers were even less impressive. By June 27, it was clear that the militia was simply outgunned and overmatched by the battle-hardened Southerners. For Lieutenant Colonel Sickles of the 20th Pennsylvania Volunteers, Hanover Junction was only the start. He was soon called twenty miles east to tangle with the Confederates again a day later and be handed yet another embarrassing defeat. As for Lieutenant Colonel White, his 35th Battalion Virginia Cavalry was one of the first units on the scene at Gettysburg four days later, on July 1. In the aftermath of the battle, over eleven thousand wounded men were processed through Hanover Junction, as was the funerary procession train carrying the remains of President Abraham Lincoln in 1865.

WHAT TO SEE: The Hanover Junction Railroad Station still stands and was added to the National Register of Historic Places in 1983.

The steam engine *York* still frequents Hanover Junction as an homage to the former North Central Railroad. (*Wikipedia Commons*)

Although it was designated a historic site, the station had fallen into disrepair. With the help of a dedicated community of local volunteers and some dutiful public officials, the station was restored to its original condition with stunning accuracy. Today a small museum is maintained there by York County Parks and the Friends of the Rail Trail detailing the history of the site from its use as a hotel, train station, and telegraph office. The exhibits include a detailed study of White's 1863 raid as well as some information on the restoration process. The highlight of any visit awaits outside the museum, as Hanover Junction is still an active railroad station.

Operated by the nonprofit group Steam Into History, Hanover Junction Railroad Station remains an important stopover for the beautiful steam engine William H. Simpson No. 17. Offering regularly scheduled rides, the No. 17 is modeled after the train that brought Lincoln to Gettysburg to deliver the Gettysburg Address. Inside the museum, visitors can see photographs of Lincoln at Hanover Junction and proceed to the No. 17's coaches to ride with a reenactor portraying the 16th president of the United States. All of the No. 17's rides depart from the station at New Freedom, Pennsylvania, and typically last two and a half hours. Depending on the dates, living historians offer battle re-creations en route and detailed interpretations of White's 1863 raid. Steam Into History offers seasonal and themed excursions, but for Civil War historians and train aficionados, Hanover Junction is truly a one-of-a-kind opportunity to experience nineteenth-century railroad travel.

22

The Skirmish at Wrightsville and the Burning of Columbia Bridge

(JUNE 28, 1863)

BACKGROUND: In June 1863, Robert E. Lee's army sent shockwaves through the Northern consciousness when it invaded Pennsylvania. Three corps of the Army of Northern Virginia spread out in a wide arch across the south central portion of the state, and great uncertainty pervaded the commonwealth as to where the marching Confederates would strike. While Harrisburg, Philadelphia, and Pittsburgh all braced for impact, the most immediate threat to the state was Lieutenant General Richard Ewell's II Corps. A division commanded by Major General Jubal Early was marching toward the Susquehanna River, and the major railroad junction and state capital of Harrisburg was his likeliest target. Early's march on the Susquehanna was one of the most critical components of the 1863 Pennsylvania invasion, but it is often overshadowed by the Battle of Gettysburg that loomed ahead.

On June 28, Major General John B. Gordon's brigade marched triumphantly into York, and a short time later the Confederates oc-

cupied the city. Before the bulk of Southerners arrived, local business owners attempted to parlay with the approaching
rebels. They put up no resistance and clar-
ified that their only ambition was to avoid
a fight at all costs. By the end of the day,
Confederates paraded throughout York and
their flag waved defiantly on flagpoles
throughout the city. Jubal Early was said to
have demanded $100,000 from the citizens
of York but was only able to collect
$25,000. Despite the capture of the city,
Gordon's most vital target lay twelve miles
east at the town of Wrightsville: the Co-

Confederate general John B.
Gordon occupied York before
marching on Wrightsville.
(*Library of Congress*)

lumbia Bridge. It was more than a mile long and was the most coveted crossing of the Susquehanna. If Lee's invasion of Pennsylvania
was to truly accomplish its strategic goals, Gordon would need to
capture the Columbia Bridge.

BATTLE: Since the Confederates had arrived in Pennsylvania, they
had been met with mixed reactions. As the farmers of south central
Pennsylvania had a much greater cultural and economic connection
to the southern city of Baltimore than to Philadelphia, there was actually a great deal of sympathy for the rebel cause. In the 1860 elections, York County voted 98 percent Democratic against Abraham
Lincoln. Therefore, when the Confederates crossed into the state,
many were met with cheers and gifts of food rather than as an invading force. Many in the region, though, did not sympathize with
Lee's men, most of all Pennsylvania's African Americans. Many of the
African American residents on the invasion route were second- and
third-generation free peoples; they were not and had never been enslaved. When the Confederates crossed into the state, over one thousand eight hundred black men and women fled northeast across the
Susquehanna River to avoid the oncoming Confederates. Many of

those who chose to stay behind paid a terrible price as Lee's Southerners took them hostage and sold them into slavery across the Mason-Dixon Line. It was a terrible reminder of what issues lay at the core of the conflict and one of the darkest legacies of the Gettysburg Campaign.

The Susquehanna River was over a mile across, and only a handful of crossing points existed for the Confederate army to pursue. One was at Harrisburg proper, which was heavily defended by a Union encampment, and the other extended from Wrightsville in York County to Columbia in Lancaster County. Known as the Columbia Bridge, it was the largest covered bridge on earth and had been crossed by such figures as future presidents William Henry Harrison and Andrew Jackson. For the Confederates, the bridge was their best available avenue to cross the Susquehanna and raid the heavily Unionist Lancaster County. If it were to be defended, it would fall on a small contingent of Pennsylvania volunteers to do so.

The men defending Wrightsville from the Confederates who occupied York were of the 27th Pennsylvania Volunteer Militia under Colonel Jacob Gilbert Frick. At the outset of Lee's invasion, President Lincoln attempted to bolster the commonwealth's ranks by asking for one hundred thousand new volunteers; twenty-five thousand from Ohio, twenty-five thousand from West Virginia, and fifty thousand from Pennsylvania. But problems arose immediately, and troop numbers as well as quality suffered. Many Pennsylvania men had already served and were reluctant to reenlist, and others were afraid to join that summer because of the impending harvest. Still more were actually Confederate sympathizers, and all of this added up to weak turnout for the Union cause. In total, one thousand five hundred soldiers defended the Columbia Bridge from Gordon's invasion force, including a company of fifty African American volunteers who abandoned the sanctuary of Lancaster County to stop the rebels from crossing the river and threatening their communities.

With York occupied, Pennsylvania forces knew it was only a matter for time before Gordon's brigade marched east to Wrightsville. In preparation for the fight, the militia created a series of defensive lines around the town allowing room to fall back toward the bridge itself if they were overrun. Although the Columbia Bridge was the most vital crossing in the region as a turnpike and railroad line connecting Pittsburgh in the west to Philadelphia in the east, both sides had committed early on to destroying it if necessary. For the Unionists, burning the structure would have been essential to keeping Lee's Army of Northern Virginia hemmed into York County and points west; for the rebels, firing the bridge meant Union reinforcements from eastern Pennsylvania could not respond to their movements when the time to engage the Army of the Potomac finally came. In York, Major General Gordon was approached by a young local woman on June 28 and presented with a bouquet of roses. Inside the strange gift was a rolled up map containing detailed sketches of the Union defensive lines at Wrightsville. Confederates had hoped that the pro-Southern sympathy of the region would work to their advantage, and it certainly did that day.

Despite having valuable intelligence regarding the position of the militia, it took Gordon all day to reach Wrightsville. Reasons for the delay are not clear, but it is likely that the Confederate leader believed the Pennsylvania volunteers to be so ineffective that the timeliness of his arrival was irrelevant to his success. By the time Gordon's brigade got to the town, it was after 5:00 PM. As was the case at their previous engagements, the militiamen were unprepared for the fire of the rebels. To be fair, there were some more experienced soldiers in the mix, but by and large the Confederates crumpled the volunteers' defense. Lieutenant Colonel William H. Sickles and the remaining soldiers of the 20th Pennsylvania Volunteers who had fled from Hanover Junction a day earlier arrived as reinforcements, but they were equally ineffective at Wrightsville. As the Southerners closed in around the Pennsylvanians, their defenses crumpled, and the bluecoats were forced to fall back.

With the city lost, the primary objective of the volunteers was now to stop Gordon's brigade from crossing the Susquehanna. To

The Columbia Bridge was the world's largest covered bridge, and its destruction kept Lee's forces from crossing into eastern Pennsylvania. (*Wikipedia Commons*)

prevent this, they turned their attention to demolishing the Columbia Bridge. In a panicked effort, the Pennsylvanians began smashing the walls and roof of the structure and cheered as parts fell into the river below. As time went on, however, it became clear that the superstructure of the bridge remained intact, and the damage was merely cosmetic. Some of the volunteers maintained fire on the Confederates to keep them at bay, and it was decided that the only way to truly disable the bridge was to burn it. After soaking it with coal oil, the volunteers set it ablaze, engulfing the western portion in flames. The Pennsylvanians understood that the entire bridge did not need to be destroyed to be rendered useless, merely a portion of it; the massive stone piers would ensure that the remainder did not collapse, allowing the structure to be repaired later. In the name of the Union and in the heat of battle, the world's longest covered bridge was set ablaze. So were any hopes of Major General Jubal Early's division crossing the Susquehanna and capturing Harrisburg; the capital city had been spared. From as far away as Harrisburg, eyewitnesses reported seeing the massive inferno from the burning bridge light up the horizon in the distance.

LEGACY: Many compelling stories have emerged from the burning of the Columbia Bridge, and all deserve their time in the spotlight. When the bridge was burning, a sudden wind swept across the Susquehanna River carrying sparks and embers toward Wrightsville. While the Pennsylvania militiamen were so focused on starting the blaze, they completely neglected to manage it. As a result, piles of lumber near the water's edge soon caught on fire, and homes in the town suddenly ignited as well. Already panicked by the arrival of the rebels, residents began to scramble to save their property from the unintentional spread of the bridge fire. John B. Gordon had received clear orders from Robert E. Lee not to destroy public property while in Pennsylvania, and the Southern general ordered his men to actually assist in saving the town. At the river, the Confederates created a bucket brigade, carrying pails of water uphill to extinguish the flames. As a result, the daughter of a local politician invited Gordon and his staff to her home the following morning and treated the invading rebels to a full breakfast. Gordon's brigade fought three days later at Gettysburg, and he lost a quarter of his men, many of whom worked to save Wrightsville from burning.

While the legacy of the skirmish at Wrightsville is often the stuff of counterfactual history, there are some interesting possibilities to consider. If Gordon's men had captured the Columbia Bridge and crossed the Susquehanna followed by the rest of Lee's army, would there have ever been a Battle of Gettysburg? Historians can only speculate, but there are some undeniable facts to consider. The fifty African American volunteers fought admirably at Wrightsville, and the only casualty of the skirmish came from their ranks. Despite wearing civilian clothes and fighting with army-issued rifles given to them that day, these men fought with great skill—an action remembered when the United States Colored Troops were established later in the war.

WHAT TO SEE: The most obvious and impressive remnant of the skirmish at Wrightsville is the leftover piers of the Columbia Bridge.

Today the new bridge runs alongside the one which burned in 1863. The original pylons remain in place. The monument at left marks the Army of Northern Virginia's easternmost point reached during the Gettysburg Campaign. (*MD Rutkoski*)

Running alongside the modern bridge, these support structures are all that remain of the original crossing. But as small as the engagement was, the town has done a wonderful job preserving the nineteenth century for visitors to see. At Constitution Square rests a large memorial from the twentieth century indicating the farthest eastern point reached by Lee's Army of Northern Virginia during the Gettysburg Campaign. Atop the monument sit two cannons that were gifts from the federal government. On Hellam Street, visitors will see the Magee Home; this was the location where Major General John B. Gordon and his staff were served breakfast the day after the battle by Mary Jane Rewalt. The three-story private stone residence is largely unchanged from 1863.

At Third and Fourth Streets is a Methodist church that was struck by a Confederate shell fragment beneath its second-story window. Continue toward the river until you see a small house advertising the "Burning Bridge" Diorama on the left side of the street. Inside, guests can see a scale miniature of Wrightsville from the day of the battle. The bridge is intact in the diorama, and the model does a fantastic job of showing the defenses established by the Pennsylvania militia on the arrival of the Confederates. Finally, end the tour of Wrightsville along Front Street. Formerly known as Westphalia, this section of the city was the location most affected by the unexpected spread of the bridge fire into town. The hill ahead was where Gordon's brigade formed into a line passing buckets of water in an attempt to extinguish the blaze.

23

The Skirmishes at Oyster Point and Sporting Hill

(JUNE 28–JUNE 30, 1863)

BACKGROUND: As the Army of Northern Virginia spread throughout south central Pennsylvania, Robert E. Lee's three corps took forage through the rich farmlands of the state. Some estimate that the region was home to over seventy thousand head of livestock and countless acres of wheat, corn, orchards, and natural springs. Worn from three years of battle on Southern soil, the Confederates feasted on the wares of the Keystone State. For the most part, they did so without fear of repercussion. The populace of south central Pennsylvania had long economic and cultural ties to Maryland more than to points east and west, and the region voted heavily Democratic during election years. In aftermath of the death of Thomas "Stonewall" Jackson earlier that spring at the Battle of Chancellorsville, his II Corps was divided into two commands; the first went to Richard S. Ewell, the second to A. P. Hill. The I Corps remained under the command of James Longstreet, and all three men rose to the rank of lieutenant general.

While Hill's and Longstreet's men were foraging west of Gettysburg near Chambersburg and Cashtown, Ewell's corps had congre-

gated near Carlisle, Pennsylvania. He occupied the city and encamped his fifteen thousand men in the former frontier town to
await a potential raid on Harrisburg. To gain a better sense of what
defenses awaited him around the capital, Ewell dispatched a brigade
of cavalrymen under Albert Gallatin Jenkins to reconnoiter around
the target and gather valuable intelligence as to the arrangement of
any Union forces nearby. On June 28, the Confederates arrived at
Mechanicsburg, where they met limited opposition, and Harrisburg
sat only eight miles away.

To curb the Confederate threat two years earlier, Pennsylvania
governor Andrew Curtain had ordered the construction of a major
encampment called Camp Union to defend Harrisburg. In time, the
tent city's population surpassed that of the capital itself, and it soon
was relabeled Camp Curtain. The camp residents were unruly to say
the least, but a first-rate major general, Darius N. Couch, commanded them. Couch had been a division commander at Chancellorsville that spring, but after quarrelling with the Union high
command was reassigned to the newly formed Department of the
Susquehanna. If the Confederates were going to move on Pennsylvania's capital city, it would fall on Couch to defend it.

BATTLE: At thirty-two, Brigadier General Albert Gallatin Jenkins was
a sight to behold. When Jenkins was on horseback, his beard touched
his belt buckle, and many believed it was the longest facial hair in
the Army of Northern Virginia. Jenkins hailed from outside of
Charleston, West Virginia, but was a dedicated rebel and unapolo-
getic slave owner despite his western roots. Since entering Pennsylvania under the command of Lieutenant General Ewell, Jenkins had
kidnapped some members of the state's free black community with
the goal of enslaving them upon his return south. When Gallatin's
cavalry arrived in Mechanicsburg on June 28, 1863, he faced some
resistance but took steps to meet the Unionists head on. After halting
his men near Peace Church, the Confederate general positioned artillery in the direction of the waiting enemy. About a mile ahead, the

Brigadier General Albert Gallatin Jenkins was forgotten by his commander on June 30th, 1863, though some speculate that he was merely a rear-guard of the Robert E. Lee's 2nd Corps. Major General Darius Couch had the unenviable duty of organizing Pennsylvania's scattered militia. (*Library of Congress*)

Carlisle Pike and Trindle Spring Road converged into a fork known as Oyster Point, and that's where Jenkins aimed his fire to scatter his enemy's ranks. Anyone going to the site with a hankering for shellfish would have been disappointed (and they were), for the region was named after the Oyster family that originally settled the location. For much of the nineteenth century, the Oyster Point Tavern stood nearby as a place of shelter, food, drink, and seemingly endless gossip.

The militiamen blocking the Confederate advance served under General William F. Smith. Smith had assigned his men to begin building earthworks to prevent a rebel approach on Harrisburg, but when shots were fired, the effort fell into disarray. Smith ordered a skirmish line to provide cover for the workers, and Jenkins eventually fell back to encamp for the evening, sensing an unnecessary stalemate developing. The following morning the Confederates once again set up their guns near Peace Church, and at approximately 11:00 AM, they charged Smith's volunteers still located at Oyster Point. Much to the surprise of the advancing rebels, the militiamen had erected a series of wooden barricades to impede their progress, and they soon opened up with artillery fire of their own. The ebb and flow of the battle continued, and despite their growing confidence, the Unionists failed to realize that the entire Confederate attack was little more than a well-timed diversion.

As the two sides sparred, Jenkins used the confusion as cover to complete his intended mission; he furtively scouted out the enemy's position and defenses around Harrisburg and concluded that the capital was primed for the taking. Jenkins was joined by three engineers who accompanied Ewell's II Corps, and from their vantage point south of the main Union encampment they saw nothing but opportunity before them. Although it was deemed a Union victory, the skirmish at Oyster Point had served its purpose; word was quickly sent back to Ewell at Carlisle to prepare for a full-scale assault on Harrisburg. When Ewell and the II Corps received Jenkins's intelligence, the lieutenant general in Carlisle began to mobilize his remaining division under Major General Robert Rodes to march on the city. As the Confederates were about to set out, a messenger suddenly arrived with instructions from Robert E. Lee. According to Lee's intelligence, the Union Army of the Potomac was entering Pennsylvania, and a great showdown seemed imminent. Per his commander's instructions, Ewell immediately abandoned his plans to attack Harrisburg, rallied his men, and proceeded south toward Cashtown to reunite with the remainder of the Army of Northern Virginia.

Communication was poor in the nineteenth century, and the II Corps learned that the hard way. As Ewell's men marched south, Jenkins's cavalrymen remained fixed across the river from Harrisburg. As amazing as it seems, it appears that in his haste to rendezvous with Lee, Ewell forgot to inform Jenkins and his horsemen. Unlike his rebel counterpart, Union major general Darius N. Couch did receive intelligence showing that the Confederates had abandoned Carlisle, and he promptly sent a detachment of New York volunteers to investigate. Couch knew that the bulk of Ewell's fifteen thousand II Corps was gone, but he hoped to pick up any stragglers and potentially gain some sorely needed newspaper accolades. The New Yorkers marched under General John Ewen, an inexperienced New York businessman, and along the Carlisle Pike, the officer received his first taste of battle. As his volunteers marched, the Southern commander Jenkins panicked. He had been left behind, and he believed that all of Couch's ten thousand men were approaching; he immediately dispatched three hundred Virginians to take up a position inside a local barn owned by the Eberly family near a prominent rise called Sporting Hill.

As the Unionists marched up the Carlisle Pike, at approximately 3:00 PM they heard the unmistakable crack of gunfire. In front of them, the rebels fired from the cover of the Eberly barn, and the New Yorkers dropped to their bellies along the road. The inexperienced General Ewen froze, and sensing weakness, a force of Southerners attempted to flank the overwhelmed Union guardsmen. Luckily for Ewen, his staff officer, Lieutenant Rufus King Jr., responded ably and dispatched a force to stop the flankers. As a stalemate emerged, the Confederates surprised their enemy with two artillery pieces and began firing. The New Yorkers were caught off guard. One private believed the smoke from the cannon to be a campfire, but as branches and debris came crashing down, chaos ensued. The scene appeared to be yet another example of hardened rebel infantrymen running roughshod over inexperienced Union volunteers. Finally, at approximately 6:00 PM, two guns from a Philadelphia light artillery unit arrived in support of the hapless New Yorkers. As the inexperienced troops attempted to load the guns, they did so improperly, causing a costly and embarrassing misfire. Again Lieutenant King came to the rescue, and after he delivered a quick artillery lesson, the gunners managed to fire a shot toward the Eberly barn. That shell exploded directly over the barn, killing a dozen rebels and causing the remaining Southerners to evacuate the structure. After some unsuccessful artillery exchanges, the rebels departed the field to reunite with the II Corps farther south.

LEGACY: The skirmishes at Oyster Point and Sporting Hill were a small part of the Gettysburg Campaign but important nevertheless. They were the farthest north that Robert E. Lee's Army of Northern Virginia had extended and also the northernmost engagement of the campaign. It was also the closest that Harrisburg came to a direct attack by rebel forces. Unlike most of their counterparts at such engagements as Hanover Junction and Wrightsville, the militiamen were highly successful at stopping Jenkins's battle-hardened brigade. Distinct from those previous battles, however, these volunteers were New Yorkers, not Pennsylvanians.

Historians hate to play the "What if?" game of counterfactual history, but it happens all the time, and it is quite tempting to speculate about the events surrounding the skirmish at Sporting Hill. If "Stonewall" Jackson had not been killed at Chancellorsville in May, he would have certainly retained command of his II Corps, now split between Lieutenant Generals Hill and Ewell. While Ewell is often criticized for his slow-moving, hesitant advances, Jackson was infamous for his lightning fast raids. Which raises the question: what if Jackson had participated in the Gettysburg Campaign? He likely would not have delayed at Carlisle as long as Ewell had, and probably would have struck at Harrisburg with vigor in the last week of June 1863. Had that offensive strike been successful, the bulk of Lee's army would have rallied around the great victory, and sketches of a smoking, ruined state capital would have been printed in newspapers around the country. The biggest question of all in the Civil War has always been, how would Gettysburg have been different if Jackson had been present? In reality, if Jackson had captured and destroyed Harrisburg, the Battle of Gettysburg would almost certainly have never happened.

WHAT TO SEE: Analyzing the skirmishes at Oyster Point and Sporting Hill makes for a wonderful day of travel in and around the city of Harrisburg. Thanks to the persistent efforts of the Camp Curtain Historical Society, numerous wayside markers and monuments have been installed and restored over the last two decades. The original site of the Unionist Camp Curtain is at Sixth and Woodbine Streets in the capital and is delineated by a Pennsylvania Historical and Museum Commission marker. Nearby, the Camp Curtain Memorial-Mitchell United Methodist Church houses many displays and

The remnants of this privately owned barn held a force of rebel sharpshooters during the skirmish at Sporting Hill. (*Wikimedia Commons*)

artifacts for public view. Across the Susquehanna River, guests can visit the community of Camp Hill to walk the site of the skirmish at Oyster Point. Located near Willow Park at the intersection of Twenty-Fourth and Walnut Streets, the site includes a detailed placard that explains the events of June 28 and June 29. While in Camp Hill, be sure to view the Samuel Albright House on Thirty-Sixth Street, which was a primary bivouac point and an artillery position. The Peace Church remains intact as well, and from this location Confederate cannons blasted Union infantry at Oyster Point.

Next, travel three miles east to Mechanicsburg to see where the bulk of the fighting took place in the skirmish of Sporting Hill. Two markers describing the battle are located near Hampden Park. A short distance away one can find the remains of the foundation of the Eberly barn that was used as cover for Confederates while they fired on Union soldiers marching along the Carlisle Pike. Also nearby is the Johannes Eberly House, one of the major landmarks used by the warring parties on June 30, 1863. While both of these sites are now private property, the barn foundation can be seen briefly from an overpass on Route 11. For the best way to experience this location, please view *Battlefield Pennsylvania*'s episode on the skirmish at Sporting Hill. Complete with detailed analysis and high-definition views of the battlefield, this episode affords viewers a detailed inspection of the site that would otherwise be off-limits.

24

The Battle of Hanover

(JUNE 30, 1863)

BACKGROUND: It's been said that the cavalry is the eyes and ears of an army, and in the Civil War it was absolutely essential. Made up of soldiers on horseback, a cavalry was utilized in long-range expeditions to locate enemy positions and movements and report back to camp. Both Union and Confederate commanders relied heavily on this ancient system of intelligence gathering, and the cavalry commanders were vital to the overall success of a campaign. Cavalry officers were the fighter pilots of their time; bold, flashy, and daring, they were often the most celebrated members of the army and relished the limelight. Their uniforms were always clean and their buttons always shined, and when it came time to parade through a town square, their flashy bravado always stole the show. During the Civil War, however, the glory melted away in the fires of combat, and horrible realities of partisan war cast aside the egos of many of North America's most famous commanders.

Brigadier General Judson Kilpatrick was the commander of the Army of the Potomac's 3rd Cavalry Division, and his task was of the utmost importance. Union officials knew that Robert E. Lee's Army of Northern Virginia was in Pennsylvania, but they had little idea where he was located. It fell on Kilpatrick's cavalry division to track down Lee's II Corps under Lieutenant General Richard Ewell and report back to the Union high command. Kilpatrick was a steady officer and up to the task, as were his two brigade commanders, Brigadier Generals Elon J. Farnsworth and George Armstrong Custer.

BATTLE: By June 30, the town of Hanover had seen enough of the Civil War. Earlier that week, a Confederate force under Lieutenant Colonel Elijah Viers White had passed through the community en route to its destruction of Hanover Junction. White's cavalry destroyed telegraph equipment and raided the town of food, supplies, and alcohol; although they did pay the residents, they did so in Confederate currency that held no value north of the Mason-Dixon Line. When Brigadier General Kilpatrick's 3rd Cavalry Division arrived, the men were greeted as saviors, and the tired townspeople showed their gratitude with a presentation of music and song. All manner of baked goods and belly-filling meals raised the spirits of the Union cavalrymen, and for a brief moment the burden of the war was lifted from their shoulders. For the last several days, Kilpatrick's cavalry had been on the trail of Ewell's II Corps, but what the federals did not realize was that they were not alone in this pursuit.

Known as "the Last Cavalier," Major General James Ewell Brown "Jeb" Stuart was one of the most recognizable figures in the Confederacy. A West Point graduate who was instrumental in the arrest of John Brown at Harpers Ferry in 1859, Stuart was the picture of a Civil War cavalry commander. Just thirty years old, he was an energetic lightning rod among the Confederate high command, drawing attention with a large ostrich plume jutting from his hat and a red rose pinned to his lapel. Famous for his liberal application of cologne and unmistakable swagger, Stuart was one of the Robert E. Lee's most trusted subordinates. On June 30, 1863, the rebel horseman was also looking for Ewell's II Corps, but for different purposes than their

Union brigadier general Judson Kilpatrick, left, tangled with the Confederates under Major General J.E.B. Stuart, right, at Hanover in one of the few examples of urban cavalry combat in the Civil War. (*Library of Congress*)

federal counterparts. A week earlier, Stuart had received orders from Lee to move his horsemen north into Pennsylvania and connect with Ewell, but the usually reliable Virginian made an uncharacteristic mistake. He elected to ride east of the Army of the Potomac instead of taking the most direct westerly route through the Blue Ridge Mountains. As he raided supplies and caused chaos, however, the federal army unexpectedly began its trek north through Maryland into Pennsylvania. Stuart was caught off guard, and the advancing Union infantry effectively cut off any hope of returning to his originally intended western route. The Last Cavalier was trapped, and Lee was cut off from receiving any intelligence regarding the position of the Army of the Potomac.

On the morning of June 30, Stuart's cavalry division began its march into Pennsylvania. Originating from Maryland, the Confederates followed established roads and planned on marching through Hanover to seek out any sign of Ewell's II Corps. As they crossed the border and moved into Adams County, however, their plans suddenly changed. At the tiny village of Gitt's Mill, the 13th Virginia Cavalry, which served as Stuart's advance guard, made contact with a small force of cavalrymen from the 18th Pennsylvania Cavalry at approximately 10:00 AM. The engagement was of little consequence, but as the federals fled, the Southerners pursued them directly into Hanover and the rear of Judson Kilpatrick's 3rd Cavalry Division. When Stuart was alerted of this startling new development, the opportunistic Virginian immediately ordered artillery to the high ground outside of town and began to shell the Unionists below. While neither side expected a fight, both temporarily paused their search for Ewell's II Corps, and the Battle of Hanover began.

The 2nd North Carolina Cavalry under Brigadier General William Henry Fitzhugh Payne was one of the first Confederate forces to storm the town. As the rebels rode through the streets, citizens fled in panic before Brigadier General Elon Farnsworth sent the 5th New York Cavalry to uproot the Southerners. The Union counterattack was successful, and the rebel commander Payne was apprehended when his horse tossed him into a tanning vat filled with vile chemicals and decaying cowhide. Brigadier General Fitzhugh Lee (nephew of Robert E. Lee) and Colonel John R. Chambliss next charged into Hanover and squared off with Farnsworth's men in the rarest of sights: urban cavalry combat. In a series of sweeping charges, the Union and Confederate horsemen coursed through the streets of Hanover, fighting with pistols and sabers in between buildings and alleys. In what was certainly a dramatic scene, the two sides even collided in the town's center square.

During the scrum, Stuart himself was nearly surrounded south of Hanover as the fighting spilled from the town, and he famously leaped his steed over a fifteen-foot ravine to escape. As the combat continued to spread, Stuart realigned his forces south of the city along a high ridge running from the Mount Olivet Cemetery to the Keller Farm. Once posted on the high ground, the Confederates again turned to their artillery to pound the federals with gunfire. As the heavy gun barrage continued, Brigadier General Custer and his Michigan cavalry rushed into the fray. Anxious to break the stalemate that was developing, Custer's Wolverines dismounted from their horses and maneuvered dangerously close to Colonel Chambliss's artillery position. By best estimates, the men of the 6th Michigan Cavalry had closed to within three hundred yards of the Confederate left flank. The sun was setting over Hanover, and it became clear to the rebels that they had little to gain from a prolonged engagement with the federals. Every minute they spent at Hanover was a minute that could have been used to reunite with Ewell's II Corps. A whole day had been wasted, and while both armies raced unknowingly toward the Battle of Gettysburg, these moments were precious. Stuart was unaware that Lee and the Army of Northern Virginia were only fifteen miles away. Using skirmishers to slowly detach from the Battle of Hanover, Stuart abandoned the fight and ordered his men north toward the Susquehanna River.

LEGACY: The fighting at Hanover was inconclusive, but it reverberated through the South for years to come. At face value, Hanover was one of the rare examples of urban street combat between cavalry forces in the entire Civil War. The discipline and control required to direct a horse takes years to master, but to do so in narrow streets and alleys is even more impressive. To Jeb Stuart's overall objective, though, Hanover was a critical error. As the eyes and ears of the Army of Northern Virginia, his cavalry had to reconnect with Lee as soon as possible. But with the actions prior to the battle and the engagement itself, Stuart's cavalry lost valuable time. Without his intelligence, Lee was effectively marching blind regarding the location of the Army of the Potomac, and by the time he discovered its location, he was pressed to rally his three corps at Gettysburg.

After the Battle of Hanover, Stuart was clueless about the location of Lee's army. As he read in a local newspaper that Ewell's II Corps was last spotted north of Hanover, he ordered his men toward the Susquehanna River. Reports indicated that Major General Early had occupied York, but by the time Stuart began his march, he was already chasing ghosts. Because Kilpatrick's 3rd Cavalry Division was still nearby, Stuart moved with even more caution. As he strode north, the Southern general had no idea that Ewell was already on his way to the Gettysburg-Cashtown area to reunite with the remaining corps of Lee's rebel army. By this time his men were exhausted, and as Stuart attempted to keep their spirits up with talk of locating Ewell, he had no idea that he was actually moving farther away from his intended objective. The next day, the Battle of Gettysburg began; it would become the largest engagement in the history of the Western Hemisphere. When Robert E. Lee needed him the most, Stuart was nowhere to be found.

WHAT TO SEE: A visit to this battlefield is a visit to downtown Hanover. Go to the town square and first look at Boston artist Cyrus E. Dallin's impressive statue *The Picket*. Funded by the government of Pennsylvania, it depicts a cavalryman on horseback. Around the square can be found a number of artillery pieces associated with the battle, including an original Parrott rifle mounted on a restored carriage; this rifle is famous for bearing the serial number 1. As visitors walk the town square, interpretative plaques detail the battles development on June 30, and four horseshoes embedded in the sidewalks indicate the position of Brigadier General George Armstrong Custer's headquarters. As you stand near *The Picket*, look directly across Carlisle Street to see the white and blue brick building that was the former Central Hotel. Still in its original form, this building was the headquarters of Brigadier General Judson Kilpatrick on June 30. In 2005, Hanover invested in a series of interpretative markers that expanded on the existing ones, and the state added some placards as part of the Pennsylvania Civil War Trails initiative. Now, a visit to this Civil War community offers a full analysis of the battle from start to finish.

One of the most unusual points of interest in Hanover sits at the base of *The Picket*. Next to the cavalryman is a statue of a dog known as *Iron Mike*. Hanover native George Washington Welsh had the casting made to memorialize his beloved hound, and when Welsh died in 1879, it was subsequently moved to Mt. Olivet Cemetery. *Iron Mike* stood guard over his master's grave, but problems arose when

A Union Cavalryman, dedicated in 1905, is forever on guard in the center of Hanover. (*Wikimedia Commons*)

horses carrying mourners would startle at the sight of the dog statue. Finally, in 1905, *Iron Mike* was placed alongside *The Picket* in Hanover's Center Square, and it has remained there ever since. It is an interesting local story, but the dutiful pup had nothing to do with the Civil War or the battle that occurred nearby.

25

The Siege of Carlisle

(JULY 1–2, 1863)

BACKGROUND: By June 30, 1863, Confederate major general J. E. B. Stuart was badly off course. As the eyes and ears of the Army of Northern Virginia, Stuart's cavalry was ordered to shadow the Union Army of the Potomac out of Maryland and alert the Confederate high command as to its whereabouts. After crossing over to the eastern flank of the federals, Stuart was caught off guard when the enemy began moving north. Unable to go back across to the western flank of the Northern army, Stuart was effectively cut off from Robert E. Lee, and his misfortune left the rebel army blind as to where the oncoming enemy was. As part of his foolhardy decision to cross to the Union's right in June, Stuart captured and requisitioned approximately 125 wagons filled with goods and supplies. With Stuart now terribly out of position, these spoils were becoming increasingly burdensome for the thirty-year-old officer known for his speed and readiness.

After battling with Brigadier General Judson Kilpatrick's 3rd Cavalry Division at Hanover, Stuart lost more valuable time. He never intended to spar with the Northern horsemen but believed it to be prudent after running into them in York County. The fighting lasted a whole day, and the results were inconclusive; the only certainty was that the Last Cavalier was no closer to locating Richard Ewell's II Corps of the rebel army. Following outdated newspaper accounts, Stuart ordered his men north toward York, but with the II Corps nowhere to be found, he made camp at Dover, Pennsylvania. He soon received word from friendly locals that Ewell had already departed, and Stuart guessed that he was likely to find at least part of the Confederate army twenty-five miles west at Carlisle.

BATTLE: The town of Carlisle has a deep, historic connection to the development of Pennsylvania as well as the United States. Originally founded by Scots-Irish settlers in the eighteenth century, Carlisle grew to become the last major community east of the Allegheny Mountains; once travelers left Carlisle, it was understood that they were in the vast Ohioan frontier. Originally laid out by John Armstrong prior to his Kittanning raid, it hosted a veritable who's who of colonial America: Henry Bouquet, John Forbes, Benjamin Franklin, and George Washington all used Carlisle as a last stopover before venturing into the wilderness. During the American Revolution, the community was the primary storage place for the Continental army's supplies and ordnance, for though it was lightly defended, patriot leaders believed that it sat out of the reach of the British armies in the east. In 1838, Carlisle played host to the US Army's primary cavalry school, and many officers in both the Blue and the Gray had lived in the barracks before the war began. For some of the Confederates who ventured through the town in summer 1863, a return to Carlisle was akin to a homecoming celebration. Stuart himself had never been stationed at Carlisle, but many of his subordinate officers had; even Lieutenant General Ewell did his time there.

On the morning of June 30, Richard Ewell's II Corps abandoned Carlisle, and that night a force of Confederates under Albert Gallatin Jenkins briefly rode through the town. Therefore, on the morning of July 1 there was a great feeling of uncertainty and fear among its citizens regarding when the rebels would return. That day the townspeople were delighted see blue coats, not gray, marching toward Carlisle. As the commander of the 1st Division of the Department of the Susquehanna, Brigadier General William F. "Baldy" Smith dispatched two brigades to seek out any rebel forces that remained in Pennsylvania; when they arrived in Carlisle, the townsfolk greeted the Union troops as heroes. They provided food, water, and supplies as a show of gratitude and were totally unaware that Jeb Stuart's Confederates were closing in on the city. The Union forces at Carlisle consisted of the 4th and 5th Brigades of the 1st Division, as well as four volunteer militia regiments. Among them were the 28th and 33rd Pennsylvania Militias and the 22nd and 37th New York Militias. As was the case at previous engagements with the men of Ewell's II Corps, the New Yorkers were among the best infantry in the volunteer forces. Not knowing where or when the Confederates may strike next, Baldy Smith arranged his men in a defensive perimeter around the city and hoped for an uneventful stay in Carlisle.

Stuart's cavalry division arrived at Carlisle on the evening of July 1. Unbeknownst to him at the time, the whole Army of Northern Virginia, numbering over seventy-one thousand men, was battling the Army of the Potomac thirty miles south at Gettysburg. One of the earliest actions at Carlisle occurred on the east side of town when four companies of locally raised home guard troops attempted to fend off a party of troopers from Major General Fitzhugh Lee's brigade; locals were no match for the hardened Confederate veterans, and as they fell back in retreat, they exposed the whole US Army barracks to attack. But instead of striking the town outright, the Last Cavalier believed that since the men defending Carlisle were only volunteer militia, they would likely give up the city if offered a peaceful resolution. Lieutenant Henry C. Lee, the younger brother of Fitzhugh Lee, was escorted to Baldy Smith with a message from the rebel commander. Lee stated that the Confederates were prepared to let the militiamen walk away from the fight under the condition that

The Saturday, July 4, 1863, *Philadelphia Inquirer* ran a story and map describing the bombardment of Carlisle, Pennsylvania. (*Dickinson College Archives and Special Collections*)

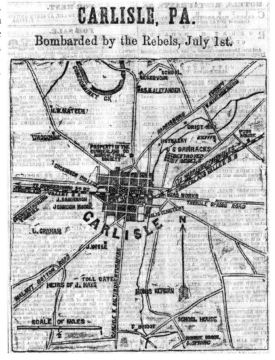

the town be handed over. If the federals chose to make a stand, Stuart promised a heavy cannonade from his artillery outside of town. The deal was offered under the flag of truce, and Stuart believed that it would be readily accepted. On hearing the offer, Brigadier General Smith defiantly stated that he would never surrender Carlisle, adding famously, "Shell away and be damned!"

True to his word, Stuart placed Captain James W. Breathed's battery on a high ridge above Carlisle. Making sure that the Unionists saw the heavy guns, he once again sent a messenger to ask Smith to surrender. With the gun barrels pointed in their direction, Stuart hoped Carlisle would fall without a fight. But for a second time, Smith stood his ground. As negotiations seemed hopeless, Stuart opened fire. For three hours, the rebels blasted artillery shells into the town, damaging homes and public buildings. Although the shelling was steady, it inflicted only minor damage, to the courthouse

The Old Cumberland Courthouse was a witness to J.E.B. Stuart's siege on July 1, 1863. Close examination of the courthouse reveals damage caused by Confederate shells. (*Author*)

façade and the buildings at Dickinson College. Not content to watch from afar, some of the more rambunctious rebels set fire to the army barracks and a local gasworks. As a final statement to the siege, the gasworks exploded, igniting a bright flame across the night sky. Stuart's victory was complete, but it came at a heavy cost that would haunt the American South for generations.

LEGACY: As Jeb Stuart tangled with union forces at Carlisle, the Army of Northern Virginia was simultaneously engaged with the Union army thirty miles south at Gettysburg. Stuart had been one of Lee's most reliable and consistent lieutenants since the start of the war, and now, in the largest battle of the conflict, the cavalry commander was nowhere to be found. Day one of the Battle of Gettysburg saw some of the fiercest fighting of the entire engagement; starting northeast of the town, it eventually spilled into the streets until moving to the famous ground to the south of the community. There is much to consider regarding how Stuart might have aided Lee during the initial phase of the battle, but the only certainty was his conspicuous absence. While the federals and rebels jockeyed for control of the high ground south of Gettysburg, Stuart's cavalry was celebrating its futile shelling of Carlisle.

By the time Lee's army was located by Union scouts at Gettysburg, Stuart's assault on Carlisle was winding down. After midnight, he received word that the Army of Northern Virginia was locked in a titanic struggle at Gettysburg. Suddenly, the entire day's efforts had become a fool's errand. Despite having the federals bogged down within the city, Stuart's one and only mission now was to untangle his men from Carlisle as quickly as possible. By 1:00 AM on July 2, he began withdrawing his horsemen from the town, and he immediately directed them south to Gettysburg. They rode the whole night, and by the time they arrived at the battle in late afternoon, his men were exhausted. Stuart was met with a cold greeting from Lee. According to Colonel Edward Porter Alexander, the old commander merely uttered, "Well, General, you are here at last."[1] For much of the next 150 years, Stuart's tardiness was highly criticized, and it has made him a primary scapegoat for the eventual Confederate defeat at Gettysburg on July 3.

WHAT TO SEE: Carlisle is one of Pennsylvania's most historic cities. Walking its streets is a tour through America's colonial, Revolutionary, and Civil War past. Begin your tour at the historic intersection of High and Hanover Streets. Here visitors can see three hundred years of history piled into a single city block. At the center of the square is the Cumberland County Courthouse, constructed in 1846. As you stand at the front of the building along Hanover Street, a careful examination of the massive stone pillars reveals the unmistakable damage caused by an artillery round. These were the result of the shots fired by Jeb Stuart on July 1, 1863. As the home of the US Army War College, Carlisle also has an impressive collection of military artifacts and an extensive archive on campus that is open to the public for inspection.

1. Porter Alexander, in Stephen W. Sears, *Gettysburg* (New York: Houghton Mifflin, 2003), 258.

Remaining in the main square of the city, walk to the First Presbyterian Church. George Washington attended services at this centuries-old landmark, and it was established as the first heart of the city by the Scots-Irish settlers of the eighteenth century. For more Civil War history, walk south along Hanover until you reach the new courthouse building. It was here in 1847 that Carlisle residents rioted when three runaway slaves from Maryland were returned to their former owners. As a result of the chaos, two were rescued from the return to bondage in the South. Finally, continue to South Street to visit the Old Graveyard. Here visitors can pay respects to such giants of Pennsylvania history as Molly Pitcher, John Armstrong, Hugh Henry Brackenridge, and Charles Seebold, drummer boy for the 1st US Cavalry. The Old Graveyard is the final resting place for 550 Civil War veterans.

26

The Battle of Gettysburg

(JULY 1–3, 1863)

BACKGROUND: On the evening of June 30, 1863, few of the one hundred eighty thousand men in the armies of the North and South had any idea that the greatest battle of the Civil War was only a day away. Robert E. Lee's Army of Northern Virginia was spread out like a fan across the Pennsylvania countryside, and the freshly appointed Major General George Gordon Meade's Army of the Potomac stretched from Hanover south to Emmitsburg, Maryland. Lee had been uncomfortable with his lack of intelligence regarding the position of the Union army, and his chief reconnaissance officer, Jeb Stuart, had failed to alert him that Meade's men had crossed the Potomac River. By June 29, the federals were already within striking distance, and Lee urgently ordered his tripartite army corps to reunite at Cashtown some eight miles west of Gettysburg.

On June 30, a series of seemingly nondescript activities ushered the tidal wave of history upon the sleepy Pennsylvania community. Once Lieutenant General A. P. Hill's III Corps joined Lee at Cashtown, a brigade of rebels under Brigadier General Johnson Pettigrew marched into Gettysburg to look for supplies they could pilfer. As they had done so often in the preceding days, they planned to resupply courtesy of the Keystone State's intimidated populace. When they arrived north of the town, they were startled to see Brigadier General John Buford's Union cavalry scouting in the area, and the rebels quietly decided to return to Cashtown and report their findings. With the news of federal cavalry in hand, Major General Henry Heth believed them to be simply more of the listless Pennsylvania militiamen who had proven to be so feeble at Wrightsville, Sporting Hill, and Hanover Junction. Confident that he could rout the volunteers, Heth ordered two brigades into Gettysburg on the morning of Wednesday, July 1.

BATTLE: In anticipation of a potential showdown to come, Buford arranged his men across a series of defensive ridges northeast of Gettysburg. Because of Buford's local intelligence and familiarity with the network of roadways nearby, the cavalry officer anticipated an attack along the Chambersburg Pike. By the time Heth's division arrived at 7:30 AM, Buford's suspicions had been validated, and shots were immediately exchanged—the Battle of Gettysburg had begun. As Heth believed that the federals in Gettysburg were merely Pennsylvania militia, there was little expectation of a major engagement, but time would reveal these scattered musket pops to be the opening stanza of the largest battle of the Civil War. Buford's dismounted cavalry provided a stubborn resistance along McPherson's Ridge northwest of the town and held back the rebels long enough for Major General John F. Reynold's I Corps to arrive in force at 10:00 AM. Reynolds, considered to be one of the finest officers in the Army of the Potomac, had rushed his men toward the fighting from distant Maryland and was killed almost immediately after he arrived at Gettysburg. The fighting was the result of a classic meeting engagement, and as the day wore on, more and more participants arrived. Confederate lieutenant general Richard Ewell's corps came from the north, and fellow rebel lieutenant general A. P. Hill's from the west. By the time Union general Oliver O. Howard's XI Corps reached the

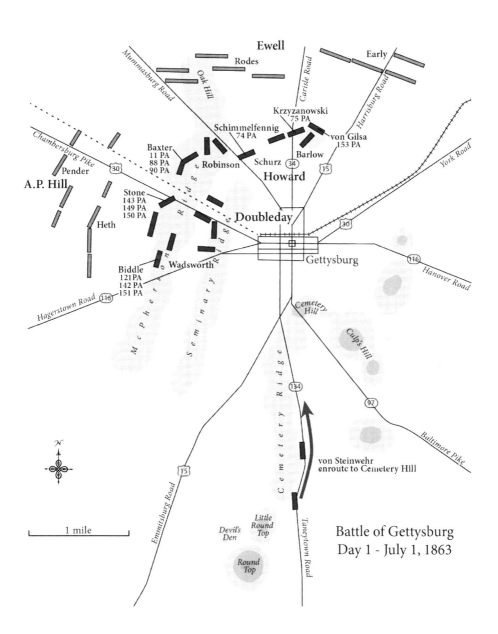

Ewell

Rodes

Early

Mummasburg Road

Oak Hill

Carlisle Road

Harrisburg Road

Chambersburg Pike

Krzyzanowski
75 PA

Schimmelfennig
74 PA

von Gilsa
153 PA

Baxter
11 PA
88 PA
90 PA

Robinson

Schurz

Barlow

Pender

Howard

30

York Road

A.P. Hill

Stone
143 PA
149 PA
150 PA

Doubleday

30

Heth

Gettysburg

116

Biddle
121 PA
142 PA
151 PA

Wadsworth

Hanover Road

Hagerstown Road

116

Cemetery
Hill

McPherson Ridge

Seminary Ridge

Culp's Hill

Cemetery Ridge

134

97

Baltimore Pike

N

von Steinwehr
enroute to Cemetery Hill

1 mile

15

Emmitsburg Road

Devil's
Den

Little
Round
Top

Taneytown Road

Round
Top

Battle of Gettysburg
Day 1 - July 1, 1863

town, it was clear he was outmatched. Instead of engaging the Southerners, Howard directed his men to retreat east through Gettysburg, and this soon turned the tiny community into a maelstrom of urban warfare. By the end of the day, the federals had established a powerful defensive line south of town on Cemetery Ridge, and as both sides received reinforcements, it appeared the Union Army possessed the best ground on the field.

By the next morning, both armies saw their ranks swell as reinforcements arrived, and the coming battle began to define itself. Both armies were aligned south of the town on opposite ridgelines. In the east, the Army of the Potomac occupied Cemetery Ridge from Culp's Hill on the north to a pair of hills known locally as Big and Little Round Top on the south. In the relative shape of a fishhook, this position was the most advantageous available and offered lines of interior communication for confronting the rebel threat. Over the previous two years, Lee had succeeded in taking the best ground before nearly every major battle, but at Gettysburg it appeared that the script had finally flipped. Across from Meade's army, the Confederates occupied a long parallel crest called Seminary Ridge; while it was clearly an inferior position, it was the most direct location from which to crush the Union right and left flanks when the battle began.

On the morning of July 2, Lee commanded Lieutenant General James Longstreet to focus his attack on the Union left flank. He was to launch his divisions along the southern end of the federal line in waves while Hill and Ewell attacked the center and right respectively. The entire maneuver depended on strategic timing, and if successful, it would have crumpled the Army of the Potomac in on itself and left the road to Washington, DC, open and undefended. The attack never developed as Lee had envisioned it. Before the fighting began, Union major general Daniel Sickles grew dissatisfied with his position along the southern end of the line and moved his men west toward a high knoll along the Emmitsburg Road. In doing so, Sickles created an enormous bulge in the southern end of the fishhook and compromised the entire position. By the time Major General Meade

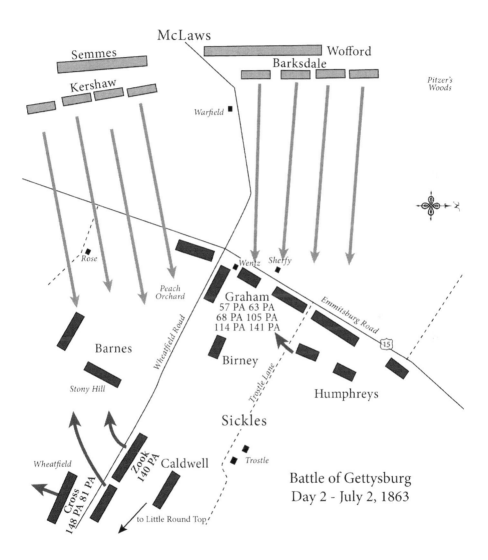

McLaws

Semmes

Wofford

Barksdale

Kershaw

Pitzer's
Woods

Warfield

Rose

Wentz   Sherfy

Peach
Orchard

Graham
57 PA 63 PA
68 PA 105 PA
114 PA 141 PA

Emmitsburg Road

Barnes

Wheatfield Road

Birney

15

Stony Hill

Trostle Lane

Humphreys

Sickles

Wheatfield

Zook
140 PA

Caldwell

Trostle

Battle of Gettysburg
Day 2 - July 2, 1863

Cross
148 PA 81 PA

to Little Round Top

Devil's Den is an iconic location on the Gettysburg battlefield. Here during the second day of fighting, the Confederates wrested control of these rocks from Union forces. (*Wikimedia Commons*)

discovered this insubordination, he realized it was too late to reposition the III Corps and instead reinforced it with twenty thousand more men. When Longstreet's great attack on the Union left flank finally came, Sickles's realignment had caused a great deal of confusion for both warring armies. Ordinary locations became scenes of terrible carnage: Sherfy's Peach Orchard, the Rose Wheatfield, a natural rock formation known as Devil's Den, and Little Round Top all saw extraordinary waves of back-and-forth combat. Each time the rebels charged with great resolve, but the federals held the position and fended off the attacks. To the north, the attacks on the Union right flank also failed to achieve their goals. Hill's attack succeeded in opening a hole in the enemy line but fell to pieces when important members of his division command were killed and night fell. At Culp's Hill, Ewell managed to capture a significant portion of the breastworks and defenses along the bottom of the hill but was never able to topple the Union defenders from its crest.

After failing to capture the Union right and left on July 2, Robert E. Lee made one final assault on the fishhook on July 3. As the edges

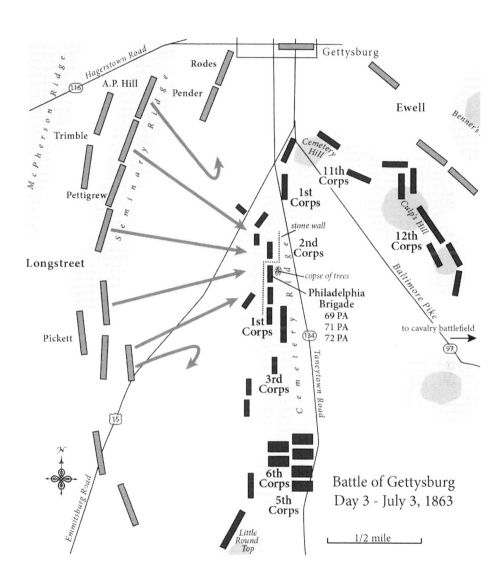

Battle of Gettysburg
Day 3 - July 3, 1863

1/2 mile

The Union positions at Gettysburg facing Pickett's Charge. The Union repulse of the futile Confederate charge was a turning point in the entire war. (*Wikimedia Commons*)

of the federal line had taken the bulk of the damage the previous day, Lee believed that the center would now be the weakest as Meade would have likely moved reinforcements outward toward the north and south. Earlier that morning, Ewell was pushed off Culp's Hill, undoing the successes of July 2 and placing an air of desperation among the Southern ranks. At 1:00 PM, Lee ordered his artillery to open fire on Meade's center in an epic and historic show of force. Using upward of 170 heavy guns, the bombardment was likely the largest of the Civil War and lasted nearly two hours. For all of its bluster, though, the cannonade largely overshot the Union line, and at 3:00 PM, Lee initiated the second phase of his final attack. Believing the center to be sufficiently weakened from his artillery barrage, Lee ordered thirteen thousand infantrymen to march across almost a mile of open ground directly into the heart of the Union army. Led by Major Generals George Pickett, James Johnston Pettigrew, and Isaac Trimble, the ill-fated attack was cut to pieces by the waiting federals troops, and the casualty figures were staggering. The event, which was labeled Pickett's Charge, became synonymous with the disastrous defeat of the Army of Northern Virginia at Gettysburg.

While the traditional story of the battle ends there, major cavalry duels occurred throughout July 3. After arriving late to Gettysburg, the crestfallen braggart Jeb Stuart was eager to regain his commander's faith. After being ordered to defend the Confederate left and harass Union wagon trains behind the main body of the army, Stuart found himself in a large battle with the horsemen of Brigadier Generals David McMurtie Gregg and George Armstrong Custer. Now known as the Battle of East Cavalry Field, the affair was a hand-to-hand and saber-to-saber slugfest three miles east of Cemetery Ridge. The engagement ended when Custer's Wolverines charged the Southerners and forced Stuart to flee the battlefield. Now defeated, Stuart ordered his cavalrymen to rejoin the rest of Lee's Army of Northern Virginia to begin their long retreat south to the Potomac River.

LEGACY: The Battle of Gettysburg can only be described in superlatives. It stands as the single greatest engagement of the war, produced the most casualties, and remains the largest battle in the history of the Western Hemisphere. By the time the sun rose on July 4, both armies limped away suffering a combined forty-five thousand to fifty thousand killed and wounded. The Gettysburg Campaign was considered a high-water mark for Lee's Army of Northern Virginia in that it never traveled farther north, and it stands as one of the few times the Virginian was truly defeated on the field of battle. While the rebels fled south in the days immediately following the three-day engagement, they did battle with pursuing federals seventeen more times over the next two weeks. When the campaign finally ended in mid-July, the Confederates escaped to the safety of the Potomac's southern banks, and the war continued for two more bloody and costly years.

For a brief time, the victory invigorated Union spirits across Pennsylvania, leading the *Philadelphia Inquirer* to declare Gettysburg the new "Waterloo,"[1] but those good feelings subsided. The death tolls of the three-day battle were catastrophic, and the realization hit that

1. Edgar Williams, "A Brief History of the Inquirer," *Philadelphia Inquirer*, September 25, 2009.

The statue of Union general John Reynolds dedicated in 1899. Reynolds was killed on the first day of the battle. There are more than 1,300 monuments and markers commemorating both Union and Confederate subjects on the Gettysburg battlefield. (*Wikimedia Commons*)

because Lee's army had escaped ultimate defeat, the war was guaranteed to continue. From the earliest days of the conflict there was a strong belief among Unionists that capturing the Confederate field armies would immediately end the war, and many federal commanders were criticized and demoted for not being aggressive enough in their pursuit of this end. When Lee's rebels escaped back across the Potomac after Gettysburg, many Northern politicians and commentators deemed the victorious Meade just another failed commander in the quest to capture the Army of Northern Virginia's high command. Further undermining Meade's triumph was Major General Ulysses S. Grant's unconditional capture of Vicksburg, Mississippi, just one day after Gettysburg, on July 4. Grant's rising fame, coupled with the legitimate criticism of Meade, served to temper the initial excitement brought on by the Union victory at Gettysburg.

WHAT TO SEE: The best way to experience Gettysburg is with a guided tour of the battlefield. The National Park Service tour is a fine way to experience the park for first timers and returning guests alike, and each tour offers something different. The rangers and guides employed by the park service at Gettysburg are some of the finest in the field, and their rigorous standards ensure only the finest of experiences for visitors. As the most studied battle in human history, Gettysburg offers opportunities to hire licensed battlefield guides who can offer precise, step-by-step analysis of every inch of the battlefield. In short, Gettysburg National Military Park has an army of the finest guides in the world—use them. If you are unable to take a tour or hire a guide, countless driving tours can direct you to the major hot spots of the tour: Culp's Hill, Peach Orchard, Wheat Field, Little Round Top, the Angle, and East Cavalry Field are all readily marked on the battlefield tour road.

Gettysburg can be fully experienced by most guests in three days. After the battlefield tours are complete, there are many locations nearby worthy of investigation. Begin your extended tour at the Cashtown Inn due west of Gettysburg. This home was not only present in 1863 but served as a temporary headquarters for Robert E. Lee. It's since been converted to a bed and breakfast that faithfully interprets its role in the battle using informational signs and placards. In the town square, be certain to visit the David Wills House. Marked by an unmistakable life-size statue of Abraham Lincoln on its sidewalk, this historic location was the site where the president completed his draft of the legendary Gettysburg Address. Its rooms have been restored to their nineteenth-century state, and it is complemented by a museum that offers a tangible connection to 1863. Finally, the locals are very helpful, but refrain from asking them how to get to the battlefield. They will be quick to note that fighting engulfed the entire town, pointing out many buildings and homes still riddled with bullet holes and artillery damage.

27

The Battle of Monterey Pass

(JULY 4–5, 1863)

BACKGROUND: The Battle of Gettysburg ended on July 3, 1863, and was the largest engagement in the history of the Western Hemisphere. Nearly fifty thousand Americans were killed or wounded, and after three days of horrendous fighting, both armies were looking forward to a long rest. The Union Army of the Potomac under Major General George Gordon Meade was victorious, but the damage to the army was enormous. For the losing general, Robert E. Lee, his battered army was forced to retreat back to the safety of Virginia with its wounded carried off in a long train of bumping and bouncing wagons; the scene was a macabre testament to the brutality of the Civil War.

Lee was presented with two primary routes for his evacuation from Pennsylvania, and he chose to use both. One of the paths began on the road through Cashtown, over South Mountain, and finally crossing the Potomac River at Williamsport, Maryland; this route would be used to transport the eleven-mile wagon train of wounded soldiers. The secondary route was more treacherous and better suited for moving the Army of Northern Virginia's supply train. It ran southwest to Fairfield and ultimately passed over South Mountain and through Monterey Pass.

Not content to have his enemy merely limp away from the battlefield, Union commander Meade dispatched Brigadier General Judson Kilpatrick's 3rd Cavalry Division as well as one thousand three hundred horsemen of the 2nd Cavalry Division under Colonel Pennock Huey in pursuit of the rebels. By the evening of July 4, federal scouts had spotted the Confederate supply train rolling through the mountains, and the Union cavalry was in hot pursuit. It appeared that the Southern army would not escape Pennsylvania without one last fight.

BATTLE: Although the Army of Northern Virginia was in enemy territory in Pennsylvania, it was by no means lost. To cross over into the state, Robert E. Lee would have needed to be intimately familiar with any available roads and passages through the great South Mountain, and because of the long history of interstate trade in the region, the best routes were apparent. After their defeat at Gettysburg, the Confederates were devastated, losing nearly a third of their seventy-five thousand men to death or injury. For the rebels, a safe retreat across the Mason-Dixon Line was essential, and history revealed that Monterey Pass was one of the best options available. Monterey Pass was a difficult piece of ground; it was high in the mountains and marked by extremely narrow roadways. Historically, the pass was the former route of the Great Wagon Road, which carried countless thousands of America's first settlers into the west. Unlike in the modern age, when massive earth-moving equipment allows engineers to place roadways virtually anywhere they choose, during the Civil War era, travelers often had to use the passages nature provided. For that reason, navigable roads through the mountains were well-known and heavily trafficked. For Lee, who recognized that control was the greatest measure of safety for the fleeing army, the gap was unique, as it contained a tollhouse that was anchored to several roads. In short, there was no better route with more options of retreat through South Mountain than Monterey Pass.

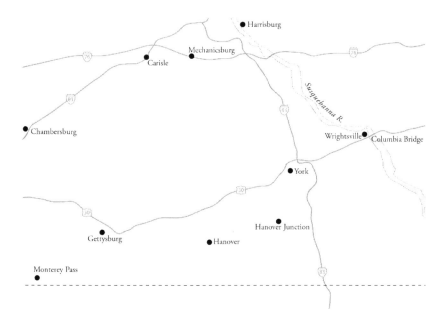

On July 4, Lee commanded Brigadier General William "Grumble" Jones to escort a Confederate train of hundreds of wagons through the narrow corridors of South Mountain. Marching alongside were cavalrymen from Maryland, Virginia, and North Carolina. Seven miles east, at the small town of Emmitsburg, Brigadier General Kilpatrick arrived with hopes of locating the valuable wagon train as it bounced and bumbled through the mountains. While the Confederates rolled cautiously over the alternating rising and falling ground, local farmer Charles Buhrman spotted the rebels. He immediately rode east to inform the federals that the wagon train was close and could be ensnared in the wilderness. Ambushing the Confederates would require climbing up the steep grade of the mountains, and Brigadier General Custer's 5th Michigan Cavalry was the first to answer the call. As the Unionists scaled the hill, a hard driving rain began to envelope the area; the sun was setting at the same time, and visibility was virtually gone. As the Wolverines climbed, they were suddenly knocked back by the blast of a Confederate cannon. After two more booming shots, the horsemen of the 5th Michigan

Brigadier General George Armstrong Custer, right, and his Michigan Wolverines were critical players in the Battle of Monterey Pass. Confederate general William "Grumble" Jones, left, was responsible for hundreds of Confederate wagons attemting to retreat across the Mason-Dixon Line. (*Library of Congress*)

turned in retreat. As they fled, they soon discovered that federal artillery had been positioned behind them and they quickly regrouped alongside the artillery battery for yet another attack.

Knowing the danger that the sudden Union attack presented, Captain George Malcolm Emack of Maryland rushed to protect the Confederate wagon train. By the time of the 5th Michigan's attack, more than half the train had made it through the pass, and Emack hoped to move the remainder to ensure its survival. As the Southerners attempted to organize their forces in the inky blackness of night, Custer's men charged again. The fighting was intense; with rain pouring down, the Blue and the Gray fought in a confusing scrum, with the only light coming from the occasional flash of lightning or blast of a musket. Using the chaos to his advantage Kilpatrick ordered the 1st Vermont Cavalry to break from the fighting and focus its efforts on destroying the rebel wagon train as it rolled off of South Mountain. At approximately 3:00 AM, Custer's horsemen dismounted and charged Emack's Confederates near the tollgate house where the various roads of Monterey Pass intersected. The fighting was at close quarters and intense, and Captain Emack was wounded. Despite the overall raucous nature of the fight, the Southerners were able to maintain a nearby artillery piece that persistently cut down the federals. Before long, Custer's men were trapped, but the 1st West Virginia Cavalry arrived just in time to push the rebels back and drive the Confederate gun backward down the side of the mountain. Before long, Grumble Jones ordered all his men, even staff, to pick up a gun and fight.

Once liberated by the Mountaineers, Custer's Wolverines went on the rampage. Focusing their efforts on the Confederate wagon train, they burned, looted, and turned over the lumbering transports. Horses panicked and fled, and with nowhere to run, many tumbled fatally down the mountainside. In the cold rainy night, residents in nearby towns saw the unmistakable orange hue of a great fire at Monterey Pass; it was the burning wreckage of dozens of rebel supply wagons that had toppled down into the ravines and valleys below. With few defensive forces to stop them, Custer's men traveled up and down the train, damaging vital stores and taking prisoners whenever possible. In the black of night and a torrential downpour, they became a force of almost unspeakable destruction. To support the raid, Lieutenant Alexander C. M. Pennington's federal battery blasted the wagons with cannon fire. For the next 150 years, locals would find the charred remnants of wagon hardware in the ravines of Monterey Pass.

With over 250 wagons captured and approximately one thousand four hundred prisoners taken, the Battle of Monterey Pass was winding to a close. The rebels had sought a speedy path to the Potomac, not to defend a mountain pass in enemy territory. Nevertheless, the 6th Virginia Cavalry and a brigade of North Carolinians arrived near daybreak on July 5, and Brigadier General Kilpatrick elected to move on. The battle was sprawled out over many miles, and his cavalry was divided across the length of it. Rather than tangle with superior forces at Monterey Pass, Kilpatrick ordered his men to continue across the Maryland border in an attempt to head off the Confederates in the days to come. While the Confederates met almost no resistance at

The road through the mountain pass is still visible in select parts of the wilderness. (*John A. Miller*)

the beginning of their great invasion of Pennsylvania, abandoning the state proved to be far more difficult.

LEGACY: The Battle of Monterey Pass holds the distinction of being one of the only battles during the Civil War to be fought on both sides of the Mason-Dixon Line. It was also the second-largest battle of the Gettysburg Campaign. One of the true axioms of traditional warfare prior to the twentieth century was that it was never prudent to fight in the rain or after dark; Monterey Pass is a shining example of the chaos that can result. As the battle was fought during a torrential downpour, both Union and Confederate officers wore dark-colored gum blanket raincoats. In the heat of battle, the two sides became virtually indistinguishable, and the result was mass confusion. During the fight it was not uncommon for Confederate officers to accidently blunder into federal troops thinking they were friendly only to find themselves taken prisoner. A veteran of the battle recounted that at one point, an entire battalion of the 10th Virginia

Cavalry was proceeding up a wet, dark road and unexpectedly encountered a federal officer. When the Union commander saw the rebels, he raised his pistol in defiance and demanded that they surrender immediately. With no hesitation the Southerners threw up their hands, only to discover that the entire battalion had surrendered to a small group of federal troops.[1]

Robert E. Lee's escape from Gettysburg remains one of the most understudied aspects of the campaign. With so much focus on the three-day battle itself, the greater narrative and consequences of the fighting are often lost, even to experienced historians. In many ways, the most precious details of moving a nineteenth-century army during a military campaign are discovered when studying the least-attractive aspects of the march. Despite the general belief that fighting ended at Gettysburg, the Army of Northern Virginia and the Army of the Potomac squared off several more times before the official conclusion of the campaign. Among the greatest engagements were Fairfield on July 3, Smithsburg on July 5, Hagerstown on July 6, Boonsboro on July 8, and Funkstown on July 10. Fighting continued even after Lee crossed the Potomac, until the campaign finally came to an end following the Battle of Manassas Gap on July 23.

WHAT TO SEE: The Monterey Pass Battlefield Park and Museum is a sprawling 125 acres in the mountains of Franklin County, but it still preserves only a tiny portion of this massive battlefield. When visiting the site, first stop in the museum to take in its collection of artifacts and exhibits highlighting the retreat from Gettysburg.

From there guests can either participate in a guided tour of the park or follow along a self-guided walking tour. Highlights include the location of a firefight between North Carolina sharpshooters and the men of Pennington's battery, as well as the intense hand-to-hand combat pitting federal troops and the 1st Maryland Cavalry. The last stop on the tour is one of the most impressive, as it highlights the

1. J. David Petruzzi and Steven A. Stanley, *The Gettysburg Campaign in Number and Losses* (El Dorado Hills, CA: Savas Beatie, 2012), 155–159.

The Monterey Pass Battlefield Museum sits directly on the battlefield. (*John A. Miller*)

exact location where the 5th and 6th Michigan Cavalries formed a battle line that allowed the 1st West Virginia Cavalry and the 1st Ohio Cavalry to charge the Confederate line and attack the Southern wagon train. For the ultra-adventurous, the battlefield also provides a two-and-a-half-hour driving tour covering the entire engagement, from the place where Brigadier General Judson Kilpatrick first encountered the rebel pickets of Captain George Emack to the end of the battle in Leitersburg, Maryland.

One of more unusual sights at the Monterey Pass Battlefield is found directly beside the museum. Because of the extraordinary efforts of Wolverines like George Armstrong Custer during the battle, the Michigan Historical Commission has placed a state-sponsored historic marker in the park. One side tells the story of the battle, while the other highlights the brave actions of the Michigan cavalry brigade on July 4 and 5, 1863. Because the Monterey Pass Battlefield Park and Museum covers such a broad swath of Franklin County, large portions of the battleground are private property. Many parts of it are yet to be identified, and the ground is still rich with archaeological remains. Handling these objects is strictly prohibited, and maintaining the sanctity of the site is a responsibility that falls on all of us.

28

The Burning of Chambersburg

(JULY 30, 1864)

BACKGROUND: By 1864, the war had turned decidedly in favor of the Union, and both sides were suffering from the grind of combat. Although the federals found success in Tennessee, Georgia, and Virginia, the fighting was far from over, and Northern administrators were feeling the strain. For President Abraham Lincoln, the war was growing costly, and he believed that short of a major victory, he might lose his reelection to Democratic challenger and former Army of the Potomac commander George B. McClellan. Campaigns were under way across the South, but nasty stalemates were developing, and thousands of lives were lost with little victory to show for it. A military success would speak volumes across the North, but a loss would reverberate even more.

When Robert E. Lee's Army of Northern Virginia first invaded Pennsylvania in June 1863, the general understood that political ramifications loomed large. In his grander view of the war, Lee hoped to win a series of victories on Northern soil to send shock and fear through the Union populace. If done correctly, the Southern commander foresaw a political wave emerging against Lincoln that would cost him his presidency. As an important part of this effort, Lee gave his subordinates strict orders regarding the treatment of private property during their campaign in the Pennsylvania backcountry. Lee insisted that his men pay for every scrap of food taken and that the wanton destruction of Northern homes be avoided at all costs. If money could not be provided, then slips of reimbursement should be dispersed. In short, Lee took careful measures to ensure that the reputation of the "Southern gentleman" was upheld at all costs. Lee wanted the Gettysburg Campaign to be evidence of the South's chivalry, which would play heavily into the debates surrounding the 1864 presidential election.

One of the most recent defeats suffered by the federals had occurred in the Shenandoah Valley of Virginia. Since the beginning of the war, the beauty and agricultural prosperity of the Shenandoah had been devastated by war. In 1864, Major General David S. Hunter was defeated there by Major General Jubal Early's rebels, but the Union commander still managed to leave a permanent scar on the landscape. As his men trekked through the Shenandoah, Hunter allowed them to pillage and plunder homes across western Virginia. They stole food, looted goods and alcohol, and set fire to homes with little regard for the families who lived there. To Early, the depredations were a personal assault on his home state, and he ordered a swift retaliation to show the federals that these offenses would not go unpunished. Recalling his earlier experiences in the Gettysburg Campaign, Early selected Chambersburg as the city he would use to exact his revenge. As the commander known as "Old Jube" wrote, "it was time to open the eyes to the people of the North to this enormity, by example in the way of retaliation."[1] The commander called on Missouri-born, Virginia-raised brigadier general John McCausland to lead the raid back into Pennsylvania. One year after the Battle of Gettysburg, the Union was invaded one final time.

---

1. Jubal Early, *Lieutenant General Jubal Anderson Early, C.S.A: Autobiographical Sketch and Narrative of the War between the States* (Philadelphia: J. B. Lippincott, 1912), 401.

BATTLE: By summer 1864, the fighting had devolved into a war of attrition. Lee felt as though his Army of Northern Virginia was constantly on the defensive, and Northern newspapers were referring to Grant as "the Butcher," as thousands of Union troops were sacrificed under his command. In many ways, the worst of both armies was yet to be revealed. Union major general Hunter had famously allowed his soldiers to ransack towns and plantations across Virginia's Shenandoah Valley, and reports of the raids shocked the South. There had always been a sense in Dixie that its soldiers were gentlemen warriors, while their Northern counterparts were senseless brutes; the wanton destruction of private property validated their belief that to the federals, nothing was sacred. In July 1864, Major General Early decided that a retaliatory message must be sent, and he commanded Brigadier General McCausland to deliver the bad news. Remembering his time in Pennsylvania from the previous summer, Early chose to bring down his wrath on Chambersburg.

When the five thousand citizens of Chambersburg received word that the rebels had once again crossed the Mason-Dixon Line and were headed in their general direction, there was little initial panic. The Confederates had been there in 1862, when rebel horsemen raided the countryside, and again during the Gettysburg Campaign of 1863. Both times the Southerners were restrained occupiers, taking special care not to cause excessive damage to local farms and homes; most of the locals believed that McCausland's stopover would be no different. Originating out of the newly formed state of West Virginia's eastern panhandle, McCausland's brigade was joined by other rebel forces totaling two thousand eight hundred men. They arrived in Chambersburg at approximately 5:30 AM. To signal his arrival, McCausland ordered a cannonade over the city, and by the time his horsemen rode into town, the citizens of Franklin County knew this visit would be very different from before. McCausland and his staff ate breakfast at the Franklin House, and after the meal he began to implement the conquest of the city. He first ordered any prominent civic leaders apprehended and then proceeded to demand a ransom from the community. To pay for the damages suffered in the Shenandoah, the rebels asked for $100,000 in gold or $500,000 in currency. If it was not provided, the town would be destroyed.

Using the captives as mouthpieces, McCausland's demands were read aloud to the townspeople. One of the prisoners was lawyer J. W. Douglas, and when he informed the community of the ransom, he claimed that most people simply laughed and shrugged them off: "They generally laughed at first . . . they said they were trying to scare us, and went into their houses."[2] When it became clear

Missouri-born, Virginia-raised brigadier general John McCausland was selected to lead the Confederate raid back into Pennsylvania. (*Library of Congress*)

that the people of Chambersburg were not going to pay the Confederates, McCausland ordered the bell rung that sat atop the courthouse and called the townspeople to the center of town. In a show of defiance and fueled by revenge, the rebel commander ordered his cavalrymen to burn the city. Terror gripped the citizenry, and one Southerner recalled, "It was impossible at first to convince the people . . . that their fair city would be burnt. . . . Terror was depicted in every face, women, refined ladies and girls running through the streets wild with fright seeking some place of safety."[3] The rebels began their assault by kicking in doors and piling furniture in the streets; they used these to start the blaze. Sources estimate that by 8:00 AM, the entire center of Chambersburg was in flames.

The Confederates withdrew soon after starting the fire, and although a Union cavalry force under William Averell arrived, it was far too late to save the town. The damage was shocking, and amaz-

2. J. W. Douglas, in Steven Bernstein, *The Confederacy's Last Northern Offensive: Jubal Early, the Army of the Valley and the Raid on Washington* (Jefferson, NC: McFarland, 2011), 114.
3. Liva Baker, "The Burning of Chambersburg," *American Heritage* 23, no. 5 (1973): 171.

The burned out ruins of Chambersburg. The Chambersburg Courthouse, right, was completely destroyed in July 1864. (*Library of Congress*)

ingly, only one person was killed in the city of five thousand. The destruction of Chambersburg sent a shocking message to the North that was received loud and clear. It also signaled that although the Civil War was winding down, there was still a great deal of fighting to come.

LEGACY: Chambersburg was the only Northern city destroyed in the Civil War. The damage was catastrophic, but the only death suffered was as a result of smoke inhalation from the fire that engulfed the community. The citizens of Chambersburg suffered terribly, as two thousand were left homeless and five hundred buildings were burned. The exact cost of the damage is difficult to calculate, but estimates set the sum at approximately $1.5 million in 1864. The reaction across the Northern states was swift and outraged; images of the ruined town were published in newspapers and became lightning rods of public sentiment. As a result of McCausland's raid, calls for revenge swept across the North (while the earlier depredations committed by federal troops throughout the South were ignored). The response to the burning was typical of America's natural disaster response in the modern age: food and shelter were offered to Chambersburg's five thousand residents, and the Cumberland Valley

Railroad offered free train service to and from the city so refugees could reconnect to family in distant parts of the country. The city was rebuilt quickly, and most of the damage was repaired by 1866. In 1878, the Memorial Fountain was erected in the center of the city, and a parade was held to honor the event; it was attended by over fifteen thousand people.

In the wake of the raid, national humanitarian fundraisers swelled Union coffers, and politicians demanded a more aggressive strategy to finish the war. That fall, Major General Phillip Sheridan waged total war on the Shenandoah Valley and burned countless acres of farmland. Major General William Tecumseh Sherman next put the torch to Atlanta, Georgia, and burned much of the city to the ground. Riding high on these victories, President Lincoln was elected to a second term in November 1864 and given the consent of the people to finish the conflict by any means necessary. Lincoln took the oath of office for the second time on March 4, 1865; on April 9, General Grant accepted the surrender of Robert E. Lee at Appomattox Courthouse. The Civil War was the first American conflict to end in a surrender rather than a negotiated peace and was the bloodiest conflict in the nation's history to that point.

WHAT TO SEE: Chambersburg is filled with history from the eighteenth, nineteenth, and twentieth centuries, and guests are encouraged to enjoy it all during their stay. Each summer, the city hosts its annual Chambersfest, which has everything one would expect from a community festival. For historians, though, it offers an added bonus: *The Burning*. Hosted as a full theatrical reenactment of McCausland's raid, *The Burning* uses special effects to simulate the burning of the city as portrayed on the courthouse steps. Including simulated fire and smoke, this portrayal must be seen to be believed. Also included are numerous guided walking tours that highlight the diverse history of the town. If you cannot make it for the summer festivities, Chambersburg has a great variety of sites worth your attention.

The Chambersburg Town Square was devastated by McCausland's Confederates. Today it is a historic and beautiful place. (*Chambersburg Chamber of Commerce*)

Begin your exploration of the city by visiting the Chambersburg Heritage Center on the aptly named Lincoln Way. Here can be found exhibits highlighting the city's role during the colonial and Civil War eras as well as its architectural, industrial, and transportation history. Heading west on Lincoln Way brings you to a bronze statue of a Union soldier placed as a quiet sentinel to defend the city. Next, venture to the Greenawalt House, where McCausland kept his headquarters during the raid, and tour the nineteenth-century property. On East King Street is Mary Ritner's Boarding House, where abolitionist John Brown resided in summer 1859 and formulated his attack against Harpers Ferry. Conclude your tour of Chambersburg by visiting the famed courthouse that was burned in 1864 but rebuilt in 1866, and pause for quiet reflection at Memorial Fountain and Statue in Memorial Square.

PART FIVE

THE MODERN ERA

In the aftermath of the bloodiest war in American history, the United States attempted to rebuild its fractured republic. As soldiers laid down their arms and returned home on both sides of the Mason-Dixon Line, all sought to find a place in the restructured America. In Pennsylvania, the rich natural resources made it a land of opportunity for immigrant and native workers alike. All across the state, manufacturing centers rose up, and tens of thousands of people entered the workforce as part of the rising tide of the Industrial Revolution. From the coal fields of the east to the steel mills of the west, the rapidly approaching twentieth century appeared as a new birth of freedom and economic opportunity for all willing to work toward a better life.

As new technologies grew, though, new means of production developed. Machines made manufacturing goods cheaper and more efficient, and highly valued skilled craftsmen were steadily replaced by automation. Profits soared for the industrialists who financed the operations, but workers suffered dramatic losses in wages, workable hours, and advancement opportunity. The result was a staggering series of strikes led by labor unions across the state, and with little government oversight they often resulted in shocking displays of violence and bloodshed. Again America was experiencing the hardships of balancing a changing society with traditional democratic values, and while these struggles occurred throughout the country, the shift was most dramatic in Pennsylvania.

The twentieth century was also the beginning of America's new role in the larger realm of global geopolitics. At the outset of World War I, the United States attempted to remain an impartial observer, but the position of neutrality became untenable if the nation wanted to be considered a true player on the world stage. Once joining in the effort to suppress authoritarianism across Europe, America became an inseparable ally of Europe's democratic superpowers. By the time World War II began, the United States was again forced to choose between action and indifference. But the December 1941 attack on Pearl Harbor, Hawaii, demanded a swift and immediate response. When the world needed it the most, Pennsylvania answered the call. The great mills and foundries that made the state a global powerhouse of industry immediately turned their efforts toward producing weapons, ships, and ordnance. President Franklin Delano Roosevelt dubbed the massive wave of national production "the Arsenal of Democracy."

The postwar world was a very different place than anything seen previously, and with Europe devastated, America found itself as the preeminent global superpower. In the great rush to rebuild the Western world, the United States and the Soviet Union fought around the planet to install and support their own unique worldviews in developing nations. Countries like Korea and Vietnam transformed into battlegrounds for global domination, and the Keystone State provided tens of thousands of soldiers to uphold America's values abroad. When the Soviet Union finally collapsed in the 1990s, the world looked to the United States and its allies to continue in their role as the guarantors of freedom and democracy in the modern age. Still, some sought to upend this world order, and the twenty-first century presented Earth's greatest superpower with unprecedented challenges.

29

The Homestead Steel Strike

(JULY 6, 1892)

BACKGROUND: The industrial prowess of western Pennsylvania is often posed as a chicken-and-egg proposition: did Pittsburgh make steel, or did steel make Pittsburgh? Historians now know this question to be easily answerable, and a simple glance at the natural resources of the region reveal the solution. Rivers provided cheap and easy transportation for manufactured goods, and Pittsburgh had not one or two waterways but three. Along with its multidirectional river traffic, Pittsburgh had an abundance of coal, one of the most critical components for creating steel. These gifts of nature, combined with a heavy influx of cheap immigrant labor, made western Pennsylvania an ideal location for large-scale manufacturing; an ambitious industrialist could produce wares in another place, but nowhere as cheaply or efficiently as Pittsburgh.

The shores of the Monongahela, Allegheny, and Ohio Rivers offered hundreds of miles of usable land, and large steel mills dominated those areas. One of the most impressive sat approximately eight miles from downtown Pittsburgh at the city of Homestead. Known as the Homestead Steel Works, the site was a collection of multiple factories and foundries powered by some of the most skilled workers in America. In 1883, wealthy Scottish industrialist Andrew Carnegie purchased the operation with hopes of folding it into his existing steel empire. By the time the Carnegie Steel Company acquired the works, automated manufacturing fueled by technological innovations had made the creation of steel much easier and required far less-skilled workers to produce a higher quality product. Suddenly, for the men who had mastered the art of steelmaking, Carnegie's commitment to automation put their livelihoods at risk.

BATTLE: From its earliest stages, making steel was a battle. Creating it required a constant fight against the elements of nature: heat and oxygen were a steelworker's greatest ally but also one of his worst enemies. The process of creating steel developed slowly, and western Pennsylvania brought together all the essential components of natural resources, people, and capital to make it the largest manufacturing hub on the planet. By the middle of the nineteenth century, Pittsburgh was not the Steel City but the Iron City, more specifically famous for its wrought iron. More malleable than cast iron, which was hard but relatively brittle, wrought iron was created in 100-pound batches at a time by master craftsmen. No machine existed that could replace the hands of a master ironworker, and Pittsburgh proved its value when it produced thousands of pieces of heavy artillery for the Union effort during the Civil War. The cannons, muskets, howitzers, and mortars that won the war were not pumped out by an assembly line or a machinist but by a skilled and experienced craftsman. As the war era passed, America experienced a technological boom, and Englishman Henry Bessemer created a new blast furnace that offered the ability to control heat, pressure, and chemical input with extreme accuracy and only limited operator training. By the 1880s, wrought iron was replaced with the far more durable product of steel, and creating it was dramatically easier with the technological innovations of the day.

Before the arrival of these innovations in manufacturing, a successful career in the iron industry was considered one of the great jobs in the United States. The creation of high-quality iron was an art and a science, and master craftsmen were some of the most sought out individuals in the industrial marketplace. Because they held so much leverage over the manufacturing process, the ironworkers dictated nearly all the terms of production: they handled all the hiring and firing, controlled when and how often they worked, and most importantly negotiated their wages. For the industrialists who owned and financed the operations, the arrangement was uneasy. Ironworkers were paid by how much they produced rather than how long they worked per day, giving them a tremendous amount of leverage in the manufacturing process. In short, there were ample incentives for labor and capital to prosper. However, with the emergence of the Bessemer converter and other automation innovations, the power gradually slipped from the hands of the ironworkers and into those of ambitious capitalists. By the 1880s, steelmaking had the potential of being highly profitable, and the workers controlled less of the process than ever before.

By 1883, the name Andrew Carnegie was synonymous with steel. That year, the Carnegie Steel Company bought the Homestead Steel Works as yet another piece of his manufacturing empire. Carnegie and his business partner, Henry Clay Frick, were well aware of how automation shifted the balance of production power in their favor and believed that the Homestead works could be on the front lines of that change. When Carnegie Steel acquired the operation along the Monongahela River, it also purchased its existing labor contract with the Amalgamated Association of Iron and Steelworkers; the terms were unfavorable to the industrialists, but with the contract set to expire in June 1892, they believed that the problem would extinguish itself. In February 1892, negotiations opened with the union, and despite near-record profitability, Frick and Carnegie offered the workers a 22 percent wage *decrease*. Negotiations stalled, and by the end of June, the company officially announced that it no longer recognized the union. Frick had fostered a reputation for ruth-lessness, but the actions taken on June 29, 1892, were beyond any-thing witnessed before in western Pennsylvania. That day, Frick officially locked the entire Homestead works, and he ordered barbed wire fencing around the perimeter of the site, accompanied by snipers in towers and pressurized water cannons. That day the workers began their strike, and the entire site became known colloquially as "Fort Frick."

As a preventative measure, Frick employed the services of the Pinkerton Detective Agency to provide private security forces to pa-trol the plant. The Pinkertons, as they were known, were famous for their dark coats, bowler hats, and heavy-handed methods. The union workers knew of this development shortly after the contract with Pinkerton was signed, and they prepared for the security agents ar-rival by patrolling the Monongahela River on small boats and a steam launch. Though debate continues as to who was to blame for the in-tense animus between the workers and the company, there was a dan-gerous air of tension surrounding the Homestead Steel Works. On the evening of July 5, 1892, the newly arrived Pinkertons boarded two barges at the Davis Island Dam north of Pittsburgh with hopes of slipping past the union's patrols and securing the Homestead site. They never made it. At approximately 2:30 AM, the strikers onboard the steam launch spotted the arriving security agents and opened fire. Doing little damage, they blared their steam whistle, and thousands of angry workers from the city of Homestead pushed down the barbed wire fencing and rushed to the river's edge.

The Battle of Homestead had begun, and it was a catastrophe for both sides. The Pinkertons landed their barges, but gunfire from the mills kept them aboard. The security agents fired back in spurts, but they were effectively stuck along the shoreline. Fighting raged from 4:00 AM to 4:00 PM, but there was no method to the madness. Spo-radic shots from both sides rang out throughout the day, but most of the event was a chaotic mix of shouting and riots. At multiple times on July 6, the strikers attempted to burn the barges holding the security agents, but each time they failed. They first sent a burning, oil-soaked raft downriver to collide with the Pinkertons, but it incinerated itself before reaching its target. They next loaded a railcar with oil drums, set it ablaze, and pushed to toward the docks; it simply stalled and burned innocuously in front of the strikers. They finally resorted to throwing sticks of dynamite at the Pinkertons, which had limited effect. By 4:00 PM, the hired guns aboard the rafts had had enough and signaled for a surrender. As the workers made way for the Pinkertons to exit the barges and the steelworks, the women of Homestead surrounded the defeated security agents in a long line and beat them as they passed.

The July 14, 1892, *Frank Leslie's Illustrated Weekly* featured the "attack of the strikers and their sympathizers on the surrendered Pinkerton men." (*Library of Congress*)

LEGACY: Before the events of July 6, 1892, the American public had generally supported the union movement. After the violent images of the Homestead strike were published in newspapers, however, public opinion turned drastically against the workers. As scenes of combat and bloody Pinkerton agents became public, the Homestead workers were labeled extremists and ruffians; public support waned, and before long it became nonexistent. The American Federation of Labor launched a campaign to boycott all Carnegie steel, but it fizzled out quickly. Within days of the battle, Eastern European immigrants crossed the picket lines to work, and the Amalgamated Association of Iron and Steelworkers' strike collapsed. In November, the union members voted to end the holdout, and the men of Homestead returned to work for far less than their prestrike wages.

On July 23, 1892, anarchist Alexander Berkman traveled from New York City to Pittsburgh with hopes of murdering Henry Clay Frick. After arriving in the city, Berkman ventured to Frick's office and claimed to be a representative of a New York hiring agency; he was turned away with no hesitation. The following day he returned using the same ruse, and before he could be sent away for a second time, he leaped into the industrialist's office and launched his attack. Berkman fired twice at Frick and missed both times, but before he could be removed he managed to stab his target three times. The anarchist was arrested and sentenced to twenty-two years in prison, and although he had no connection to the Homestead strike, the attack was used as a political wedge against the greater unionization movement.

In many ways, the Homestead strike was the high-water mark of the union movement in the nineteenth century. In the years that followed, industrialists used political and economic pressures to deunionize manufacturing facilities across the country. Mills in Illinois, Indiana, Ohio, and Pennsylvania all took steps to phase out their resident labor associations. Carnegie Steel's facility in Mingo Junction, Ohio, forty miles west of Pittsburgh, was one of the last unionized steel plants in America. The US labor movement recovered during Franklin Delano Roosevelt's New Deal, but for forty years after the events at Homestead, it was lost in the wilderness.

WHAT TO SEE: Today the former site of the Homestead Steel Works is operated and maintained by the Rivers of Steel National Heritage Area. As with most of the sites discussed in this book, the modern world has encroached considerably on the former steelworks location. With most of the sprawling operation now consumed by the posh shopping centers and restaurants known as The Waterfront in Pitts-

This water tower is modernized and unrecognizable, but it was present in this location during the 1892 strike. The Homestead Strike site is littered with clues from its industrial past. (*Author*)

burgh, only a few scant buildings survive. As you approach the city from Pittsburgh, you'll first cross the famous Homestead Bridge. Proceed past the busy shopping locations on East Waterfront Drive until arriving at the Pumphouse on the left side. The Pumphouse is preserved and operated by The Battle of Homestead Foundation and is an original structure that was present during the battle; it was here that a striker named John Faris was shot and killed by a Pinkerton agent while he peered through a window. Outside the Pumphouse sit a number of interesting pieces of equipment from the mills that have been landscaped and highlighted to be permanent additions to the historic site. Proceed to the water's edge along the walking trail and read the placards there. Each details a different phase of the battle, which is easily reconstructed in the mind's eye. If you glance down into the water, you can see the remnants of the pier pylons the Pinkerton agents used to tie off their barges prior to the battle. For the remainder of the day, walk through the streets of Homestead, being sure to visit its cemeteries and its wonderful library, all of which contain tangible connections to the battle. End your exploration at the Bost Building on East Eighth Avenue, which is operated by the Rivers of Steel National Heritage Area. This is the former headquarters of the Amalgamated Association and is maintained as a full museum and archives pertaining to the history of the event and the site.

Rivers of Steel National Heritage Area provides a free driving tour map that guides travelers throughout western Pennsylvania focusing on the development and fall of the steel industry for all points north, south, east, and west. One of its greatest resources sits directly across the Monongahela River from the Homestead site known as the Carrie Blast Furnace. Standing ninety-two feet above the river's edge and constructed of 2.5-inch steel plate, the Carrie Furnace was a marvel of its time; personal tours are offered from May until October.

30

The Crash of Flight 93

(SEPTEMBER 11, 2001)

BACKGROUND: Following the conclusion of the Soviet-Afghan war that raged from 1979–1989, an extremist jihadist militant organization known as al-Qaeda emerged on the world stage. Fueled by secretive foreign investors and a doctrine of hate, al-Qaeda (The Base) began a campaign of terror across the globe; its leader, a wealthy Saudi named Osama bin Laden, became the most wanted man on earth for his crimes. In 1998, al-Qaeda claimed responsibility for the bombing of American embassies in Tanzania and Kenya that took the lives of 224 people and injured more than four thousand. On October 12, 2000, the terrorist organization struck the USS *Cole* as it refueled in Yemen, killing fifteen and wounding thirty-nine. By the end of 2000, bin Laden was considered to be the vilest mass murderer on the planet, and al-Qaeda's leaders spent their days hiding deep in the caves and mountains of Afghanistan.

On the morning of September 11, 2001, al-Qaeda struck the United States with the worst terrorist attack in human history. At 7:59 AM (EDT), American Airlines Flight 11 took off from Boston's Logan International Airport carrying eighty-seven passengers and crew. After a brief time in the air, five hijackers took control of the plane and redirected it toward New York City; at 8:46 AM, the terrorists flew the plane into the North Tower of Manhattan's World Trade Center. At 8:14 AM, United Airlines Flight 175 took off from Logan carrying sixty passengers and crew, and after a second hijacking, was crashed into the South Tower of the World Trade Center at 9:03 AM. A third aircraft, American Airlines Flight 77, departed Dulles International Airport outside of Washington, DC, at 8:20 AM for Los Angeles, and it too was hijacked and rerouted. At 9:37 AM, the plane and its fifty-nine passengers and crew were flown into the Pentagon in Arlington, Virginia. Finally, in what would be the last of the four aircraft hijacked that morning, United Flight 93 departed Newark International Airport at 8:42 AM with thirty-three passengers and seven crew members onboard.

BATTLE: The September 11 attacks were developed at the highest levels of al-Qaeda's command structure and originally entailed the hijacking of at least ten flights on both the East and West Coasts of the United States. After it was determined that such a venture would be too difficult to execute, the decision was made to use just four planes, all originating in the Northeast. While the overall attack involved nineteen assailants from across the Middle East, the figure most vital to the hijacking of United Airlines Flight 93 was 26-year-old Ziad Jarrah. Jarrah was born in Lebanon and raised in a secular household; it was not until he moved to Hamburg, Germany, that he was converted to the ultraconservative sect of Islam known as Salafism. As part of his extreme interpretation of the Qur'an, he was indoctrinated and radicalized before officially joining al-Qaeda in 1998. As part of his involvement in the September 11 attacks, he legally took up residence in Florida, where he engaged in flight training from June 2000 to January 2001. When Jarrah boarded United Flight 93 at Newark International Airport at 7:48 AM, three other terrorists were already on the plane. Ahmed al-Nami, Ahmed al-Haznawi, and Saeed al-Ghamdi planned to capture the aircraft while Jarrah acted as pilot.

Flight 93 had only thirty-three passengers that morning. Although the aircraft had many unsold seats (and therefore would likely have been canceled today), the killers had no idea what type of situation they had walked into. The passengers of Flight 93 came from all walks of life and were of all ages, and they possessed an impressive array of athletic prowess that proved to be critical as the day went on. Jeremy Glick had been an all-state high school wrestler in New Jersey and a national collegiate judo champion. Attorney Linda Gronlund was a brown belt in karate who had once reset her own dislocated knee. Mark Binghman was a two-time national collegiate champion in rugby at Berkeley and had participated in the famed running of the bulls in Spain. Andrew "Sonny" Garcia had been a wrestler and sprinter at San Jose State University. Joe Driscoll had served four years on a US Navy destroyer, and Bill Cashman had been a US Army paratrooper in the 101st Airborne Division (he was also an ironworker who had helped to construct the World Trade Center). CeeCee Lyles was a former police officer and detective in Fort Pierce, Florida, and was noted for tackling much larger male suspects. Each person onboard had a unique skill set and full lives ahead of them, and all were brought together on September 11, 2001.

For the terrorists who planned the attacks, timing was essential. All four planes were chosen because they were slated to take off within twenty-five minutes of one another. While Flights 11, 77, and 175 took off on time, Flight 93 was delayed at Newark for forty-two minutes. When it finally left New Jersey at 8:42 AM, it proceeded across Pennsylvania toward Cleveland, Ohio. At 9:28 AM, the hijackers stormed the cockpit and took control of the aircraft. It is not known why they waited so long to begin their attack, but it bought the passengers of Flight 93 valuable time to respond as the plane turned east above Cleveland toward Washington, DC, at 9:37 AM. Details remain unclear about the timeline of events onboard, but calls made from air phones gave investigators information about who was sitting where, when. During these calls, loved ones on the ground informed the passengers of Flight 93 about the tragic events at the World Trade Center. After holding a quiet vote among themselves, the forty men and women began their counterattack to reclaim the plane. At 10:00 AM, a man's voice was heard saying in English, "In the cockpit. If we don't, we'll die." As the hijackers attempted to keep the cockpit door closed, it was clear that the heroes of Flight 93 had every intention of retaking control of the plane and attempting to land it safely; passenger Donald Greene had a small-plane pilot's license. At 10:02 AM, the passengers broke into the cockpit, and screams in Arabic were heard over the voice recorder as well as shouts of "Give it to me!" In a final attempt to shake the revolting passengers off them, the terrorist pilot Jarrah rolled the plane before slamming it nose first into the ground outside of Shanksville, Pennsylvania.

As the plane hit the earth at 563 miles an hour, some of its wreckage was driven nearly forty feet into the ground. A common sight in Somerset County, the field in which Flight 93 crashed was a former strip mine. The soil was loosely compacted and very soft. Investigators knew they would find the most physical evidence at Shanksville rather than in New York City or at the Pentagon. Forensic analysis showed that the front one-third of the plane snapped off and flew into a grove of hemlock trees nearby. Because of that immediate impact, many personal effects from the hijackers were readily identified, and both of the aircraft's black boxes were located. Eyewitnesses claim that when Flight 93 crashed, a massive fireball blasted into the air but quickly vanished; because the plane hit the ground and not a building, the fire had nowhere to spread and dissipated after only a few seconds.

LEGACY: The crash of United Flight 93 was the result of an ultimate act of heroism and sacrifice. Just one hour and seventeen minutes after American Airlines Flight 11 struck the North Tower of the World Trade Center, Americans were already fighting back in the skies above Pennsylvania. While the forty passengers and crew were the smallest contingent on any plane hijacked that terrible morning,

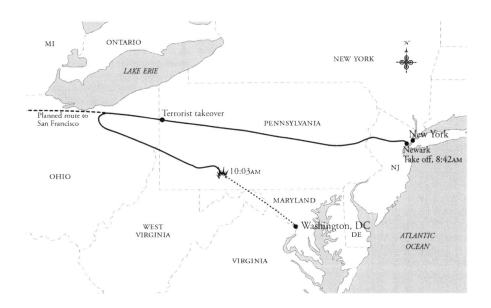

they selflessly charged the cockpit with little hesitation. Unlike those on the other planes that day, the passengers of Flight 93 had the benefit of time and telecommunications to inform them of the hijackers' intentions. In an act of true evil, the hijackers of Flights 11, 175, and 77 told their hostages they were going to land the planes and negotiate a ransom. The souls onboard had no intuition of what lay ahead.

As Flight 93 reached Cleveland and turned east for Washington, passengers received calls from loved ones via cell phones and air phones relaying the shocking scenes in New York and at the Pentagon. Though historians can only piece together the story onboard from calls made to family members and from the plane's flight recorder, it appears the passengers fully intended to retake the plane and attempt to land it themselves. In a close examination of the cockpit recorder, a hijacker is clearly heard stating, "Yes, put it in it, and pull it down . . . pull it down! Pull it down!" This is followed by a voice responding, "Turn it up!" and then finally, "Pull it up." With the plane unable to be saved, the heroes of Flight 93 gave their lives to save countless more. In 2014, the forty men and women of Flight 93 were posthumously awarded the Medal of Honor for their efforts.

WHAT TO SEE: The Flight 93 National Memorial in Shanksville is hallowed ground and remains the most gut-wrenching, tear-inducing, prideful experience one can find in the commonwealth. Beginning as a mere chain-link fence filled with mementos immediately following the crash, it has since grown into an impressive, multimillion-dollar memorial and interpretive site. Beginning with a long, somber drive down a paved road off historic Route 30, guests will arrive at the Visitor Center Complex. In the exhibit area, visitors can see wreckage and personal effects found on-site as well as profiles of the men and women onboard. Audio-visual equipment allows guests to hear the phone calls and flight recordings made on September 11 and see how the memorial has evolved over the last seventeen years. Stepping outside, one can travel down a suspended walkway built precisely along the flight path the aircraft was on when it crashed at 10:03 AM, and a balcony offers a bird's-eye view of the entire memorial park.

After experiencing the museum, return to your vehicle and drive back down the paved road until signs appear for the Memorial Plaza. Here guests can walk along a path toward the crash site and either take a guided tour or listen to audio cues from a mobile device. At the end of the path is the Wall of Names offering an individual memorial to each of the forty men and women who made the ultimate sacrifice for their country on September 11; it will be the most moving and emotional experience of the entire visit.

In the years to come, a ninety-three-foot-tall Tower of Voices will be completed housing forty different chimes, one for each passenger. The individual chimes will have their own unique resonance and offer a daily reminder of the events that occurred close by. The Flight 93 crash site will be a different experience for each generation, and like all other historic sites, its value will change over time. For those who remember September 11, 2001, the site will always rekindle deep emotions; for those yet to come, it will be a place of reverence—just as Gettysburg Battlefield began as a memorial for lost loved ones after the three-day battle but today, for modern Americans, offers invaluable lessons of leadership, bravery, sacrifice, and patriotism.

A common field one day. A field of honor forever.

A glass panel at the end of the Flight Path Walkway at the Flight 93 Visitors Center provides a view of the Memorial Plaza at the crash site.(*National Park Service/Brenda Schwartz*)

The place where the Flight 93 National Memorial stands is some of America's most sacred ground, and the forty men and women who fought there join the pantheon of this nation's greatest heroes.

Recommended Reading

GENERAL OVERVIEW

Pencak, William A., Christian B. Keller, Barbara Gannon. *Pennsylvania: A Military History*. Yardley, PA: Westholme Publishing, 2016.

THE SEVEN YEARS' WAR ERA

Anderson, Fred. *Crucible of War: The Seven Years' War and the Fate of Empire in British North America, 1754–1766*. New York: Vintage Books, 2000.

Barr, Daniel P. "Victory at Kittanning? Reevaluating the Impact of Armstrong's Raid on the Seven Years' War in Pennsylvania." *Pennsylvania Magazine of History and Biography* 131 (2007): 5–30.

Betts, William W. *Rank and Gravity: The Life of General John Armstrong of Carlisle*. Westminster, MD: Heritage Books, 2011.

Calloway, Collin G. *The Scratch of a Penn: 1763 and the Transformation of North America*. New York: Oxford University Press, 2006.

Crytzer, Brady J. *Fort Pitt: A Frontier History*. Charleston, SC: History Press, 2012.

———. *Major Washington's Pittsburgh and the Mission to Fort LeBoeuf*. Charleston, SC: History Press, 2011.

Dixon, David. "A High Wind Rising: George Washington, Fort Necessity, and the Ohio Country Indians." *Pennsylvania History* 74 (2007): 333–353.

———. *Never Come to Peace Again: Pontiac's Uprising and the Fate of the British Empire in North America*. Norman: University of Oklahoma Press, 2005.

Dowd, Gregory A. *A Spirited Resistance: The North American Indian Struggle for Unity, 1745–1815.* Baltimore: Johns Hopkins University Press, 1993.

Kelsay, Isabel Thompson. *Joseph Brant, 1743–1807: Man of Two Worlds.* Syracuse, NY: Syracuse University Press, 1984.

Kenny, Kevin. *Peaceable Kingdom Lost: The Paxton Boys and the Destruction of William Penn's Holy Experiment.* New York: Oxford University Press, 2009.

Kopper, Kevin, ed. *The Journals of George Washington and Christopher Gist: Mission to Fort Le Boeuf 1753–1754.* Old Stone House series, vol. 5. Harmony, PA: Historic Harmony, 2009.

Kopperman, Paul. *Braddock at the Monongahela.* Pittsburgh: University of Pittsburgh Press, 1977.

Loudon, Archibald. *A Collection of Some of the Narratives of Outrages Committed by the Indians in the Wars with the White People, Vols. 1–2.* London: Loudon, 1808.

O'Meara, Walter. *Guns at the Forks.* Pittsburgh: University of Pittsburgh Press, 1965.

Preston, David L. *Braddock's Defeat: The Battle of the Monongahela and the Road to Revolution.* New York: Oxford University Press, 2015.

Soderlund, Jean R. *William Penn and the Founding of Pennsylvania: A Documentary History.* Philadelphia: University of Pennsylvania Press, 1983.

Wallace, Paul A. W. *Historic Indian Paths of Pennsylvania.* Harrisburg: Pennsylvania Historical and Museum Commission, 1952.

———. *Indians in Pennsylvania.* Harrisburg: Pennsylvania Historical and Museum Commission, 1981.

Washington, George. *The Diaries of George Washington.* Vol. 1, March 11, 1748—November 13, 1765. Edited by Donald Jackson. Charlottesville: University Press of Virginia, 1976.

———. *Journal of Colonel George Washington.* Edited by J. M. Toner. Albany, NY: J. Munsell's Sons, 1893.

THE AMERICAN REVOLUTIONARY ERA

Allen, Thomas B. *Tories: Fighting for the King in America's First Civil War*. New York: Harper, 2010.

Brubaker, Jack. *Massacre of the Conestogas: On the Trail of the Paxton Boys in Lancaster County*. Charleston, SC: History Press, 2010.

De Crevecoeur, J. Hector St. John. *Letters from an American Farmer and Sketches of Eighteenth Century America*. New York: Penguin Classics, 1986.

Drake, Samuel G. *Indian Captivities: A Collection of the Most Remarkable Narratives of Persons Taken Captive by North American Indians*. Boston: Antiquarian Bookstore and Institute, 1839.

Engels, Jeremy. "Equipped for Murder: The Paxton Boys and the Spirit of Killing All Indians in Pennsylvania, 1763–1764." *Rhetoric and Public Affairs* 8, no. 3 (2005): 355–382.

Fischer, David H. *Washington's Crossing*. Oxford: Oxford University Press, 2006.

Franklin, Benjamin. *The Papers of Benjamin Franklin*. Vol. 13, January 1, 1766–December 31, 1766. Edited by Leonard W. Labaree. New Haven, CT, and London: Yale University Press, 1969.

Graymont, Barbara. *The Iroquois in the American Revolution*. Syracuse, NY: Syracuse University Press, 1972.

Harris, Michael C. *Brandywine: A Military History of the Battle That Lost Philadelphia but Saved America, September 11, 1777*. El Dorado Hills, CA: Savas Beatie, 2014.

Jasanoff, Maya. *Liberty's Exiles: American Loyalists in the Revolutionary World*. New York: Alfred A. Knopf, 2011.

Lengel, Edward. *General George Washington*. New York: Random House, 2005.

McGrath, Tim. *Give Me a Fast Ship: The Continental Navy and America's Revolution at Sea*. New York: Dutton Caliber, 2015.

McGuire, Thomas J. *Battle of Paoli*. Mechanicsburg, PA: Stackpole Books, 2000.

———. *The Philadelphia Campaign: Brandywine and the Fall of Philadelphia, Vol. 1.* Mechanicsburg, PA: Stackpole Books, 2006.

Middlekauff, Robert. *The Glorious Cause: The American Revolution, 1763–1789.* Oxford: Oxford University Press, 2005.

Minutes of the Provincial Council, Colonial Records of Pennsylvania, Vol. 9. Harrisburg: State of Pennsylvania, 1852.

Newman, Andrew. "The Black Boys Rebellion of 1765." *Franklin County Historical Society Kittochtiny: A Journal of Franklin County History* 27 (2015): 7–20.

Savas, Theodore P., and J. David Dameron. *A Guide to the Battles of the American Revolution.* New York: Savas Beatie, 2006.

Shannon, Timothy. *Iroquois Diplomacy on the Early American Frontier.* New York: Penguin, 2008.

Williams, Glenn F. *Year of the Hangman: George Washington's Campaign against the Iroquois.* Yardley, PA: Westholme, 2005.

THE REPUBLIC'S FIRST TESTS

Borneman, Walter R. *1812: The War That Forged a Nation.* New York: Harper Perennial, 2004.

Frew, David. *Perry's Lake Erie Fleet: After the Glory.* Charleston, SC: History Press, 2012.

Hogeland, William. *The Whiskey Rebellion: George Washington, Alexander Hamilton, and the Frontier Rebels Who Challenged America's Newfound Sovereignty.* New York: Simon and Schuster, 2006.

Howarth, Stephen. *To Shining Sea: A History of the United States Navy, 1775–1998.* Norman: University of Oklahoma Press, 1999.

Mackenzie, Alexander Sliddell. *Commodore Oliver Hazard Perry: Famous American Naval Hero.* New York: MacLellan, 1907.

Milano, Kenneth W. *The Philadelphia Nativist Riots: Irish Kensington Erupts.* Charleston, SC: History Press, 2013.

Rybka, Walter P. *The Lake Erie Campaign of 1813: I Shall Fight Them This Day.* Charleston, SC: History Press, 2012.

Slaughter, Thomas P. *The Whiskey Rebellion: Frontier Epilogue to the American Revolution.* New York: Oxford University Press, 1986.

THE CIVIL WAR ERA

Baker, Liva. "The Burning of Chambersburg." *American Heritage* 23, no. 5 (1973): 165–173.

Bernstein, Steven. *The Confederacy's Last Northern Offensive: Jubal Early, the Army of the Valley and the Raid on Washington*. Jefferson, NC: McFarland, 2011.

Brown, Albert Gallatin. *Speeches, Messages, and Other Writings of the Hon. Albert Gallatin Brown*. Edited by M. W. Cluskey. New Orleans: H. D. Maginiss, 1859.

Brown, Kent Masterson. *Retreat from Gettysburg: Lee, Logistics, and the Pennsylvania Campaign*. Chapel Hill: University of North Carolina Press, 2005.

Cameron, Christopher. *The Abolitionist Movement: Documents Decoded*. Santa Barbara, CA: ABC-CLIO, 2014.

Coddington, Edwin B. *The Gettysburg Campaign: A Study in Command*. New York: Touchstone, 1997.

Early, Jubal. *Lieutenant General Jubal Anderson Early, C.S.A: Autobiographical Sketch and Narrative of the War Between the States*. Philadelphia: J. B. Lippincott, 1912.

Horton, James O., and Amanda Kleintop. *Race, Slavery and the Civil War*. Richmond: Virginia Sesquicentennial of the American Civil War Commission, 2011.

Mingus, Scott L. *Flames beyond Gettysburg: The Gordon Expedition, 1863*. El Dorado Hills, CA: Savas Beatie, 2009.

Petruzzi, J. David. *The Complete Gettysburg Guide: Walking and Driving Tours of the Battlefield, Town, Cemeteries, Field Hospital Sites, and Other Topics of Historical Interest*. El Dorado Hills, CA: Savas Beatie, 2009.

Petruzzi, J. David, and Steven A. Stanley. *The Gettysburg Campaign in Numbers and Losses*. El Dorado Hills, CA: Savas Beatie, 2012.

Petruzzi, J. David, and Eric J. Wittenberg. *One Continuous Fight: The Retreat from Gettysburg and the Pursuit of Lee's Army of Northern Virginia, July 4–14, 1863*. El Dorado Hills, CA: Savas Beatie, 2011.

————. *Plenty of Blame to Go Around: Jeb Stuart's Controversial Ride to Gettysburg.* El Dorado Hills, CA: Savas Beatie, 2011.

Sears, Stephen W. *Gettysburg.* New York: Houghton Mifflin, 2003.

Wingert, Cooper H. *The Confederate Approach on Harrisburg: The Gettysburg Campaign's Northernmost Reaches.* Charleston, SC: History Press, 2012.

————. *Harrisburg and the Civil War: Defending the Keystone of the Union.* Charleston, SC: History Press, 2013.

Wittenberg, Eric. *The Devil's to Pay: John Buford at Gettysburg.* El Dorado Hills, CA: Savas Beatie, 2014.

————. *Gettysburg's Forgotten Cavalry Action.* El Dorado Hills, CA: Savas Beatie, 2011.

THE MODERN ERA

Burgoyne, Arthur. *The Homestead Strike of 1892.* Pittsburgh: University of Pittsburgh Press, 1979.

Kahan, Paul. *The Homestead Strike: Labor, Violence, and American Industry.* New York: Routledge, 2013.

McMillan, Tom. *Flight 93: The Story, the Aftermath, and the Legacy of American Courage on 9/11.* Guilford, CT: Lyons Press, 2015.

Standiford, Lee. *Meet You in Hell: Andrew Carnegie, Henry Clay Frick, and the Bitter Partnership That Changed America.* New York: Three Rivers Press, 2006.

Wright, Lawrence. *The Looming Tower: Al-Qaeda and the Road to 9/11.* New York: Vintage, 2007.

Acknowledgments

In many ways this book is the product of three years of travel, interviews, production, and on-location shoots. After three seasons of creating *Battlefield Pennsylvania*, we have had the wonderful opportunity to sit down with dozens of guests. I would like to express my gratitude to all of them. Their tireless efforts resulted in the creation of countless books, documentaries, and articles, and it has been my pleasure to help them share their research with the world. I would also like to thank Pennsylvania Cable Network President and CEO Brian Lockman as well as Vice President of Programming Francine Schertzer for greenlighting our show. I would like to thank Producer Todd Abele for his tireless efforts helping to make this all possible. Finally I would like to thank my publisher Bruce H. Franklin and everyone at Westholme Publishing.

Index

Lincoln, Abraham
 attempts to bolster the commonwealth's ranks and, 188
 call for seventy-five thousand military volunteers to suppress
  the Southern rebellion and,
  168
 David Wills House and, 225
 elected to a second term and, 239
 funerary procession train and, 183
 Gettysburg Address and, 184, 225
 railroads as vital arteries to war effort and, 177
 reaction across the South to 1860
  election and, 167
 York County vote and, 187
Little Round Top, 218, 220, 225
Lochry, Archibald, 133-134
Logan, Benjamin, 170
Logan International Airport, 253-
 254
Logan, James, 110, 112
Longstreet, James, 194, 218, 220
Louis XV, 5, 7, 14, 65
Loyalhanna Creek, 46-47, 54, 56
Luzerne County, 128-129
Lyles, CeeCee, 255

Mackay, James, 22, 25
Madison, James, 151-152, 155-156
Marshall, John, 108
Martin, Joseph Plumb, 121-122
Martin's Tavern, 96
Maryland Battalion, 56
Mary Ritner's Boarding House, 240
Mason-Dixon Line, 188, 202, 227,
 229, 231, 236, 243
Maxwell, William, 108
McCausland, John, 235-238, 240
McClellan, George B., 173, 234
McFarlane, James, 146
McGinnis, Richard, 127
McGraw, Mary McCandless, 172
McPherson's Ridge, 216
Meade, George Gordon, 215, 218,
 222, 224, 226-227

Memorial Fountain, 239-240
Memorial Plaza, 258-259
Memorial Square, 240
Messner, Robert, 36
Michigan Historical Commission,
 233
Military Railroad Department, 183
Miller, Oliver, 146, 149
Mingo, 7, 14, 37, 50, 65, 134
Mingo Creek Presbyterian Church,
 149
Mississippi River, 55, 144
Mohawk River, 124
Monongahela, battle of, 28-36, 146
Monongahela River, 22, 31, 33-34,
 52, 245, 247-248, 252
Monterey Pass Battlefield, 233
Monterey Pass Battlefield Park and
 Museum, 232-233
Monterey Pass, battle of, 226-233
Montgomerie's Highlanders, 47
Montresor, John, 117, 122
Morgan, Daniel, 35
Mount Olivet Cemetery, 204, 206
Mount Parnell, 86-87
Mud Island, 115, 117-118, 121
Mud Island Fort, 117
Murray, John, 136

Nanny Goat Market, 160, 164
A Narrative of a Revolutionary Soldier
 (Martin), 122
National Park Service, 27, 224
National Register of Historic Places,
 183
Nesbert, Vincent, 52
Neville, John, 145-146
Neville, Pressley, 146, 149
Newark International Airport, 254
New Deal, 250
New France, 3-5, 7, 16-17, 26, 28-
 29, 31, 35, 37, 42, 45, 51,
 55, 58, 63, 65-66
New Orleans, battle of, 156
Niagara, 153-154, 157